ROSES IN DECEMBER

Carter G. Woodson Institute Series
DEBORAH E. MCDOWELL, SHAWN LEIGH ALEXANDER,
AND ROBERT T. VINSON, EDITORS

Roses in December

*Black Life in Hanover County
from Civil War to Civil Rights*

Jody Lynn Allen

UNIVERSITY OF VIRGINIA PRESS
Charlottesville and London

The University of Virginia Press is situated on the traditional lands of the Monacan Nation, and the Commonwealth of Virginia was and is home to many other Indigenous people. We pay our respect to all of them, past and present. We also honor the enslaved African and African American people who built the University of Virginia, and we recognize their descendants. We commit to fostering voices from these communities through our publications and to deepening our collective understanding of their histories and contributions.

University of Virginia Press
© 2025 by Jody Lynn Allen
All rights reserved
Printed in the United States of America on acid-free paper

First published 2025

1 3 5 7 9 8 6 4 2

LIBRARY OF CONGRESS CATALOGING-IN-PUBLICATION DATA

Names: Allen, Jody Lynn, author.
Title: Roses in December : Black life in Hanover County from Civil War to civil rights / Jody Lynn Allen.
Other titles: Carter G. Woodson Institute series.
Description: Charlottesville : University of Virginia Press, 2025. | Series: Carter G. Woodson Institute series | Includes bibliographical references and index.
Identifiers: LCCN 2024031214 (print) | LCCN 2024031215 (ebook) | ISBN 9780813952482 (hardcover) | ISBN 9780813952499 (paperback) | ISBN 9780813952505 (ebook)
Subjects: LCSH: African Americans—Virginia—Hanover County—Social conditions. | African Americans—Virginia—Hanover County—History. | Hanover County (Va.)—Race relations.
Classification: LCC F232.H3 A44 2025 (print) | LCC F232.H3 (ebook) | DDC 305.896/0730755462—dc23/eng/20240826
LC record available at https://lccn.loc.gov/2024031214
LC ebook record available at https://lccn.loc.gov/2024031215

All photos from the Louis Hyme Freeman, Jr. Collection, courtesy of the Library of Virginia.

Cover art: Students at John M. Gandy High School (Louis Hyme Freeman, Jr. Collection, courtesy of the Library of Virginia); map of Hanover County, Virginia (Thong Thai LLC)
Cover design: TG Design

In Memoriam

Dorothy Tobias Parker, Daisy Wright Tobias, Bessie Allen Ellis,
Flossie Parker, Juanita Barrett, Gloria Allen Davis, Mary Gatling,
Frances Williams Jackson Jones, Johnnie Little, Gladys Maxwell, Lydia Porter,
Theresa Powell, Bernice Savage, Pearl Walker, Westina Parker Walker

In honor of Sandra Bailey, Kordella Allen Jolivet,
Helen Tobias Walker, and Katherine Wright

CONTENTS

Preface	*ix*
Introduction: A Place for Everything and Everything in Its Place	1
1 | Seeking and Embracing Freedom	13
2 | The Politics of Reconstruction and the *Entente Cordiale* That Never Was	33
3 | An Uneasy Citizenship: The Path to Disfranchisement	55
4 | Disfranchised: The First Generation	81
5 | The Great Depression, New Deal, War, and Ordinary Acts of Resistance	113
6 | The Heat of Change	146
Epilogue: Black Life in Hanover County, Virginia, Today	175
Notes	*181*
Bibliography	*205*
Index	*213*

PREFACE

It was November 8, 2005, election day. The weather was beautiful, and there was a steady turnout of people voting in Virginia's most hotly contested gubernatorial campaign since 1989, when L. Douglas Wilder became the first elected African American governor in the United States. It was late morning in Ashland, the only incorporated town in Hanover County, Virginia, and I observed a Black man in his late 70s or early 80s, leaning on his cane, as he exited the public library where he had just cast his ballot. As he approached a campaign volunteer distributing information for the Democratic Party candidates, he proudly pointed to the sticker on his jacket that read, "I Voted." The white campaign worker, who appeared to be his contemporary, beamed back at him and said, "You're a good boy." The man's steps hesitated, and his already slow forward movement slowed even more. While he never stopped smiling, he remarked, almost to himself, that he was just remembering the old days when people used to call men boys. The campaign volunteer, noticeably embarrassed, hastily explained that she had not meant to be offensive. The man replied, "I know. I was just remembering," and he continued on his way. The volunteer's immediate response and red face indicated that she too, remembered—at least when events jogged her recollection.

The woman's turn of phrase carried the man back to a time when his manhood was questioned by virtually an entire nation, especially white southerners. He remembered when legalized segregation and overt racism severely restricted the lives of African Americans. He probably never heard Black adults referred to or addressed as Mr. or Mrs. outside his community. It was a time when most African Americans were not allowed to vote in elections—when public schools for Black children, while prized by the communities they served, were substandard and lacked basic equipment. On the other hand, like his contemporaries interviewed for this book, the old man might have also remembered Black and white farmers sharing tools and other equipment, and Black and white children playing together, at least before the first grade.

He was remembering the early twentieth century when a white employer could weep at the funeral of a Black woman who had worked for them or raised them but would decline an invitation to join her family at her home after leaving the cemetery. It was a complex time. It is chiefly the period of this man's earlier memories, the Jim Crow Era or what I refer to here as the era of disfranchisement that this book explores.

Like many first books, this one began as a dissertation. While still in the early writing stages, I did not have a title for the dissertation. The more I wrote, however, the more I felt that the title should reflect what I was learning about Black Hanoverians. In short, it seemed to me that the women and men appearing on the pages before me were tenacious, hardworking people who, despite their circumstances, seemed to be able to find the silver lining. About this time, I attended a Black History Month program at the Ashland Public Library entitled "Growing Up Black in Ashland." The panel included three participants—Inez Winston Gray, Alvin Jackson, and Frances Williams Jackson Jones. When discussing the challenges of growing up during the era of segregation, Jones shared how difficult it had been to obtain a textbook for school. She explained that she had to borrow a book from a classmate, copy the assignment, and return it. Continuing, Jones asserted that while times were hard, she and her family always had good memories, and it was these memories that got them through. According to Jones, "God gave us memories so we could have our roses in December." Black Hanoverians had their roses in December which stirred their resilience and their determination to maintain the fight for their rights as citizens of the United States of America.

This book is dedicated to my husband, Anthony E. Keitt, who never balked when I quit my good-paying job to pursue my dream. He has supported, encouraged, read, commented, listened, gently pushed, and ducked when I have thrown him the "look." Thank you for loving me when I was not lovable and for believing in me no matter what.

First and foremost, I thank God and his angels for always running interference for me. I have learned a lot of history, and I have also come to fully understand from whence cometh my help.

Thank you to my dissertation committee: Melvin Patrick Ely, Leisa Meyer, Kris Lane, and the late Theodore DeLaney. Thank you to Nadine Zimmerli, Brian Daugherity, Hilary Green, Adrienne Petty, William Sturkey, Brent Tarter, Robert Trent Vinson, and Craig Steven Wilder. I'm also thankful to my William & Mary and Sewanee friends, especially Susan Kern, Rick Mikulski, Woody Register, Courtney Thompson, Shannon White, and James P. Whittenburg.

Most of my research took place at the Library of Virginia, and I am thankful for the phenomenal staff who answered my questions, made suggestions, and brightened my day with a smile. They will never know how much they helped. I am also grateful to the taxpayers of Virginia for the library, which is an inspirational place to think and write. I have also spent a considerable amount time examining the government records of Hanover County and the Town of Ashland, the Maggie Walker Historic Site, the Virginia Museum of History and Culture, and the National Archives and Records Administration. I appreciate retired Ashland police chief Douglas Goodman, who shared with me how he used my dissertation. Finally, my gratitude for those who shared their life stories with me has no bounds. Their trust humbles me.

I thank my friends who have stuck by me no matter what and have laughed, cried, loved, and encouraged me. This group includes: Evelyn Barnes, Warren and Cate Buck, Kathy Benham and Chris Clark, Charles

Preface

and Patricia Brown, Heather Brown and Stan Webb, Ruby and Tommy Campbell, Reber Dunkel, Beth Edwards and Bill Koppersmith, Jean Folly and the Hickory Hill Team, Leah Glenn and Steve Prince, Stacy Gill, Fanchon Glover, Linda Hunter, Barbara Johnson, Jajuan Johnson, Lydia Johnson, Timothy Jones, Phyllis Slade Martin, Valerie McAlister, Jacqueline McLendon, Hermine Pinson, Lewis and Adah Randolph, Ajena and Lewis Rogers, Michael and Deborah Shannon, Francis Tanglao-Aguas, Chinua Thelwell, Sarah Thomas, my students, and my Shiloh family.

I am grateful to my family, who for some reason think I can do anything, and whose trust in me makes me work hard not to disappoint: my parents, Dorothy T. Parker and the Rev. James O. Parker Jr.; my siblings, James and Brenda, Carl and Tishawna, Jezmon and Nickkol, Frank Keitt, Willie Keitt, Patrick O'Neal, the Hatchers, the Josephs, the Aleongs, the Millers, and the Whites; my cousins, the Adams, Allens, the Parkers, and the Tobiases; and my nieces, nephews, and godchildren—Brittney, Tiffany, LaVanne, Jimmy, Tiffany, Jody, CJ, Nic, Rachelle, William, Zaria, Christina, Charles Jr., Christoper, Mike, Brandon, Danielle, Amber, Nathaniel, Rasheam, Sheri, and Deborah, our "oldest" godchild. You all inspire me, and I am proud to know you. I am thankful for the support of the women of Delta Sigma Theta Sorority, Inc., with a special shout out to Mu Pi, Pi Delta, and Williamsburg (VA) Alumnae Chapters.

Simply, I thank you all.

ROSES IN DECEMBER

Introduction
A Place for Everything and Everything in Its Place

AS A TEENAGER, in 1945 Robert Grimes worked at the five-and-ten-cent store owned by the white Flowers family in Ashland, Virginia. His coworker was a white girl about the same age. Both typically arrived at work early and, though they attended different schools, they studied together and developed a friendship of sorts. One day, Mrs. Flowers approached Grimes and told him that, since the girl was about to turn 17, he would have to start calling her Miss Stanley. Mrs. Flowers was attempting to force Grimes into his place in the racial order, but Grimes pushed back, replying that he would call his colleague Miss Stanley when she called him Mr. Grimes. The older woman answered that she would have to tell her husband; to this, Grimes responded that she could tell anyone she wanted, and he walked out. As it turned out, Mr. Flowers was not as concerned about the situation as his wife, or he found the young man to be too good a worker to let go, so he talked him into coming back to work.[1]

The circumstances Robert Grimes faced were not unusual ones. Rather, they were rules related to the social order in twentieth-century America, rules put in place by the twisted logic of white supremacy. Some were spelled out in the law while others were unwritten but every bit as potent and harder to delineate and therefore harder to avoid breaking. At times, it must have seemed like the rules changed overnight, as when Robert Grimes was required to change the way he addressed his co-worker. He knew the societal rules, but—most importantly—there was a line that he refused to cross. To his mind, he and his fellow worker were equals, and he was not going to allow her the greeting of adulthood, a form of respect denied to Black people regardless of age, if she did not return it. He understood the consequences, and he was ready to accept the loss of his job.

The young Grimes faced a twentieth-century situation that had roots in the post-slavery era. At the end of the Civil War, white people could have accepted that slavery was over and that, from that point forward, Black people and white people would live together as citizens of the republic. This did not happen. Instead, the vocal majority of white Southerners accepted the end of slavery but not the end of white supremacy, and tried to enforce the subjugation of Black people who were to remain in their assigned place, and that place was on the bottom rung. In this book, I write comprehensively about Black people in one Virginia county, people like Robert Grimes who learned the rules by observing his parents and other adults yet still, as a high school student, stood up to the demands of white supremacy.

The oppression engendered by white supremacy in the Upper South typically did not involve bodily harm or the destruction of property, yet Black people in the upper south, like Robert Grimes, contended with countless everyday aggressions designed to keep them in their place. Often they were unable to label what was happening to them, but well aware that they were fighting an enemy that was difficult to define but always present. In *Roses in December*, I chronicle the Black experience in Hanover County, Virginia, from the end of the US Civil War until the desegregation of county schools during the Civil Rights Movement to spotlight Black Virginians like Grimes who knew their assigned place and resisted it.

The great majority of the civil rights scholarship via books, articles, documentaries, etc. has focused on the Deep South and features a level of violence that was not as prevalent in Virginia. This has led many people in the public to assume that Black people in the upper south failed to resist the system of white supremacy. The scholars who have focused on the upper south, like William Chafe and Matthew Lassiter and Andrew Lewis have provided great insights into the white power structure.[2] This book focuses on the Black response to white supremacy.

This is a story of resilience and resistance in the Upper South. While the great majority of scholarship on this time period focuses on the deep South, this work brings attention to Black life in a largely unknown Virginia county and challenges anyone who believes that Black residents of the Upper South contributed little of importance to the struggle for civil rights.

Rather, across America during the era of disfranchisement, African American parents focused on two major childrearing goals: to shield their children from the realities of being Black in the United States while simultaneously preparing them for those same realities. Black parents knew that the day would come when their children would be tested, and they desperately wanted them to pass the test with as little harm, physical or emotional, as possible. They also prayed for the time when the testing would end—and the praying continues today. Charity Earley, a World War II veteran, wrote about this aspect of Black childhood in general that "as we grew older there came a gradual awareness of a Black social order and a white social order, each interdependent but separate and unequal."[3] Deborah Dabney Joseph, who grew up in segregated Ashland, Virginia, explains that there were just certain things you knew: For example, you knew where to go and not to go, where to sit and not to sit. She understood that if she was first in line at the drugstore a white person who came in after her might be served first. Of the public busses she said that "I never had anybody to tell me you gotta get up so I that can sit down, but you were just accustomed to doing that." According to Joseph, "Some things, you just knew."[4]

Under this form of oppression, those attacked lived with a sense of foreboding that was difficult to define but felt at every turn. Parents wanted their children to have access to the best education, but they knew that, while the teachers in Black schools would do their best, they were working in poor conditions with few resources. This oppression lived in the minds of Black parents as they tried to explain to their children why they did not have school buses, up-to-date books, and indoor toilets at school. So, while there were few instances of physical violence in Hanover County, there are many stories of Black people thriving despite the consistent, daily, subtle violence that weighed down the soul at every turn. Covering a full century, including the Civil War, Reconstruction, disfranchisement, and Civil Rights eras, *Roses in December* shows how Black life in a rural Virginia county centered on organizing, education, religious faith, and employment. From the end of slavery through the eventual desegregation of public schools, Black Americans in Hanover County remained resilient in the face of a system that consigned them, daily and in countless ways, to a place of inferiority, largely born out of and sustained by white supremacy. Chronicling their resilience is important because it adds a previously neglected dimension—that of an Upper South Black community in a rural environment coping with and even thriving in the face of quotidian oppression—to our understanding of the history of Black life in America.

Founded in 1720, Hanover County was once a part of New Kent County to the east. It is located in the Coastal Plain region of Virginia and directly adjacent to the rolling hills of the Piedmont. It is the largest county, as measured by land area, in the Richmond area. During the period covered here, the county was largely rural with the majority of the land dedicated to farming and very little to manufacturing. Before the Civil War, the over 9,000 enslaved people living in the county labored on farms, small and large. After slavery ended, most Black people, whether owners, renters, or sharecroppers, continued to work the land. From the slavery era until 1870, there was a Black majority in Hanover, but scholars have largely overlooked the county's Black population. Ashland, Hanover's only incorporated town, is home to Randolph Macon College, which provides a comparison between town and country life. While Hanover is a historically rural county, today it increasingly contains suburban neighborhoods, light industry, office buildings, warehouses, and distribution centers, along with considerable remaining rural areas. In essence, Hanover is one among many such communities across the South with similar profiles past and present, which adds to the importance of the story told here.

According to the 1860 census, there were 148 counties in Virginia and only one, McDowell County in what is now West Virginia, had no Black residents. Indeed, at the start of the Civil War, 34 percent of the state's population—including enslaved and free men, women, and children—was Black; east of the Blue Ridge mountains, the percentage was more than half Black. Demography and patterns of wealth, poverty, and slaveholding varied greatly from one region of the state to the next.[5] Each local study provides a piece of the puzzle that is Virginia and enhances our understanding that there is not one uniform South. The community I chronicle in *Roses* differs from most that have been written about in the past, and I hope this book provides a model for future place-based studies.

From the last days of slavery through Reconstruction, and from the onset of the era of disfranchisement to the Civil Rights Movement, *Roses* depicts both change and consistency. Some of the biggest changes were the US Constitutional amendments of the Reconstruction Era, which abolished slavery, defined citizenship, and applied the franchise to Black men for the first time. Public schools were established across the South and Virginia in 1870.[6] Black men sought public office and were elected to Congress and to local posts. In the twentieth century, lawyers chipped away at segregation laws to establish pay equalization for teachers, integrate the military, and declare that separate but equal was a fallacy and unconstitutional.

While these federal changes boded well for African Americans, many white southerners opposed them. In the South, many people saw them as threats to society as they knew it. White people believed these changes would lead to social interaction, therefore engendering "race mixing." Indeed, the fear of miscegenation fueled much of white supremacist ideology. White people understood that if their children went to school with Black children, they would become friends; they might then realize how much they had in common, fall in love, and have children, and this would dilute and eventually extinguish the so-called white race. White people resisted every measure promoting Black people's participation as equals. In some places, this resistance took the form of physical violence—church bombings, lynchings, arbitrary arrest, and more. In Virginia, Black people endured threats and trickery at the polls, the lack of adequate funding for education, and the blocking of employment opportunities beyond the service and agricultural sectors. While physical violence was less frequent in the upper South, the threat of physical violence was always a possibility reinforced by people's awareness of what was happening in other locales. Yet the most common form of violence that Black Hanoverians faced daily was violence against the psyche. The constant slights,

Introduction

the constant fight for better schools, to participate as citizens. It was the attack on their soul, mind, and spirit that was unrelenting but an attack that they fought and overcame in ways big and small.

The history of Black Hanover falls into three distinct historical periods—Reconstruction, disfranchisement, and Civil Rights. For my piecing together the story of Black resilience in Virginia across these three eras, I owe much to the work of Black scholars of the early twentieth century including W. E. B. Du Bois, Carter G. Woodson, and Luther Porter Jackson, who each in his own way showed Black resilience, resistance, perseverance, and ingenuity and they recorded where they saw it in others.[7]

In addition, John Kneebone's *Southern Liberal Journalists and the Issue of Race, 1920–1944* allowed me to understand how Black people and white liberals approached life during disfranchisement. Studying white journalists, Kneebone argues that white liberals sought and found a way to address racial oppression and render it less jarring without ever jeopardizing the social barriers between the races. Kneebone considers what he labels "vertical segregation," a form of separate-but-equal that provided a means by which Black and white people of similar class ranking could work together to eradicate racial injustice without raising concern among those white people who feared social mixing.[8] To his insight I add that Black Hanoverians developed "parallel lives" as a means of coping during segregation. Vertical segregation and parallel lives both allowed for necessary interaction between the races, but neither required nor sought social equality.

Roses also draws on recent studies by historians Heather Andrea Williams, Hilary Green, Nicole Myers Turner, and William Sturkey. With freedom came educational opportunities in the former states of the Confederacy. Some Black adults wanted to read and write so they could understand God's word for themselves, but they also wanted their children to learn because they desired a better life for them and saw education as the pathway to full citizenship. In *Self-Taught*, Heather Andrea Williams addresses the strong desire on the part of Black men, women, and children to learn to read and write. Instead of focusing on particular communities, Williams covers a broad swath of the South. She uncovers how Black people sought and obtained education before and after Reconstruction and finds copious evidence of their agency. Rather than depending on white people to provide an education for them, they acted on their own behalf to obtain the skills they desired.

Hilary Green argues in *Educational Reconstruction* that African Americans understood the importance of education and knew they would have to fight to gain and maintain access to this important avenue to citizenship. Comparing two urban areas—Richmond, Virginia, and Mobile, Alabama—Green finds that Black people understood that education was the key to full citizenship. This realization led Black people in these two cities to persevere despite obstacles placed before them. Indeed, Green describes Black people as victorious despite efforts of white people to curtail their educational opportunities.[9]

In *Soul Liberty: The Evolution of Black Religious Politics in Postemancipation Virginia,* Nicole Myers Turner takes on the intertwined roles of religion, politics, and community organizing in post-emancipation Virginia. Indeed, churches were "vehicles for participation and self-determination."[10] Like other historians, Turner finds that church leadership was mostly male, but she argues that this pattern was not inevitable and chronicles avenues open to women such as fundraising.

Recovering the perspectives of Black and white people from the late Reconstruction era through the Civil Rights Movement, William Sturkey focuses on Hattiesburg, Mississippi. Migrants looking for a better life converged on Hattiesburg from locations within and outside of the South. They sought employment and they organized political and social goals. In doing so, the Black people of Hattiesburg found ways to coexist with their white neighbors and enriched their own lives as they exercised their agency.[11]

Like these books, *Roses* finds Black agency, resilience, and resistance to white supremacy and confirms that Black people were not defeated by slavery or by the nation's retreat from Reconstruction. To the contrary, despite their previous circumstances, they were empowered by freedom to establish communities despite what white people wanted or expected. *Roses* also differs from these other studies by providing a comprehensive and braided narrative of church life, battles over education, the evolution of employment, and the nature of organizing in a rural Black community over a one-hundred-year period. Crucially, I find that the avenues to full citizenship chartered during the Reconstruction period remained a part

Introduction

of the Black experience in this rural Virginia county well into the Civil Rights era.

The church was a constant presence in Hanover County throughout the period covered here. It was a space that was at once spiritual and political. It was the one place where African Americans could operate unmolested, providing spiritual guidance and political clout. In the earliest days of freedom, the building was sometimes a school. Indeed, from that time until the integration of public schools, education was another key factor in Black rural life and proved the key factor in the struggle for citizenship. Black parents and other community members raised funds to pay the teachers, extend the school year, and add on to school buildings. Expanding opportunities to work and improving working conditions also became major concerns among Black people in Hanover County. Throughout the century of Black life that it examines, *Roses* finds the Black citizens of Hanover County organizing to achieve better schools and employment using the church building as a gathering space and as a spiritual guide, creatively braiding the three pillars of rural Black life—church, school, and work—to advocate for a better tomorrow.

As mentioned above already, *Roses* also disputes the popular notion that the concentration of physical violence against Black people in the lower South meant that the experiences of Black people in the upper South were less traumatic or less devastating. *Roses* argues that there are several types of violence, and all deeply affect individuals, families, and non-blood-related kin. While the continued study of the physical violence that Black Southerners endured in the era of disfranchisement and into the Civil Rights era (and arguably today) is laudable, it is just as important to understand federal, state, and local laws written to safeguard white supremacy as violent interruptions into daily life; to understand that living in constant fear, as Black Hanoverian Robert Grimes did, takes a huge toll; and that the Black parents who want their children to get a good education are also traumatized by the reality that this might not be possible because of factors beyond their control.

Each chapter of *Roses* considers Black life in Hanover County through the overlapping lenses of religion, education, employment, and organizing. Chapter 1 tells the stories of how, after generations of slavery, newly free men, women, and children embraced their circumstances with vigor and excitement. They did not cower, nor did they seek the supposed comfort of the "old" world they and their ancestors had known. They embraced freedom with ideas of what it could mean. While the vast majority of the formerly enslaved, male and female, worked the land as farmers or farm laborers, they also found employment as domestics, railroad hands, sawyers, shoemakers, carpenters, brick masons, and even a potter. In 1870, Hanover boasted over 130,193 acres of improved land being farmed or ready to farm, and farms and farm equipment valued at $3,346,486 was second only to Henrico County to the south, valued at $3,967,748.[12] The newly free also established churches so they could worship God in their own way. Shiloh Baptist Church was established in Ashland by 1866, first under a brush arbor and, according to the church history, they used a shack located at Langsford Crossing.[13] Black men and women also sought formal education through the Freedmen's Bureau and religious organizations, taking advantage of the opportunities presented, and forging their own way when nothing else was available. They embodied the line from a Phillis Wheatley poem that says, "In every human Breast, God has implanted a principle, which we call Love of Freedom; it is impatient of Oppression, and pants for Deliverance."[14] They were ready for deliverance—prominently including *self*-deliverance.

Once the Fifteenth Amendment enfranchised Black men, Black Hanoverians participated in state and local politics while simultaneously establishing a place for themselves in the governance of the county. Focusing particularly on political agency, chapter 2 features Black men, and by extension, the women in their lives, embracing the opportunity to participate in the franchise. They actively sought information, and one man ran for office. Chapter 2 argues that resilience, capability, hopefulness, and most importantly involvement in the shaping of their freedom remained the markers of success for Black Hanoverians despite forces exhibiting contempt for and resistance to the lives they were building. At every opportunity, they acted on their rights as citizens. challenging their designated "place" as they actively worked to build a future for themselves and their descendants.

Chapter 3 examines the forces outside Hanover County that affected Black life throughout Virginia. Attacks on the franchise heralded a bleakness that clouded the political future of Black Virginians throughout the

1880s and 1890s. Despite this reality, Black Virginians, including Black Hanoverians, continued to pursue avenues that they believed would lead to full citizenship with all its rights and responsibilities. They embraced self-help in myriad ways and pursued economic strength by buying land and establishing financial security for future generations. They opened businesses, educated their children, and leaned on their spirituality for strength.

Between June 1901 and June 1902, the state of Virginia held a constitutional convention, the main purpose of which was the elimination of most, if not all, Black male voters. Chapter 4 considers how Black Virginians, and especially Black Hanoverians, responded to the revocation of a right enumerated in the Fifteenth Amendment to the US Constitution. In the face of flagrant white supremacist ideology, Black Hanoverians organized, worshipped, sought better schools, and worked hard. Still aware of their role as citizens, they even took up arms to fight for democracy and worked on the home front during World War I. Ever resilient and willing to work against and within a deeply unjust racialized structure foisted upon them, Black Hanoverians shaped lives that ran parallel to those of white people and enabled them to continue moving forward in the 1910s and 1920s.

Chapter 5 finds Black Hanoverians on the global stage as they responded to economic depression and another world war. Once again, they stepped up and played their role as citizens against the backdrop of constitutionally guaranteed but unfulfilled rights. Despite the challenges of systemic racism, Black Hanoverians took advantage of opportunities presented by the New Deal and once again fought a war to safeguard democracy for others.

Lastly, chapter 6 looks at postwar Black Hanover and how Black people in the county responded to the call for Civil Rights, in step with people across the South, by participating in state and local action. There were no marches or boycotts in the county, but Black Hanoverians worked to improve the segregated education system and then to eliminate it in favor of desegregation. In 1950, they organized and happily celebrated the establishment of John M. Gandy High School, the first high school for Black students in the county.

By examining closely, the rural and ultimately quasi-suburban setting of Hanover County, Virginia, we can learn a good deal about the Black experience in America over the century between the end of the Civil War and the desegregation of public schools. This first study of Black life in Hanover County sheds light on a largely unstudied population and finds resilience and resistance to circumstances imposed on them from without. From the early days of freedom through the desegregation of Hanover County public schools, Black Hanoverians were productive citizens of the county, the state, and the nation. Through the lenses of religion, education, employment, and organizing we see a Black community built by people who sought to be active citizens, and who, when they met resistance to their involvement in civic activities, built lives parallel to whites in the county and continued to act as citizens. They constructed lives around their friends and families, lives that fostered their involvement in the larger community but that were not dependent on that community. As in the case of Robert Grimes, they resolutely carried on with their lives and exhibited resistance when it was necessary. They were resilient; they got it done.

Following Emancipation, the amendments to the federal Constitution, and the Reconstruction Acts, Black Hanoverians, like all Black Americans, desired and expected full citizenship, but they soon found that this goal remained out of reach. Instead, citizenship came via avenues of their own making. In the end, through their actions they taught their descendants that citizenship asserts itself from within the individual and the community, and this legacy has proven to be something that no one can take away. That descendants understand this history is more important than ever before. As avenues to full recognition of citizenship are once again being challenged, it is vital that all Americans, especially Black Americans, recognize what they have contributed to this country and what they deserve.

It is my hope that this history will serve to inform readers across the United States. Locally, the story told here has already been used in support of two national register nominations, for Brown Grove and Berkleytown, two historically Black neighborhoods in Ashland. It has also been shared with the Ashland Police Department as a means of introducing officers to the history of the town and county and to give them a better understanding of the historical events that might still color their interactions with Black Hanoverians. *Roses* is also an important addition to understanding the African American experience at the state, regional, and national levels. *Roses* adds to the genres of Southern Studies, Virginia Studies, the Long Reconstruction, and African American History by illustrating that the story of the South is layered and that all the versions need to be considered when telling "southern" history. At the national level, I hope that it encourages researchers all over the country to find and illuminate county-level studies.

Importantly, these Black Hanoverians were not an anomaly. There are comparable untold stories waiting to be uncovered in other counties throughout Virginia, across the South, and indeed the nation at large. *Roses* serves as a model for others willing to take the time to find the people, in all their diversity, who have faced unspeakable odds with grace, dignity, and resilience. Together these works will tell the untold stories, so that scholars can finally draw, with greater accuracy, a collective picture of the history of the United States. Historians must do this work so that textbook writers have the information necessary to write a history of the nation that is reflective of "we the people"—all the people.

1
Seeking and Embracing Freedom

"No child, it is not thunder but the Yankees is coming." Day after day this thunder seemed more distinct and so insistent that it seemed it was only a very few miles away. Many of the colored people grew frantic with fear because of the stories told to them by the owners to keep them from going away with the Yankees. They said they would cut off their noses and eyes and ears and fingers. Said the Yankees had only one eye and that was in his forehead. But mother said, "I don't care what they look like, God is going to take care all my children and me."

—George Washington Fields, Hanover Courthouse

AT THE START of the US Civil War, 16,965 people resided in Hanover County, Virginia, and of that number, 9,483 or 56 percent were African American. Of this Black majority, 257 were free. Most Black people lived and labored on one of the farms or plantations in the county. While there are no reports of uprisings in the area, given the opportunity, Black people self-emancipated well before the war. Between 1763 and 1803, 185 enslaved people ran away from their enslavers, and this number only includes the people for whom ads were placed in newspapers. County lore suggests that Negrofoot, Virginia, located in the Beaverdam District of the county, was the site where habitual runaways were punished by the cutting off of a foot, putting it on a stake and placing the stake along a well-traveled road so that enslaved people would be reminded of the fate of runaways.[1]

The stories of self-emancipating Black people are telling. Martha Ann Fields, George Fields's mother who rightly identified the sounds that George heard as the approaching Union Army, left Hanover County in March 1863 with George and five of his siblings.[2] Later in 1863, William Henry Winston, who was enslaved at North Wales also known as Broadneck, on the eastern end of the county, also walked to freedom behind the Union Army. A boy of fifteen, Winston soon found himself at City Point, Virginia, and by December 1863, he was in Norfolk, where he enlisted in the 2nd Cavalry, Company E, United States forces, commanded by Captain Tucker. Martha Ann and her children ended up at Fortress Monroe, in Hampton.[3]

Like young Winston and the Fields family, men, women, and children walked to freedom as soon as the opportunity presented itself. As an old man, a member of the Hanover County planter class recalled witnessing a large number of Black people leaving his family's plantation following a nearby battle. He remembered that the advance Union scouts rode by first, followed by the guard, then soldiers on horses carrying their dead, and next the wounded in wagons. Bringing up the rear was a large group of people referred to by the storyteller as "our colored people."[4] This group consisted of Black people with little more than the clothes on their backs and a desire to be free.[5]

This chapter will tell the stories of how, after generations of slavery, the newly free men, women, and children embraced their circumstances with vigor and excitement. They did not cower, nor did they seek the supposed comfort of the "old" world that they and their ancestors had known. They wanted to be free, and they had ideas of what freedom should and would mean. Through the eyes of Black people living in wartime Hanover County and those who remained in the county after the fall of Richmond, their first steps into freedom will shed light on their mindset and desires. In this chapter, I will highlight their resilience and argue that contrary to the myths, they were ready, willing, and able to live as free productive citizens of the county and state. In the early days of freedom, they made decisions for themselves and their dependents.

Roses in December

They sought paid employment, the freedom to worship God in their own way, and formal education. And just as important—they organized. They had already learned what slavery meant and how to navigate that institution. Now, they wanted to learn about freedom and the rights and responsibilities of citizenship.

Divided in two parts—wartime and the immediate post-war Hanover County (1861–68)—discussion of the wartime experiences will feature William Henry Winston, Hannah Johnson, Mildred Graves, Peter and Amy Storrs, and the Fields family. A picture of postwar Hanover will develop through the eyes of these same people with the added experiences of Dick and America Denton and the people of Hickory Hill.

Virginia seceded from the Union on April 17, 1861, and everything changed for Hanoverians, Black and white. The once quiet rural county and Ashland, its only incorporated town and a popular resort, faded into the background. One of the largest counties in the state, Hanover was the scene of many battles—Cold Harbor, Beaver Dam Creek, Gaines's Mill, Hanover Courthouse, Old Church, to name a few. Lying between Richmond and Washington, DC, the county's main roads were often filled with Union and Confederate troops on their way to or from battle. Ashland saw its share of transient soldiers and officers since the railroad and the Washington-Richmond Highway ran through the town proper. While Ashland was spared from any major battles and occupations, Union and Confederate troops—intent on disabling rail lines, obtaining supplies, or both—did visit. Many of the town's homes and churches served as hospitals for the wounded of both armies.[6]

The US Civil War was a total war, which meant attacking enemy resources on all levels, including personnel, food, shelter, and infrastructure. In addition to risking their lives in battle, soldiers also scavenged for supplies. Hannah Johnson, a formerly enslaved woman, remembered these scavenging Union soldiers when interviewed in the 1930s by a Works Progress Administration (WPA) staff person. Johnson, along with the family who enslaved her, moved from Richmond City, about fifteen miles to the south of Hanover, to Ashland. Johnson recalled that early one morning, men attached to General Philip Sheridan's forces knocked on the door and demanded the key to the smokehouse. According to Johnson, they took what they wanted and left a guard behind to keep the family out.[7]

Seeking and Embracing Freedom

While Hannah Johnson might have been appalled at the actions of Sheridan's men, taking provisions from homes throughout Hanover County was commonplace. Of course, if a battle was pending or taking place, the loss of food was the least of the landowner's worries. Sometimes soldiers on both sides took farm animals, tools, wood from house exteriors, and fencing. While these losses might be categorized as acceptable or at least understandable during wartime, some instances of physical injury or material loss are not as easily understood.

Mildred Graves, interviewed by the WPA in 1937, was a field worker and midwife who lived on the highway, now known as Route 1, that ran between Washington and Richmond. She described three encounters with northern soldiers. She wore her long hair in a braid that hung low on her back. One day, while working in the field, six federal soldiers attacked her. She resisted, but they succeeded in cutting her hair.[8] On another occasion, Union soldiers attacked Graves and as many as five other young women cutting their arms, legs, and backs with razors. The third time Graves encountered the Union army, the soldiers took her gold earrings.[9]

Graves believed that her encounters with Union soldiers were a consequence of living on the highway. Undoubtedly, accessibility was a factor, but the resentment of northern white working-class men, drafted to fight a war to free enslaved people, a cause that they might not have embraced, must be considered. Indeed, the men probably believed that they were superior to Black people and resented risking their lives for people who, when free, might take their jobs.

Today, many people labor under the misconception that most, if not all, northerners were abolitionists.[10] In reality, abolitionists were in the minority. In Graves and the others, the soldiers saw Black women and girls. Their gender conveyed weakness and their skin color inferiority. In short, Union soldiers viewed them as easy targets and deserving of punishment.

Mildred Graves alone or with female friends represented no real threat but did present a real opportunity for stress relief for Union soldiers, and these women became tangible objects to blame for the war, scapegoats of a sort. While treated badly, Graves' remembrances indicate that she might have escaped the fate of many Black women and girls raped by their supposed deliverers.[11]

Roses in December

Indeed, regardless of region, the vulnerability of Black women and girls was a persistent theme throughout the slavery era. From the time they were captured on the African continent, transported, and sold to enslavers, Black females were at the mercy of white men. Whether the men stealing them from their villages and marching them to the coast, the guards in the so-called castles or pins, or the seafarers transporting them to their future enslavers, Black women and girls were, in most cases, powerless against these rapists. The codification of their vulnerability in 1662 made a common practice into a way to increase wealth. Under English common law, the child followed the status of the father, but in 1662, the law changed so that the child inherited the status of the mother. In short, the children of the women they raped became the enslavers' property. Black women and girls were no longer simply a vessel through which the enslaver could exercise power, lust, and hatred, but also as means of increasing their wealth.

While the circumstances differed, Peter and Amy Dustry Storrs also encountered soldiers during the war. Free by the start of the war, Peter Storrs had been an enslaved shoemaker. Largely allowed to live on his own, Storrs paid his enslaver a certain amount at an agreed upon time while keeping fifty dollars a year for himself. Over time, Storrs saved enough money to buy land. As an enslaved man, he could not own land, so his wife, Amy Dustry, purchased the land. By 1858, Storrs had saved enough to purchase his freedom, and he and Dustry, along with their children, set up housekeeping. They built a two-story, four-room house, and acquired the necessary tools for running a successful farm. They seem to have built a comfortable life. This all changed in June 1864 when the Union Army camped on the Storrs's land.[12]

One Sunday evening, Union troops crossed the Pamunkey River; the next day, they came to Storrs's place and stacked their arms in a line a few paces from his house. The captain informed Storrs that the house was between the lines of the two opposing armies, and that battle would soon commence. He explained that he could not let the Storrs family pass to rebel lines, and if they tried to cross into Union territory, the rebels would probably try to shoot them. Storrs and his family had no choice but to hide in the potato cellar, and soon the firing began; it lasted about half an hour. When the Storrs family surfaced, the rebels had been pushed back, but the Storrs home was destroyed. The Storrses left the area in the company of the Union soldiers and spent the remainder of the war in Washington, DC.[13]

The Civil War in Virginia ended on April 9, 1865, and much of Virginia and the rest of the former Confederacy lay in ruins. The infrastructure—roads, railroads, canals, and bridges—was severely damaged. Farmers' fields—littered with human, animal, and material debris—looked as though they would never produce crops again. Sometimes, only chimneys remained where homes once stood. This was the lens through which white southerners viewed their circumstances. On the other hand, Black people saw freedom at the end of a very long tunnel.

Across the South, Black people defined freedom in different ways. Some found freedom in the ability to move throughout the region looking for family and friends sold away during slavery, others moved to a neighboring plantation, and still others, tired of the agricultural life, moved to the nearest city. For example, between 1860 and 1870, the number of African Americans in Atlanta, Georgia, increased from 1,900 to 10,000. While migration within the region was commonplace, migration out of the South during this time was minimal largely because of the lack of employment opportunities in the North.[14]

For the most part, the Black population in Hanover remained. On the eve of the Civil War, there were 9,740 Black people in the county, outnumbering the white population by just over 2,000. Of that number, 9,483 people were enslaved. In 1870, there were 8,562 Black people,[15] a decrease of 1,178, but Black people were still in the majority. Most African Americans remained on the land they knew best. They might have remained in Hanover because of the county's proximity to Richmond, which gave people access to the city without their having to move there. Black men and women traveled between Richmond and Hanover regularly for meetings, church events, and socializing.

While Black people were ready to embrace freedom, they also needed and deserved support. After accepting the idea that freedom for the enslaved was a war goal, the federal government then accepted the idea that it owed support to Black people and white refugees. In anticipation of the end of the war, the federal government established the Bureau of Refugees, Freedmen, and Abandoned Lands (Freedmen's Bureau)

Roses in December

in March 1865. A temporary agency, the bureau was housed within the auspices of the War Department and was to remain in place for one year after the end of the war. The bureau was unfunded, and it was to obtain funds through its management of abandoned property. The bureau was understaffed, and what staffing there was consisted mainly of former Union officers.[16] In hindsight, the bureau was set up to fail. It was the first government agency of its type, and there was no blueprint. There was also a lack of goodwill on the part of some of the agents assigned to work with the newly freed people. Some agents were corrupt and out only to make money for their personal coffers. Others resented Black people and resisted providing real assistance. Despite this reality, the agency did do some good.

One of the greatest horrors of slavery was the precarious nature of family life. Indeed, their families were not their own. While some enslaved people were in committed relationships, the "marriages" were not legal and could be pulled asunder at the whim of the enslaver. Enslaved people understood that death, debt, marriage, anger, greed, jealousy, etc. could lead to the breakup of family units. Black people often spoke of the dread and reality of this situation in narratives of the time and after.

One of the first tasks of the Freedmen's Bureau was to establish a marriage registry, enabling formerly enslaved couples to record pre-war marriages in a legal document. These reports put an end to the notion that the enslaved did not understand or care about the sanctity of marriage. In Hanover County alone, 199 couples reported their marriages, and three of the 199 had been together since 1816.[17]

While some white people argued that the formerly enslaved would not work without the leverage of slavery, the zeal with which the newly free sought paid employment put an end to that notion. Some found work as railroad hands, blacksmiths, domestics, and cooks, but in Hanover County, the great majority found work in agriculture. The county was largely agricultural before the war. According to the 1860 census,[18] local farms produced several agricultural products, the largest of which were orchard products, garden products, and butter. There were a few free Black people who owned and farmed land before the war. After the war, Black farmers owned, rented, sharecropped, or worked as farm laborers. Regardless of who owned the land, farming was a family affair for

Seeking and Embracing Freedom

African Americans, with the wives and children noted in the census as farm laborers. Along with their neighbors, Black farmers contributed to the production of buckwheat, orchard and garden products, butter, hay, hops, and wine in 1870. In 1880, farmers, including Black men and women, continued to produce similar products with the addition of tobacco, honey, Canadian peas, and cords of wood.[19]

Some Black people left the county for different employment opportunities or for other reasons. Hannah Johnson and Mildred Graves, the women who related their wartime encounters with Union soldiers, are two examples. Johnson returned to Richmond after emancipation, found work as a domestic and married James Johnson. Graves, who moved to the city for the first time, also married and found work as a domestic. Black women also found work as domestics in Hanover, but urban life might have been the enticement for Johnson and Graves.

In some instances, Black people were able to find employers worthy of their trust and therefore established agreements. On the other hand, they were at the mercy of former enslavers who resented the change in circumstances and refused to deal with them fairly. It was under these situations that Black people sought the assistance of the agents of the Freedmen's Bureau.[20]

Black men and women were now able to choose among employers based on financial reward and the potential employer's reputation regarding Black workers. By all accounts, the freedmen and women were ready, willing, and able to work for a living. The Hanover Freedmen's Bureau agents regularly acknowledged a willingness on the part of Black people to work. In 1866, one agent wrote that there were few destitute Black people because they wanted to work and support themselves and their families. He went on to say that the biggest challenge was finding employers who did not want to "tyrannize" Black people. Indeed, some whites would have re-enslaved people if they had not feared military intervention. Black people seemed to know who those whites were, and they typically refused to work for them. Those who treated Black people fairly had no trouble securing workers.[21]

Sometimes on their own and sometimes with assistance from a Freedmen's Bureau agent, Black people willing to work and white people willing to hire established sound and fair contracts. Unfortunately, white employers sometimes took advantage of Black people looking for work. In his May 1866 monthly report, Hanover County agent, Ed Murphy,[22] lamented that the freed men and women would be fine if not sabotaged by white people. Since most Black people were illiterate, they were at the mercy of employers to read and explain contracts. Murphy regularly received complaints from Black workers who believed they had been misled or lied to outright about the terms of contracts. The agent was usually able to mediate, but if he was not successful, the case might be referred to the Freedmen's court.

On September 27, 1865, Orlando Brown, the assistant commissioner for the Freedmen's Bureau for the State of Virginia, issued a circular regarding the establishment of a body to settle civil disputes and criminal cases between white people and freed men and women, as well as controversies between Black people. This body, which became known as the Freedmen's Court, consisted of three men. While the record does not explain how Hanover County selected the men, it does provide their names. The white citizens chose Williams C. Wickham, who was from an old Hanover family.[23] The freedmen chose Charles Morris.[24] It is not clear whether Morris was Black or white. The third man on the court was the assistant superintendent of the Freedmen's Bureau, Lt. Ed Murphy.[25]

The labor disputes most likely to reach the Freedman's Court involved Black men and women who entered into contracts without the aid of an agent and where oral agreements were reached. Such arrangements often led to non-payment of wages.[26] This was the case with America Denton and two other women who opted to remain on the plantation where they had been enslaved before the fall of Richmond. Choosing to remain on the plantation where they had been enslaved was not unusual for men or women.[27]

Because of their decision, Denton and the other two women entered into an oral agreement on April 3, 1865, with their former enslaver.[28] This agreement called for each woman to be paid five dollars per month. When she had not been paid by September, Denton approached her employer asking payment for services rendered. The farmer claimed that she had not been promised pay and that her services were not worth any more to him than the one dress annually, food, and medical care that she had received while enslaved.[29] America Denton left the farm.[30]

Seeking and Embracing Freedom

In April 1866, a year after the contested oral contract was established, Denton's husband and the husbands of the other two women took their case to the Freedmen's Court. The cases were heard separately, with Dick Denton[31] going first. Dick testified that all he knew about his wife's contract was what she told him. When questioned by the former enslaver, who, like Dick Denton, functioned as his own counsel, Denton admitted that he had also been in his employ and that his contract had been honored.

When questioning America Denton, the landowner asked her how many times a day she left the field to feed her baby and how much time she lost working compared with the other women. She responded that she worked as much and as hard as women who did not have children to feed. The farmer then questioned Jesse Brown, a Black man and employee, to ascertain Brown's opinion of America Denton's work habits.[32] Next, Dick Denton cross-examined Brown who testified that, when in the field, America Denton worked as hard as a man named George, but he clarified that America did not come to the field as early as George. Dick Denton then asked Brown to compare his wife's time in the field with that of a woman named Maria who also had a baby. According to Brown, Maria only left the field at dinnertime and therefore worked longer hours than America. Following Brown's testimony, the farm owner rested his case. Curiously, Dick Denton did not call any witnesses other than his wife. Theoretically, he could have called the other women to confirm the verbal agreement. After deliberations, the court found the employer innocent of having violated a contract with America Denton. The record does not indicate the rationale for the court's decision in this case, nor does it offer an account of how the three men voted, but the lack of a written contract, and the testimony suggesting that Denton did not put in the same hours as other workers, may have convinced the court that the employer was justified in not paying America. The court did not consider that the farmer acknowledged that America Denton had worked for him. Indeed, she had worked for him for five months without compensation.

Seeing the writing on the wall, the other two men withdrew their suits. In previous instances, when Freedmen's Bureau agents felt that Black people were treated unfairly by the legal system, they passed the evidence on to their superiors with the hope of finding justice in that arena; however, there does not seem to have been a formal appeals process. The fact that the agent did not refer this case to his superior might be an indication that he believed the ruling fair.[33] Also, the other cases in question involved males. While all Black people were free, Black women still had fewer rights than their male counterparts.

The Denton case raises questions about the judicial system as it concerned women, whose legal status after the Civil War was complex. In general, married women, regardless of race or class, had few rights that were not conveyed to them by men. Before and, for a time, after the Civil War, married women in Virginia lived under the coverture umbrella, meaning that at marriage, their husbands gained control of their property. This allowed men to buy, sell, encumber, and use as payment of debts, land brought into the marriage by their wife.[34] This ability left women vulnerable. Even before the Civil War, some wealthy fathers had begun to will land to daughters, married or single, and some husbands left control of their assets to the wives they named executors. Some men, concerned about the welfare of their wives, set up separate estates, by a trust deed, marriage settlement, or special bequest, ensuring their wives and daughters' financial security. During Congressional Reconstruction, Congress extended new rights to women. The rights afforded men and women were still not equal, but the new opportunities granted women were significant, such as the right of married women to own property, known as the Married Woman's Property Rights Act, which Virginia adopted in 1877. These acts gave married women control over their property and earnings.[35]

Class and race played a role in how women and the law interacted. The husbands and fathers of poor women, Black or white, had no land to leave, so the question of landed property rights was moot. Like elite white women, poor women also had no vote, and thus had little to say about their own circumstances. Poor white women and Black women were also less protected than their wealthy counterparts—while the men in their lives had the right to vote, they had relatively little economic power.

A second issue raised by America Denton's case surrounds the perception of Black women in general and Black motherhood in particular. Based on the men's testimony, it appears that the farmer did not have a problem paying Black men. It was the women he refused to pay. Given the employer's line of questioning regarding Denton's child, it is obvious that her responsibilities as a mother were seen as detrimental to her role as a worker. Denton testified that she cooked and cleaned for her employer before going to the field after sunrise. She left the field two or three times a day, once for lunch, once between lunch and dinner, and sometimes between dinner and sunset, to feed her baby. While in the field, she hoed and grubbed, and "worked as hard as a man."[36] While not mentioned in the testimony, it is highly likely that the men stopped once or twice during the day to eat and take care of other needs. For five months, the farmer had a diligent worker who took care of his domestic needs as well as worked hard in the field. She received no financial compensation at all, not even a partial payment.

If the women had been paid, it is unlikely that they would have received wages comparable to the men. Gender bias was written into the Bureau's labor policies, which instructed that Black men and women were to receive compensation based on their sex and not their ability to work.[37] This policy can be seen in action in Hanover in 1867, when Black men typically earned $7-$10 per month, and the women earned $3-$4 per month for fieldwork.[38] With the exception of their ability to reproduce and add to the wealth of the enslaver, Black women had always been undervalued and unworthy of protection. Indeed, Black women were to work, giving one hundred percent, without regard to personal or familial needs.[39]

Another question concerns the Black men who appeared before the court in the Denton case. It is not clear that they felt free to question a white man and testify honestly and openly. While Dick Denton was not then currently employed by the defendant, he had been in the past, and he may have wanted to keep the option open. This would certainly explain his rather tepid testimony on his wife's behalf. Then, too, Dick Denton may have used this opportunity to establish some control over his wife—even, perhaps, as the white man asserted his authority over him. Another possibility is that the employer may have intended to pay the women when they first struck their agreement. When it came time to pay, the farmer may not have been able to pay. The postwar economy was still struggling, and he may have been unwilling to go hat in hand to people he had previously enslaved to explain his financial situation, and therefore handled matters as he would have had he still been their "master." What he failed to realize was that these women, especially America Denton, were no longer enslaved, and they now had the option of leaving or at least attempting to force him to honor his word. There is no indication of what happened to America and Dick Denton after her case was lost. Since they were young and healthy, they most likely secured employment elsewhere.

Many Black people, like America Denton, worked on the plantation where they had been enslaved but not all faced employers who refused to acknowledge contracts. There were instances where landowners, eager to move forward with reestablishing their business, honored contracts established with those they formerly enslaved. On June 7, 1865, for example, one Hanover plantation owner and nine people formerly enslaved by him entered into an agreement within a few months of wars end. Edmund and Bob were to receive $5 a month, John $4 a month, and George, Andrew, and Anthony, $2.50 each per month. Melinda and her four youngest children and Margaret and her two children were "to receive their board." Finally, Patsy was to receive her board and clothing. Additionally, the landowner agreed to provide board to all free of charge while employed by him and acknowledged in the contract that either party, employer, or employee, could end their arrangement at the end of each month. This agreement was witnessed signed by the landowner and witnessed by three other white men.

The contract does not indicate the type of work that each person would be doing, but clearly, the work that the women were to perform was not seen to be as valuable as the work of the men. In essence, Melinda and Margaret were not paid because everyone received board. Patsy was remunerated with clothes. Another issue raised by this scenario relates to Melinda and Margaret's children. While they all appear to have received board, there is no mention of their clothing. The employer takes care to mention several details, so it seems unlikely that he would accidentally overlook the children. Perhaps the children were too young to work, and they no longer added to the wealth of the employer. They cost him money instead of adding to his coffers.[40]

Remaining on the plantation where they had been enslaved was a decision that many formerly enslaved people made. Given the circumstances, it made sense that some would remain among those they knew at least until they got their bearings and could think through their best options. This was true of many of the laborers at Hickory Hill, which encompassed 3,360 acres and was reputedly one of the largest and most beautiful plantations in Hanover County before the war. Located three miles from Hanover courthouse, it was famous for its four-acre garden. After the war, the owners found themselves with limited means, but were eager to move forward. In need of a labor force, they began paying formerly enslaved families. Until around 1870, they paid the men $7.00 and the women $2.50 per month and offered former slave quarters as housing. To make sure that the workers remained all year, the workers were only paid two-thirds of the wages for each quarter and then paid the remainder at the end of the year.[41] Controlling Black people was still the end goal.

While finding employment was paramount in the minds of the newly freed men and women, establishing an independent spiritual life was also important. As early as August 1866, the Colored Baptist Convention took place in Richmond's Ebenezer Baptist Church. The convention attracted many participants. In fact, there were so many that the sanctuary and the basement lecture room were used for communion. Additionally, many individuals were baptized, signifying the expansion of the church in the community.[42]

The Black church in general and this convention were places where Black men could exercise the rights of freedom. A newspaper account explains that several northern white men were present, but they had no roles in the proceedings, and none were appointed to committees. Indeed, at least one white minister was reportedly given the "cold shoulder," and still another who "loved the [Negroes] better than any people on God's earth" failed to make any real headway into the leadership of the assembly. The actions of the Black convention leadership suggest that they saw maintaining control over their spiritual lives as vital to the maintenance of their freedom.[43] Also, there might have been some leeriness of the notion of white men "loving" them like no other people. This type of patriarchal "love" was the last thing a group of Black men seeking to establish and confirm their place in society would desire.

The following year, the Colored Shiloh Regular Baptist Association of Virginia, an organization of Black congregations met, at Manchester Baptist Church just across the James River from Richmond, for its third annual gathering.[44] At least one of the Black churches in Hanover, First Shiloh Baptist Church, was represented at the meeting.[45] Each day began with prayer and singing followed by a sermon. Cold Spring Baptist Church of Southampton County sent a letter to this assembly, which the presiding officer read aloud; he pointed out that Southampton County, located in southeastern Virginia, had been the place where Nat Turner "first struck for freedom."[46]

The Nat Turner comment caused great controversy in the press. The editor of the Richmond *Daily Dispatch* chastised the convention moderator, saying that he was misleading Black people and that "Nat Turner's massacre was the most barbarous and brutal of all human butcheries." Continuing, the editor suggested that allowing these types of comments did nothing to bring Black and white people together—indeed they served to widen the breach between "Afro-Virginians" and "those whose prosperity is theirs, and whose peace alone can give them repose."[47]

Like the refusal of the Colored Baptist Convention to allow white church folks to infiltrate the leadership, the presiding officer's decision to make the connection between the location of Cold Spring Baptist Church and the site of Nat Turner's rebellion, was another attempt to establish the bounds of freedom. Black people and white people had very different perspectives on Nat Turner and the meaning of his rebellion. To Black people, Turner was a revolutionary, a hero, and to white people, he was a "barbarian."[48] They had already forgotten or never even considered the barbarity of the institution of slavery.

Other convention business involved the discussion of several resolutions. On the second day of the assembly, the members resolved to recommend that Black churches remove the word African from their names "as we are not Africans, but Americans" with all that term endowed. Indeed, all they knew about Africa was what they had heard from white Americans who saw Africans as barbaric and useful when enslaved. There was no reason for Black people to embrace the moniker. They understood that it was their labor that had built the American infrastructure and economy. They intended to have what they had earned and deserved.[49]

The second resolution reflected the financial situation of the association. At the start of the convention, the treasury held $100.07 and with contributions, that amount was raised to $257.73. With $312.93 paid out, the total financial resources at the end was $44.87.⁵⁰ Given this status, it is not surprising that the second resolution called on each member church to take quarterly collections to help with the mission work of the forty-five churches in the association.⁵¹ It is not clear how the money was to be used, but there were six traveling male missionaries (preachers), including Burrell Toler of Hanover County, who were responsible for carrying the gospel to rural communities. Part of the funds might have covered any expenses incurred by the preachers. It might also have covered salaries if they were paid. During the convention, the men reported that they were meeting with success, and it is safe to assume that the leadership and the body of the association recognized the need to continue to fund this work.

Perhaps the most telling resolution involved a special "thank you," which read: "Resolved, That the thanks of this Association be tendered to the 40th Congress of the United States for the [Reconstruction Acts] passed by them, enfranchising us as citizens and giving us protection in the exercise of all our rights and privileges and we earnestly advise all our brethren and friends to vote for righteous men to be put into authority, for the Scriptures say that 'when the righteous are in authority the people rejoice, but when the wicked rule, the people mourn.'"⁵² This resolution offers insight into the political involvement of the leaders of the association. It also indicates that the Baptists gathered understood and appreciated their rights and privileges as citizens. Surely, this resolution, printed in the white newspaper and probably widely read, must have caused white Virginians to take notice that the Black population they had once subdued through legal and extralegal means was taking their citizenship seriously and intended to exercise their rights.

By 1870, there were between eight and ten Black Baptist churches in Hanover County.⁵³ During the era of slavery, Black people had typically worshipped under the auspices of their masters, or in biracial churches of their choosing (which, however, were led by whites), or in secret spaces outside the prying eyes of the enslaver. In short, they had not been free to express their spirituality in their own way. Freedom brought change. By 1867, most Black worshippers had withdrawn from white churches on their own or at the invitation of the white members. Either way, they were free to worship in a manner that suited them and to choose their own leadership.

For example, the minutes of the Mount Olivet Baptist Church in Hanover show that on December 3, 1865, the members resolved "that the colored members numbering about two hundred, be dismissed from that church and discharged from all obligations to the church as members thereof, and left free to act for themselves."[54] This group became Ebenezer Baptist Church of the Beaverdam section of Hanover County. Similarly, a group of thirty-two Black worshippers withdrew from Taylorville Baptist Church in 1868 to form Jerusalem Baptist Church at Bothwell, now Doswell. Neither of these congregations had the benefit of a church building when first formed. In most instances, Black congregations first worshipped in brush arbors until they could purchase land and build structures.[55]

Regardless of where they worshipped, freedom opened doors. They could now worship without oversight. Without having to listen to white preachers teach them that they were slaves because God had made them so. They could hear the Exodus stories and celebrate with their Old Testament heroes because they too had been freed by the God they had prayed to, not the one enslavers wanted them to know and revere.

Shiloh Baptist Church, also known as Shiloh Freedmen's Church, of Ashland began worshipping in a brush arbor, shortly after the end of the war. The membership soon erected a building and held a wedding there in December 1866. Like so many African American religious structures of the period, the building also housed a school.[56] Next to finding work and establishing places of worship, Black people wanted an education. Many adults simply wanted to learn to read the Bible for themselves, but they also hoped education would bring a better life for their children.

Before the war, organized education for Black people had been against the law. Some people, Black and white, violated that law, but for the most part, education remained out of bounds for Black people. As a result, at the end of the war, Black people worked from scratch as they established schools. They also worked against the wishes of some white residents who felt that educated Black people would conflict with their place in society.[57]

Regardless of these obstacles, education did become a reality for many Black Hanoverians. Between 1866 and 1870, eight schools for Black children were organized throughout the county. Some operated a few months annually for several years, while others lasted for much shorter periods due to lack of funding. Some schools were in facilities owned by Black people with the rent paid by the Freedman's Bureau. Some of the buildings were owned by white people sympathetic to the desire of African Americans to have access to education, or who were at least willing to accept rent money from the Bureau each month. In some cases, the freedmen wholly supported the school, meaning that they paid for the teacher and owned the building. In other instances, Black people partially supported the school, which sometimes meant that they boarded the teacher. Depending on the time of year and the fate of the crops, the freedmen might not be able to maintain their financial commitment to the school, which could pose a hardship to the teacher.

Many of the schools received support from northern aid societies. In Hanover, the New York Friends and the American Baptist Home Society were the major contributors. While the records do not indicate where the teachers in those schools came from, they do suggest that many of the white teachers were from outside the area and probably outside the state. The teachers who opened day schools in the county typically also opened night schools where adult pupils paid tuition, which helped to maintain the day schools. Sabbath schools were also popular, sometimes enrolling as many as 370 students but at other times as few as 30, depending on the time of year.

While records are sketchy at best, we know that a school was opened at Ashland under the patronage of the American Baptist Home Society and housed at Shiloh Freedmen's Church in October 1866. By December, the school boasted 102 students.[58] The Shiloh Freedman's Church employed a young Black man, unnamed in records of the time, who formerly had been a teacher in Richmond. He charged students fifty cents each month. The bureau helped by supplying books at wholesale rates. The bureau agent described the building as "new and very comfortable as well as very suitable for school purposes." The agent concluded his report by commending Black families for taking responsibility for their education and expressed his belief that schools organized by local Black people themselves would meet with less hostility than schools organized by northern philanthropies.[59] At the beginning of the following school year, a new agent wrote to his superiors that the freedmen and women continued to be interested in the "cause of education." He indicated that he was selling at cost, books supplied by the American Tract Society, a nineteenth-century organization that printed and dispersed religious pamphlets to the masses.[60]

The challenges faced by Black Hanoverians trying to obtain an education were like those of other African Americans across the state, but they remained undaunted. In August 1867, the superintendent of the Virginia schools operated with the support of the Freedmen's Bureau, reported that much had been accomplished by Black people across the state during the 1866–67 school year. The average number of students enrolled during the year was over fourteen thousand, and the superintendent believed that the entire number of Black students attending school during the year, including public and private schools, was over twenty-five thousand. He asserted that several thousand Blacks across the state had become readers. This success was attributed in large part to dedicated and well-qualified teachers, most of whom were associated with northern philanthropies, such as the American Baptist Home Society and the Religious Society of Friends (Quakers). Additionally, Black teachers were being trained to teach Black children.[61]

Although the Ashland school was up and running by 1866, it was not easy to maintain the student population. One reason was the poverty of the students' families. If parents paid the fee of fifty cents per child each month, they might have to do without warm winter clothes. In the winter of 1867, the bureau agent requisitioned two hundred suits of children's clothes for such families—and these were not the county's truly destitute citizens. Without the proper clothing, the children would not have been able to attend school.[62]

The response of county whites to educating Black people varied greatly, based partly on the area of the county and the year. Throughout 1868, Julia Carter, the Black teacher at the Ashland school, reported that white attitudes in the area toward educating Black people were positive. The next year, she moved to the school at Hanover Junction, and throughout her tenure there, she reported that the attitudes of white people were very bad. John Cooper and William French, both white teachers, took over the Ashland school after Carter left, in 1869 and 1870, respectively. Both men reported less than favorable attitudes toward educating Black students. The difference in the substance of these reports might boil down to the fact that Carter, a Black woman, hesitated to report trouble at the Ashland school. As a Black woman, she was vulnerable and may have felt threatened by white people in the community, whereas Cooper and French as white males may have been freer to report the true situation. Moreover, Cooper and French went to the Ashland school after the constitutional convention of 1868, when conservative white people were still reeling from the outcome of the elections and the proposed state constitution.

Black people organized to find employment, to establish churches, and to obtain an education and formed the path to survival after Emancipation, but the franchise as elaborated in the federal Constitution and the Reconstruction Acts was the key to involvement in the governing process. By March 1867, Congress enacted the Reconstruction Acts over President Andrew Johnson's veto. News spread quickly among Black southerners. By April, Black Hanoverians inquired of the Freedmen's Bureau agent about the acts. They wanted to know about their duties and privileges under the new laws. "The same concern in political matters is manifested upon the part of the colored people throughout the county," the agent reported.[63] The 9,740 Black Hanoverians enslaved before the war were free, and as the agent suggests, they intended to act on that freedom.

Whether they took their freedom like William Henry Winston when he walked off the plantation behind the Union Army or became free after the fall of Richmond, like America Denton, they all embraced their new status. While they still had to define freedom for themselves, after generations of enslavement, Black Hanoverians knew that it was the only option for human beings. Some Black Hanoverians moved away but most remained with expectations that they would join the community on a new level. In those early days, they boldly sought all that freedom meant even when they met barriers. They found jobs and participated in the local economy, tackled literacy, worshiped, organized, legalized longstanding families or began new ones, and sought assistance when needed. Most of all, they discovered what it meant to be a citizen with rights, and they exercised those rights. When they came against white supremacy they fought back, sometimes with their fists and other times through the legal system. They spoke up for themselves; they quit jobs if they were being abused. They were free men and women, and all they wanted was to be able to live with that freedom.

2

The Politics of Reconstruction and the *Entente Cordiale* That Never Was

THERE WERE PEOPLE living in the Confederate States of America who remained Unionists. Many lost property during the war, and by 1871, they became eligible to claim reimbursement for losses incurred during the war. Peter Storrs, a Black man claimed his losses.¹

Peter Storrs had been an enslaved shoemaker, largely allowed to live on his own and paying his enslaver a certain amount while keeping fifty dollars a year for his personal use. Storrs was married to Amy Dustry, a free woman, and they were parents. Over time, Storrs saved enough money, which Dustry used to buy land. Storrs then began to save to buy his freedom. He and Dustry set up housekeeping. They built a two-story, four-room house, and acquired the necessary tools for running a successful farm. They seemed to have built a comfortable life. This all changed in June 1864 when the Union Army camped on the Storrs land.²

One Sunday evening, Storrs later recalled, Union troops crossed the Pamunkey River; the next day, they came to Storrs's place and stacked their arms in a line a few paces from his house. The captain told Storrs that the house was between the lines of the two opposing armies, and that he expected to be attacked immediately. The captain explained that he could not let Storrs and his family pass to rebel lines and that if they tried to cross into Union lines the rebels would probably try to shoot them. Storrs and his family had no choice but to hide in the potato cellar, and soon the firing began; it lasted about half an hour. When the Storrs family came up from the cellar, the rebels had been pushed back. The Storrses left the area in the company of the Union soldiers.[3]

Beginning just after the passage of the Reconstruction Acts in 1867 and encompassing the start of public education in Virginia and the rise of the Funders in state politics, this chapter explores the Black experience in Hanover County, highlighting Reconstruction Era politics at the national, state, and local level.[4] Employment, spirituality, organizing, and education are the lenses through which Black people will be heard.

Black Hanoverians did not "toe the line" placed before them by white Hanoverians. Like the Storrses, they took advantage of the rights of citizenship. They exhibited resilience, capability, and hopefulness. Most importantly, their involvement in the shaping of their freedom remained the markers of their success, despite forces exhibiting contempt for and resistance to the lives they were building. Benefitting from changes at the federal level, they participated in state and local politics, while at the same time building a future for themselves and their descendants, kith or kin. At every opportunity, they acted on their rights as citizens, challenging their "place" as designed for them by white people in the county.

In July 1867, the *Richmond Daily Dispatch*, a white paper, published a letter from someone calling themself Ruta Baga. In addition to reporting the good weather and fine crops, the author shared the news of a "rather singular matrimonial alliance" between a nineteen-year-old Black woman and a sixty-seven-year-old Black man. According to the writer, Black people in the area felt that the "ebony damsel was tricked by the aged wooer." Making textual caricatures out of the couple, Ruta Baga's letter goes on to claim that Black and white people in the county were interacting on a civil basis and that "freedmen in this section, I am pleased to state, are working faithfully. The best feeling prevails between them and the whites, and I trust that the *entente cordiale* may remain unbroken."[5] There are no clues to Ruta Baga's identity or even if there was such a person. The writer might have been a foil for the paper's editor or most likely a white person who wanted to send an anonymous message to the community. The messenger could have been a Black person pointing out that Black people were working hard. It was most likely a white person, maybe the editor of the paper or a subscriber. Either way, the message

Roses in December

communicated that the freedmen were acting in accordance with their place as imagined by white people in the county.

A month later, the *Daily Dispatch* received another letter lauding the state of race relations in the county. Commending an impromptu speaker at Hanover Courthouse, this correspondent reported a large gathering of Black people hoping to hear an African American traveling preacher. The guest speaker was a no-show, so John Wallace, a native Black Hanoverian, took his place. His words were probably soothing to the white listeners in the crowd. He admonished Black attendees to be polite, honest, industrious, and sober. The white writer explained that the speaker's "plain, earnest, home-spun sentiments went right to their [Black men's and women's] hearts."[6] There is little doubt that Wallace's words went right to the hearts of the white listeners as well. Like Ruta Baga, this letter writer appreciates Black people who remained in their place—polite, honest, industrious, sober—on their face, not bad traits for anyone to exhibit. But when used by white people in the county, these traits took on the meaning of subservient people who understood that they were of inferior stock. A key question to consider is whether the *entente cordiale* that Ruta Baga touted ever existed, and if it did, was its existence contingent upon Black people acting a certain way, which is to say was it based on Black men and women acting as they were forced to act when enslaved?

The fragility of the *entente cordiale* could have been foretold in the immediate aftermath of the war on the national level. While Black Hanoverians worked toward solidifying their freedom, the country's leadership awakened to a harsh reality. The wartime president had been assassinated. While the Freedmen's Bureau was in place, there was no formal plan for post war reconstruction. The vice-president turned president, a southerner and no friend to the newly freed, tried to restore the South to the Union as quickly as possible under a plan known as Presidential Reconstruction.[7] This plan offered few real opportunities to Black people or protection against the machinations of former enslavers. White people understood that a system of labor, based on slavery would never be restored, but the white leadership that was installed in the South put in place laws aimed at reining in the actions, activities, and freedoms of Black people.[8] The states of the former Confederacy established ordinances defining where Black men and women lived and worked, how they raised their children, and how they socialized. Virginia, too, enacted these laws, known as Black Codes, aimed at controlling the state's labor force. Vagrancy and labor contract statutes were passed, as well as "anti-enticement" laws aimed at curtailing efforts on the part of employers to lure workers away from their present places of employment, which were largely tied to agricultural work.[9] In general, most white southerners wanted to maintain some approximation of the hierarchical structure in place during slavery. An article from a southern newspaper, quoted in 1865 in the New York *Tribune* noted, "We must keep the ex-slave in a position of inferiority. We must pass such laws as will make him feel his inferiority; and while we give him ample protection in his 'person and property' we are finally lost if we permit ourselves, by an abstract would-be philosophical reasoning to admit him [to] any position that [seems] of the slightest equality with the White man."[10] Some white northerners interpreted these sentiments as an indication that the former Confederates did not understand their position as the conquered party in the war. Many northern Republicans and their congressional representatives questioned whether the South had really changed its ways.

After the elections of 1866, when the Republicans obtained veto-proof control of Congress, they took steps to overturn the effects of Presidential Reconstruction. First, they put forth a bill to extend the life of the Freedmen's Bureau.[11] Second, the Congress submitted a civil rights bill to the president. This bill conveyed citizenship to all people born in the United States and established that these citizens had the right to enter into contracts and file lawsuits, and to enjoy "full and equal benefit of all laws and proceedings for the security of person and property."[12] These rights were for all individuals without regard to race. The president rejected both bills, but Congress overrode the vetoes. The term of the Freedmen's Bureau was extended and the Civil Rights Bill of 1866 became law.[13]

To strengthen the 1866 bill, Congress ratified the Fourteenth Amendment, which, among other things, encased the tenets of the bill in the Constitution. Indeed, the first section of the amendment defined citizenship and protection of civil rights. The second section explained apportionment with regard to representation. Section three disqualified officeholding by individuals who participated in insurrection or rebellion.

Fourth, covered what was and was not an acceptable public debt, and finally, section five allows Congress to enforce the amendment.

Ten legislatures in the South rejected the amendment for at least two reasons. First, most white southern voters opposed endowing Black people with equal citizenship, and the legislators reflected the views of their constituents. Second, the amendment disfranchised all men who had taken a loyalty oath to the US Constitution before the war but then aided the Confederacy by holding office under it. According to many white Southerners, this disqualified the best men from taking political leadership in the South.[14] The rejection of the Fourteenth Amendment propelled Congress into a full-fledged reconstruction of the South. Congress ratified the Fourteenth Amendment to the US Constitution on July 28, 1868.

The Fourteenth Amendment was not a plan for Reconstruction; that task still lay before the federal legislature. In 1867, Congress passed the Reconstruction Acts, dividing the South into five military districts, which required each state to hold constitutional conventions to form new governments, write new state constitutions, and ratify the Fourteenth Amendment.[15]

Under the Reconstruction Acts of 1867, Virginia became military district number one. In order to comply with the requirements of the Acts and rejoin the Union, Virginia, like each of nine other states of the former Confederacy, held a constitutional convention.[16] The idea of amending the state constitution was not alien to Virginians. In 1830, Virginia established a more equitable basis for assigning representation in the General Assembly. In 1851, a new constitution removed property restrictions on the franchise allowing all white males to vote and providing for popular election of local officials. Thomas Jefferson had even written that regular review of a document such as the Constitution was vital to the life of the document and of the country. What was novel in 1867–68 was that Black men participated in the political processes of the state.

Black men in Hanover were ready for the challenge of participating in county and state politics. Reportedly, Black people in general were becoming more and more distrustful of white politicians; at the same time however, the Freedmen's Bureau agent believed that Black men would unite behind loyal (Unionist), intelligent white men who supported the

Reconstruction measures. The voter registration process began and by June 1867, 329 Black men registered in Hanover County compared with 307 white men. White men who had not remained loyal to the Union during the war were not eligible to vote. The process went smoothly, with Black men returning to work after registering without being accosted. By July 27, 1867, 1,398 Black male Hanoverians had registered to vote.[17]

With the election scheduled to take place in October, a Republican mass meeting convened at Ashland on September 21, 1867, for the purpose of nominating men for the positions of delegate and "floater" to the constitutional convention.[18] Colonel William James and John B. Crenshaw—both white—were nominated unanimously by the mostly Black electors, but the story of the selection of delegates was far from over; more than a little drama would be revealed before the final votes were cast.[19]

On September 27, 1867, William James and John B. Crenshaw were elected delegate and floater, respectively.[20] James was an attorney by training and the federally appointed Collector of Internal Revenue for Virginia in 1865. Described in one newspaper as "disreputable" for taking a bribe, James pled not guilty before a jury of four white and eight Black people.[21] The defense must have been convincing, because the jury took only moments to find the defendant innocent. Crenshaw was a husband, father, Quaker minister, and described by his daughter as a friend to Black men and women in the community. She went on to say that before the war, her father raised money and sometimes used personal funds to help enslaved Black people purchase their freedom. Described as an eloquent speaker for the rights of Black people, after the war, Crenshaw helped open an orphanage in Richmond for Black children.[22]

Both James and Crenshaw expected to run unopposed by other Republicans. This was not to be the case for Crenshaw, however. Shortly after the meeting at Ashland, Crenshaw learned that he would be running against Burrell Toler, formerly enslaved, a carpenter by trade, and a traveling preacher.[23] Crenshaw was familiar with Toler, who initially declined to run for either delegate or floater at the mass meeting citing his lack of education and preparedness to hold either position. Indeed, Toler had thrown his support behind Crenshaw. Undoubtedly surprised to hear that Toler had agreed to run against him, Crenshaw believed that certain Hanover Republicans had urged Toler on because Crenshaw had expressed disapproval of William James. Indeed, Crenshaw believed that James's removal from government service, made him unfit to "represent the interests of the people of that noble old county."[24]

Burrell Toler was not without standing in the community. According to the 1870 census and his son's marriage registry information, Toler was born in Hanover County and most likely enslaved. His name does not appear on any of the property tax lists under the heading "free Negroes" from the 1840s through 1865, nor is he in the federal census of 1850 and 1860. The 1870 census indicates that he was a Baptist preacher and carpenter.[25] By March 1867, Toler was listed by the Freedmen's Bureau as one of the "prominent citizens" in the county, respected by Black and white residents alike.[26]

In the fall of 1867, citizens across the South cast ballots and elected 265 Black delegates to represent their districts at their respective states' constitutional conventions. Some of the Black delegates were educated; others, like Toler, had learned life lessons on farms and plantations. The African American delegates were ministers, artisans, farmers, teachers, and laborers. Some freedmen and others had spent all or part of their lives as free men in the North.

Hanover County voted in favor of the convention in voting patterns that reflect Black people as engaged citizens. Just over 1,400 Black men and 63 white men in the county voted to hold the meeting. Only 2 Black men voted against the convention along with 1,003 white men. Virginians elected 105 convention delegates, including 24 African American men. William James and Burrell Toler garnered 1,460 and 1,338 Black votes, respectively. Crenshaw was out of the running, receiving 10 Black votes and 1,057 white votes. Three Black men voted against the convention.[27] Conservative white men voted against the convention because they understood that Black men would receive the suffrage in a new constitution; that alone repelled them, fearing that the next step would be social equality. Some white people in the county believed that Black and white residents were getting along well and hoped to see this type of cooperation continue. Following the referendum on the matter of the convention and the election of delegates to that gathering, these feelings of goodwill diminished greatly. The near unanimity of Black voters dismayed white conservatives. They could not understand why Black men "should have refused to support those who, when they had the power, ground them down under the worst form of oppression," the Freedmen's Bureau agent noted sarcastically. The agent reported that Black people neither professed nor manifested any ill will toward their former enslavers, but neither did they trust them, as demonstrated by their votes. [28]

The result of the election caused at least one Hanoverian to put pen to paper. "A Citizen" writing to the editor of the Richmond *Enquirer and Examiner*, applauded the editor for asserting in a previous editorial that white citizens could and would live without Black people. He added that he had hoped that the formerly enslaved people could be made into useful members of society, but by their votes they had "proved themselves traitors to their own interests, and prefer to be led on to utter degradation and want by men who, with oaths and threats, and for a counterfeit twenty-five cent note, will lead the whole race into utter ruin and damnation."[29] A Citizen concluded by saying that the residents, presumably white people of Hanover, were raising money for "old Jack Bias," a Black man who had voted the Conservative ticket of his own accord; "in honor of his high appreciation of the White man and his fidelity to his friends, this fund is being raised," the writer reports. "Peace and quiet would [reign] if all were Jacks."[30] Bias may have been one of the three Black men who voted for the Conservative ticket. There was an African American man named John Bias listed in the 1870 census.[31] Of course, the writer may have invented Jack Bias to make a point. The point being that Black men who remained in their place would be supported.

The convention began on December 3, 1867, and by December 22, the Black renters on the Broadneck Plantation discovered the high price they would pay for not being "Jacks." Shortly after the election, the many Black renters at Broadneck were told that they would have to leave at the end of the year. A white man rented the land from a white landowner and in turn rented the land to Black farmers. He made a point to tell the men that they had no business voting the way they had. The renters had heard rumors that the landowner planned to turn them off the land without warning just before Christmas, but since no written or legal notice had been issued, the Bureau agent believed that the manager was just trying to scare the Black people and, in the end, would allow them to stay. This was not the case.[32]

The Reverend James Weatherless, who had been enslaved at Broadneck, had been a renter there since the fall of Richmond.[33] On December 22, 1867, even though his name had appeared on the bureau's list of prominent citizens respected in the community, Weatherless received a letter from the manager saying, "it will not be in my power to supply you with a house next year." When confronted by the Freedmen's Bureau agent, the manager responded that he rented the land from someone else, and that person was calling the shots in this situation. The agent wrote a letter of warning, but the record is silent as to the outcome of this situation.[34] Incidentally, the owner of the land had run for the position of delegate to the constitutional convention and exactly two Black people had voted for him; he may well have felt bitter over that result.[35]

The convention moved forward and regardless of the circumstances surrounding Toler's election to the position of floater, he went on to participate actively at the convention in Richmond. He served on at least two committees, including the Committee on Taxation and Finance and the Committee of Thirteen, which established the operating procedures of the convention.[36] Toler also presented two resolutions. One involved the institution known as the Eastern Lunatic Asylum, in Williamsburg. At the time, the US military ran the facility. Toler's resolution called for the Committee on Public Institutions to "inquire into the status, funds and present management" of the hospital with the idea of turning it over to civilian control as soon as possible.[37] Toler's second resolution charged the Committee on Internal Improvement to look into funds allocated some years earlier for a railroad line that was to extend from Fredericksburg to Gordonsville. Work on the line stopped because of the war, and Toler's resolution asked the committee to ascertain the amount of state funds already spent, whether the investment was justified, and whether the public was still committed to the project.[38]

Toler's role at the convention presents interesting questions. There is little doubt of his dedication and commitment to his job. He was present for every vote, and while his vote often matched his colleagues from Hanover, this was not always the case.[39] The questions that arise focus in part around Toler's background and ability. Considering his self-proclaimed lack of experience and training, and the obvious sophistication of the resolutions presented, might mean that Toler was under the guidance of someone else.

Of course, there may have been clerks charged with the responsibility of translating all resolutions into the appropriate legal language. Even if this were the case, questions remain. For example, why was Toler so concerned with issues that did not affect his constituents directly—constituents who, just out of slavery, might have had more pressing concerns. Were these the issues important to the Black men who elected him? The issues of the poll tax and the whipping post would seem to have been more relevant to Toler's constituents. The record does not show Toler's level of participation beyond his various votes, and it might never be clear what his role was on committees or in debates. Of course, if Toler had focused laser-like on the concerns of his constituents in Hanover, he might have been accused of parochialism. In short, his record can cut both ways.[40]

The convention of 1867–68 produced the Underwood Constitution.[41] A very democratic document, it outlawed slavery, gave equal civil and political rights to all citizens, provided for state-funded public schools, enacted the secret ballot and annual legislative sessions, and established townships with the hope of increasing the number of local elective offices, which in turn was supposed to put the people closer to their government.[42]

It is difficult to know with certainty the feelings of white Virginians regarding the Underwood Constitution, but there were definite indications of discontent at the state level. One sign was the rise of the Conservative Party in the late 1860s, a direct response to Congressional, also known as Radical Reconstruction. This party consisted mainly of individuals who resented the Black male franchise and disfranchisement of former Confederate government officials and soldiers who had been disloyal to the Union.

A level of rage existed in Hanover that took form in physical attacks by white people displeased with Black people exerting their rights as citizens. Refusing to remain in their place, Black citizens were considered unacceptable. Three recorded incidents illustrate this frustration. The treatment of John Lewis, Jacob Powell, and Andrew Jackson suggest that the *entente cordiale* had indeed been broken, if it had ever existed for noncompliant Black people.

In August 1868, a member of the family that John Lewis served before the war murdered him for the offense of giving instructions to a group of white workers. According to the employer, Lewis, who was sixty-five or seventy years old at the time of the incident, was out of bounds. After the two men had words, which must have further enraged the killer, the white man picked up a shovel and hit the older man in the back of the head, killing him instantly. The coroner determined that the killer had acted without malice or premeditation. Bail was set at $2,000. By December, the courts had declared the white man insane and acquitted him.[43]

Two months later, a similar incident, involving two laborers, one Black and one white, took place on a Hanover farm. Jacob Powell, along with two other Black men, was in the kitchen for breakfast. According to testimony, Powell joked that he could knock down any man in the room. A white man approached Powell and the two men struggled with the Black man getting the better of his enraged attacker. The white man grabbed an axe to hit Powell, but the other two men stopped him. He left briefly and returned with a brick that he threw at Powell. Still not satisfied, he left again, and this time returned with a shotgun and shot Powell, blinding him in one eye. He also accidentally shot one of the other men. The shooter went straight to the justice of the peace and turned himself in.[44] At the trial, the defendant's attorney took advantage of the racism of the jury. He pointed out that his client was an ex-Confederate soldier, a Virginia gentleman, and a white man. Powell was simply a "nigger." In the end, the shooter, found guilty of unlawful shooting, was sentenced to twelve hours in jail and fined one penny.[45] Both cases were heard by the county court, and in both cases, the local Freedmen's Bureau agent believed the decisions unjust, and he reported the outcome to his superiors for review. There is no indication that the cases were reviewed. Black Hanoverians understood that the injustice of slavery was not behind them, and these cases served as reminders that political power would be the key to bettering their lives. There are not as many details about the third incident but in December 1868, a full year after the start of the convention, a white man beat Andrew Jackson, a Black man, "over the Head with a stick."[46]

The Underwood Constitution gave Black men the franchise, free and clear, and in those counties, including Hanover, where African Americans were in the majority, conservative whites feared "black rule." The Conservatives were desperate to regain political control of the state. Since the Republican Grant was now president, they knew they were no longer able to hope for rescue from that quarter.

If the Conservatives were going to regain political control, they would first have to rid the state of the occupying military force. To do that they needed a constitution that would be acceptable to Congress. The Underwood Constitution fit the bill, and so the Conservatives voted to ratify that document even though it was described by at least one contemporary as "the liberal [arm] of a bi-racial General Assembly that was . . . composed in measure, of aliens and strangers."[47] With the ratification of this radical constitution, then, ironically the Conservative plan to retake Virginia was well underway. In 1869, the Conservatives decided to make a serious attempt to win the governorship. To do so they withdrew their candidate, backed a moderate Republican slate, and thus split the latter party's vote. The moderate, Gilbert C. Walker, won in a landslide, thus opening the door allowing Conservatives to take back local and state offices.[48] One year after the Conservatives' success of 1869, the United States Congress voted to restore Virginia to the Union, thus ending Radical rule in the state and beginning the removal of the federal army.[49]

Despite what was happening in the county and state concerning the new constitution, Black citizens continued to seek redress for wrongs committed against them. Citizens in good standing, who had lost property during the war, were now eligible to take claims to the Southern Claims Commission. While the Freedmen's Bureau was declining in visibility by 1870, the Southern Claims Commission remained important.[50] On July 4, 1864, a Congressional Act provided for the reception of claims from loyal Unionists who had lost property during the war in states not in rebellion. In the late 1860s, southern Unionists began to file claims, but it was not until 1871, when the power of northern Radicals had begun to wane, that an act was established to replace losses incurred by loyal Unionists in states that had seceded. The President appointed three commissioners who investigated each claim and reported their findings to the House of Representatives. The House then voted to approve the claim or not, and appropriate funds to pay. The Congressmen usually went along with the recommendation of the commissioners. Eleven Hanoverians applied for aid under this commission. There were two African Americans among them: Peter Storrs[51] and Frances Coleman.[52]

The application for reimbursement required that applicants explain any actions on his or her part that appeared to have aided the Confederates. Storrs admitted that Confederates demanded his services as a shoemaker for three weeks during the spring of 1864. He also acknowledged that during the war, he had traveled to Richmond on several occasions to deliver or pick up shoes. At these times, he had to get a pass—the same kind of pass he had carried while enslaved. Storrs said he had not taken an oath to obtain the pass, and he had always been a loyal Union man. When given the chance, Storrs insisted he had done all he could to help the Army of Generals McClellan and Grant. He had cooked for them, helped with the sick and wounded, and given any information he had to the Union troops.[53]

In support of Storrs's application, three others gave depositions. One was a Black man named Richard Dandridge. He testified that Storrs was a Union man and always believed that if the North won, he would get his rights. Dandridge went on to explain that, since obtaining the right to vote, Storrs had always voted Republican and was an officer in the Union League, an organization affiliated with the Republican Party, which encouraged Black men to register to vote, offered protection to Black people, and supported Republican Party candidates. Regarding the items taken by the Army, Dandridge claimed to have been present when the soldiers removed the items in question. After all was destroyed, he went, along with the Storrs family, to Washington. He returned with them in May 1866, and they found that the land was as "naked as your hand." Dandridge signed his deposition with an X.[54]

Taylor White, a Black man, also gave a deposition. White, who said "he [Storrs] believed, like all of us did, that the North would set us all free."[55] B.C. Burnett, a white man, gave the third deposition. He reported that he had known Storrs all his life and explained that someone named Truehart had enslaved Storrs. Burnett said that as long as Storrs made a certain number of shoes every two weeks, he could keep any extra money. Burnett explained that he thought that Amy Dustry had bought Storrs about 1858. Shortly after Storrs became free, Burnett added, he had bought a horse, which he kept until General Philip Sheridan's raid.[56] Storrs's application claimed that he had lost $1,145 in property. Storrs received $115.[57]

Similarly, Frances Coleman encountered Sheridan's Cavalry, commanded by General George Armstrong Custer, in the spring of 1865. Described in some accounts as a freeborn woman, Coleman was a widow at the onset of the war. At other times, she was said to have been freed by Charles Crenshaw, who sold her twenty-six acres of land. Likewise, some accounts suggest that she owned twenty-six acres of land in her own right, while others indicate that Nathaniel Crenshaw held the deed until after the war. According to Hanover County deeds, Coleman purchased the land from John B. Crenshaw and his wife Judith. The purchase was recorded in November 1868.[58]

Regardless of her circumstances before the war, Coleman insisted afterward that she had been a loyal Union woman who took pride in the fact. She declared that she did not know exactly what the war was about, but that she had always felt that the northern people were her friends. This belief may have been fostered by her Quaker employer, Nathaniel Crenshaw, who sent deserving[59] free Black people north if they wanted to go and if not, he employed them. Whenever the Union army came through Hanover, Coleman said, she provided assistance. She did laundry and cooked for the men when she had food to cook. On the occasion when Custer and his troops stayed on her farm, Coleman sacrificed far more than she had in the past. She lost food and supplies, her mule, and all the rails that had enclosed her twenty-six acres, which the soldiers used as firewood.[60]

George Coleman, Frances's thirty-three-year-old nephew, offered a deposition on her behalf. He explained that during the war he lived on her place and saw her daily. They both worked for Nathaniel Crenshaw. George said that his aunt was a strong Union woman, and that she had often spoken of hoping the Yankees would win so that she and her people could have their rights. Her "whole prayer" was that the Union would win. Frances Coleman claimed $597.75 and received $278.[61]

Frances Coleman and Peter Storrs may have exaggerated their pro-Union activities in order to gain government compensation. It is possible too, that such activities were not typical of Black Hanoverians during the war; that only two African Americans filed claims in effect defines those individuals as atypical. Even so, Storrs's and Coleman's stories suggest that pro-Union sentiment and even activity existed among Hanover's Black people—a suggestion that resonates at least in part with Booker T. Washington's reminiscences from western Virginia. Moreover, Storrs's and Coleman's attempts to obtain restitution show that they understood themselves to be citizens, and as such entitled to take advantage of opportunities enjoyed by citizens.

The treatment of these two people, first by Union forces and later by the claims commission, might or might not have been racially motivated since, as stated earlier, obtaining provisions was a key to soldiers' survival, and necessary provisions were obtained wherever they might be found. In all, there were eleven applicants to the Southern Claims Commission from Hanover County. The dollar amounts awarded to Frances Coleman and Peter Storrs seem very low, but on the surface, they do not appear to be inconsistent with awards given to white male applicants (there were no white female applicants). For instance, of the eleven applicants, seven, including Coleman,[62] received half or more of the requested amount. William Timberlake, a white man, received less than a third of the funds requested, and Peter Storrs requested almost ten times more money than he received.[63]

The difference between the amounts asked for and subsequently received by Peter Storrs is explained by the investigator, who begins his report by saying that he had talked to three white men who had known Storrs for a while. One of those white men was B.C. Burnett, who explained Storrs's circumstances and how he had acquired the money to buy land and his freedom because the agent believed that since Storrs had been enslaved up until just before the war, it was questionable that he would have had property valued at over a thousand dollars. In addition, Burnett said that Storrs did not actually own the mule he claimed but was merely in possession of it when the Union soldiers took it. Storrs received $100 of the $125 he asked for his horse and $15 of $26 he requested for three hogs. He was not reimbursed for the loss of his house, fence panels, or farming tools. There is no explanation of why these items were not allowed, especially since fencing was allowed for others, including Frances Coleman.[64] It is impossible to understand the process behind Storrs's reimbursement, except as racially motivated. If there was resentment on the part of the decision makers that this Black man had accomplished so much, Storrs was punished for stepping out of his place.

Racism might have been a factor in the attitude of the investigator. The first sentence of the interviewer's report on Peter Storrs says that the investigator had spoken with three white men. Although he did include the depositions of two Black men in the final report, he took the word of the white men, who were not on the scene, instead of accepting the Black men's accounts.[65]

Like Storrs and Coleman, many Black Hanoverians understood the value of land, but unlike those two, most did not have the opportunity to purchase or have unimpeded access to land until after the war. William Henry Winston, who walked off William Carter's plantation in 1863, purchased land in October 1866, presumably not long after returning to Virginia in the wake of his service in the Union Army. Winston bought five acres for fifty dollars.[66] Two years later, Winston and his wife Agnes partnered with Joseph Tinsley and his wife Jane, another Black couple, to purchase 25½ acres in Hanover County's Henry District. The two couples held this land until 1883, when they split it—the Tinsleys, who had paid one-third of the price for the land, received 8 ½ acres, and the Winstons received the remaining 17 acres.[67]

William Clarke and his wife Eliza were among early postwar African American landowners in Hanover County. Land records show that the Clarkes bought one hundred acres in 1867. One year later, Clarke and three others inherited land from a woman named Amy Winston. Winston's relationship to Clarke is unclear, but the others named in her will were all Winstons. Amy, listed in the 1842 tax register as a free Black person, paid property taxes over the next decade, on two to four enslaved people and one to two horses. At least two of the enslaved people mentioned were minors, possibly her children. In fact, it might well be that all of those listed as enslaved were family members; by not formally freeing them, Winston could preclude their being required to leave Virginia, as a law of 1806 ostensibly required of Black people freed after that year. In

1868, Winston bought eighty-five acres of land, the acreage that she would later leave to Clarke and the others.[68]

Burrell Toler, the former constitutional convention floater, purchased twenty-five acres of land in Hanover in 1871, shortly after his service at the convention ended. He bought the land from fellow delegate, William James.[69] Records indicate that Toler and his wife Sally sold two acres of land to another Black couple, John and Sarah Ellett, in 1873.[70] Later, Toler on two occasions borrowed money using the remaining land as collateral. He successfully repaid the initial loan, but he failed to repay the second loan and the land was auctioned off in 1881. Toler died in 1880.

Elizabeth Hogg, later Elizabeth Tinsley, described in a post-war deed as a free woman of color, was also a landowner of some note.[71] While the records are incomplete, Hogg acquired land before the Civil War. During the conflict, she sold 104 acres of land to a white man for $4,500. While she signed land transactions with her mark, it is evident that Hogg was not ignorant of the ways of business. In 1874, she sold land to Shiloh Baptist Church in Ashland.[72] Hogg also held notes on mortgaged lands, and even took the board of the Mutual Building Fund and Dollar Savings Bank to court. By the time this institution declared bankruptcy, some of Hogg's land had somehow become entangled in the bank's dealings. To regain her land, Hogg sued the bank, but lost her case in the Hanover Circuit Court. She went on to petition the District Commissioner of the United States for the Eastern District asking to join in with *A. Cappell and Company v. the Mutual Building Fund and Dollar Savings Bank of Richmond*. While she had to pay lawyers' fees, she got her land back.[73]

Elizabeth Hogg was a woman of mystery and intrigue. She was a prewar landowner, but unfortunately, the prewar land records had been taken to Richmond for supposed safekeeping and burned during the evacuation fire of April 1865. What is known provides a fascinating picture. She was a landowner, she was uneducated, and she was bold enough to take on a group of white men in court to obtain what she believed she was owed. Hogg's actions might be a sign of the confidence she attained as a free woman of color during the antebellum period. She might have always assumed the system was open to her when she had a grievance. At the same time, according to the stories that have been passed down through the generations, Hogg was extremely light-skinned and could have passed for a white woman.[74] This may have meant that she had a white father in the community, someone from whom she learned and possibly even someone who was powerful enough and willing to shield her. He might have also been the source of the land she owned.[75]

Financial wealth was not the path to full citizenship for most Black Hanoverians. While agriculture provided the greatest source of income in the county, most Black farmers did not own the land they farmed. Manufacturing was not a viable solution at that time. Indeed, according to the 1870 census, there were thirty-nine "manufacturing establishments" employing one hundred and one individuals. Just under $13,000 a year was paid in total wages in manufacturing. In comparison, over two million dollars was paid in manufacturing wages in Henrico County, Hanover's neighbor to the south. Over $130,000 was paid in agricultural wages in Hanover. Most Hanoverians, Black and white, earned their living off the land.[76]

It was during this time that a remarkable phenomenon began to take shape in Black communities throughout the South. Indeed, it began to gel almost as soon as slavery ended. Freed people organized thousands of self-help societies, sometimes in conjunction with their formerly free Black neighbors. Often these organizations were formed among friends, family, and church members who had known each other before emancipation. People banded together to address needs and promote members' welfare, a trend that had been evident throughout slavery and continued through Reconstruction and the era of disfranchisement.[77]

Evidence of Black people finding strength in numbers and in organizing can be found in the records of the Freedmen's Bank in Richmond, the financial institution resorted to by countless Black people, and in the annals of Black beneficial societies.[78] The names of some of these organizations, such as the Soldiers Aid, Laboring Mechanics, and the Sewing Circle, suggested their purposes and their membership. Many of these societies were founded by churches or at least had strong religious leanings. Examples of religiously affiliated organizations were the Sons of Simeon, the Sons and Daughters of Wresting Jacob, the United Order of Tents, Daughters of Zion, Soldiers of the Cross, and the Christian Call of Love Society.[79] Black men and women in Hanover were aware of the benefits of organizing. Burwell Toler, the former delegate to the 1868 constitutional convention, opened an account at the Freedmen's Bank in the name of the United Sons of Love of Ashland. He was the president of the organization.[80]

In many instances, these societies acted as insurance companies. Individuals contributed monthly dues in return for a decent Christian burial when the time came. As these organizations evolved, they also endeavored to teach men and women proper hygiene, attire, eating habits, and public demeanor; in short, they taught their members how to take care of themselves, their families, and their homes. A phenomenon known as the "politics of respectability" took shape. Some Black people believed the reason white people worked so hard to keep them down was that Black people did not know how to conduct themselves properly—they were not articulate enough or neat enough, they had unruly children, they spat on the sidewalk, they dressed inappropriately. Of course, with the privilege of hindsight, these concerns were not the reason white people believed Black people inferior. During the early days of freedom, hoping for acceptance as full members of society, some Black people concluded that such behavior needed alignment with normative definitions of "respectability" as constructed by the white hegemony and dominant white gender norms. Those who adhered to this philosophy believed that full acceptance would come with acceptable behavior on the part of Black men, women, and children.[81]

Fighting negative racial stereotypes became the purview of women. Generally, it was the role of the women to acquire proper etiquette and learn how to take care of their homes and families. It was then the woman's role to make sure that Black men understood how to maintain proper decorum in public and at home. This was not simply a matter of wanting the approval of white people; it was also a key to survival. The weaponization of Black sexuality provided a platform from which to attack and limit the power of Black men and women who might be tempted to step out of their place. Many white people saw Black men as a threat to the purity of white womanhood and used that canard to rationalize the phenomenon of lynching—when in fact most individuals lynched had not even been accused of a sexual infraction. Black women, perceived by many white people as oversexed and unable to control their lust, were raped and sometimes lynched by white men, typically without recourse.[82]

The Politics of Reconstruction

The new constitution's most significant contribution to the state was the establishment of public schools for all children. Black men and women saw education as a key to their freedom, opportunities, and their acceptance as citizens. Schools opened immediately following the war were typically set up by the freedmen and women themselves in collaboration with the Freedmen's Bureau and northern missionary societies. Heavily in demand, these schools were never adequate in number.

In 1871, the first year that education was available to all Virginians, more than 130,000 students enrolled, and Republican-Conservative Governor Gilbert Walker declared that the issue of public education for everyone was no longer a debatable topic. J. B. Brown, a white man, became the first superintendent of the Hanover public schools in September 1870. The county was divided into five school districts: Beaverdam, Allen's Creek, Ashland, Clay, and Henry. That year there were 5,260 students in the county schools, and half of them—2,668—were Black. There were twenty-eight schools for white students, and sixteen for Black students. There were twenty-eight white teachers and seventeen teachers for Black students. Salary breakdowns based on race are not available, but the record does indicate that male teachers earned $26.06 per month on average, and the female teachers earned $26.90. This was the only year that the female teachers earned more than the males.[83] At the end of the first school year, the Virginia superintendent of public instruction made a report, declaring the year a success. The average length of the sessions was just under five months. Statewide, the expectations were high, with school officials predicting that there would be at least two thousand schools in the state by April 1871 for Black and white youth. Yet the education of Black and white children in Hanover County and across the state would never be equitable. Annual (and later, biennial) reports from 1870 to the end of the century consistently show white schools and teachers outnumbering those for Black children.[84]

Throughout the 1870s, the Hanover superintendent reported success in the schools despite financial hardships. Indeed, Brown lamented that a lack of funds was all that kept the school system from flourishing. Even the negative attitudes of white people toward public schools in general, and toward educating Black people specifically, seemed to improve. By 1873, Superintendent Brown reported that "few intelligent persons offer any opposition to the public school system; and where we find one opposed to it, such opposition is confined to whispered insinuations among his especial friends and admirers." The following year, the teachers reported that the schools continued to grow in popularity. Brown suggested that the biggest detriment to the schools was the "threatened passage" of the proposed civil rights bill.[85]

While Black Hanoverians continued to work to establish themselves as free men and women, the political climate in the state continued to bubble with uncertainty. By the late 1860s, the Conservative Party moved to take Virginia back from the radicals but by 1871, there was another concern centering on the state debt. By 1871, the state debt exceeded $45 million and the concern over this debt crossed party lines. There were Conservatives, Democrats, and Republicans who believed that the full debt had to be paid, regardless of how that affected the state budget. Indeed, this was a matter of the state's honor and its future economic vitality. The result was the Funding Act of 1871, and its supporters were called the Funders.[86] The 1871 act did not have a great impact on the state debt. By the end of the 1870s, the Funders were losing their grip on Virginia's government. Failure to listen to the masses, especially concerning public schools, cost the Funders votes. Additionally, there was an atmosphere of "mistrust, jealousy, and intrigue" fueled by nepotism and backroom deals, which left the Funders vulnerable to the Readjusters who understood that the Funders' approach would cause financial hardship on Virginians. Not a group to give up without a fight, the Funders began a campaign of fear. They warned white voters that, if they did not stick together as a race, they would find themselves under "Negro rule." In addition to this tactic, the Funders were not above election tampering and bribery. They also instituted a poll tax and reduced popular control of the government, cutting the size of the House of Delegates and moving from annual legislative sessions to biennial sessions. The Funders gerrymandered county lines to reduce the impact of the Black vote. The township system was eliminated and the threat of restoring the prewar political system was leveled.[87] These tactics on the part of the Funders, however, succeeded mainly in pushing more of the electorate into the arms of the Readjusters, who won control of the General Assembly in the elections of 1879.

In the years from 1865 to 1879, Virginia experienced serious political and social upheaval. White Conservatives struggled to hold on to some semblance of the state they had loved before the war. They understood that the era of slavery was over but believed that there must be some way to rein in the formerly enslaved, if not by the whip, then by the law. The conservatives had not bargained for a population of Black citizens who would not be subdued. They had not counted on Black people's interest in politics. They had expected a docile labor force, lost without the firm hand of the master. What they found instead was a population of working people with minds of their own and a will to succeed.

Black men and women in Hanover County and elsewhere wanted to organize, work, worship, and learn on their own terms, and for a while they accomplished this feat, with assistance from federal authorities, despite all the forces lined up against them. Black men voted, and Black men and women participated in civic life, some bought land, they organized, and generally continued the process of building lives as citizens of the county, state, and country. They became, and remained, a force with which to reckon.

3

An Uneasy Citizenship

The Path to Disfranchisement

ALTHOUGH THE POLITICAL FUTURE of Black Virginians looked increasingly bleak throughout the 1880s and 1890s, they continued to pursue avenues that they believed would eventually lead them to full citizenship with all its rights and responsibilities. While the vote continued to be a valued indicator of citizenship, the paths to upward mobility that were more firmly controlled by Black citizens themselves had not altered much since the early days of freedom. They embraced self-help in myriad ways and pursued economic strength by buying land and establishing financial security for future generations, opened businesses, educated their children, and leaned on their spirituality for strength and for answers.

William Taylor was born into slavery in Caroline County, but by the early 1870s, he lived in Hanover County just south of Caroline. In 1874, during revival week at his church, Taylor accepted the call into the ministry. The following year, he married Rachel Waller in Beaverdam, and together they worked as sharecroppers. They met with some success, enough to be able to afford to buy a cow, but Taylor wanted more. He desired an education so that he could preach the Gospel. To this end, he and his wife sold their personal belongings, including the cow, and by 1876, Taylor was studying theology and music at the Richmond Institute.[1] When Taylor signed the Richmond Institute registrar's book, he declared that he had been born enslaved at Spring Cottage in Caroline County on April 28, 1854, and that he had been baptized by Rev. Stephen Anderson in August 1868 at Ebenezer Baptist Church in Chilesburg, VA.[2]

After his first year, he received a scholarship. Taylor's wife supported his dreams, but three years of working and raising the children took its toll, so Taylor left school before completing his studies. Initially, the family returned to farming and this time earned enough to buy two cows. Taylor also taught music at Union, Jerusalem, and Bethany Baptist churches in Hanover. By 1883, he was teaching in the Hanover County Public Schools.[3]

The Taylor family's success might have been aided by the existence of the Readjuster Party. From 1880 until 1884, the Readjusters, supported by the votes of Black men and many white men, did much to improve the living condition of Black Virginians, but by the mid-1880s, the political scene had changed in favor of Conservative Democrats who were not inclined to offer many benefits to the state's Black population. As a result, Black Hanoverians, along with their compatriots in Richmond, began to shift away from an emphasis on advancement through political channels and concentrated their efforts around self-help through large-scale formal organizations and other avenues established at the end of slavery.

The Readjusters—an odd coalition of white and Black people, former Conservative Democrats, and Republicans—supported the civil and political rights of Black citizens in the state in exchange for their vote. During the Readjuster period, there were thirteen African Americans in the General Assembly. They, along with their colleagues, provided a mental health facility in Petersburg for Black Virginians, banned the whipping post as a punishment for crimes, and repealed the poll tax.[4] While the Readjusters experienced electoral success in 1879, the Funders, who received 42 percent of the vote that year, continually nipped at their heels. Two years later, in 1881, the Funders garnered 47 percent of the vote, but their numbers were still too low to overthrow what some of them viewed as the "middle class 'riff raff' that had taken charge of the government." The Funders stepped up their efforts to regain control of the state government.[5]

By 1882, the Readjuster Party had begun to lose its tenuous grip on state politics. The fabric of the improbable coalition was beginning to show signs of wear and tear, yet the Readjusters went on to accomplish perhaps their greatest achievement on behalf of Black Virginians. In 1882, the Readjuster legislature passed a bill establishing a state college in Petersburg for Black citizens. Alfred Harris, an African American representing Dinwiddie County near Petersburg and known as a great debater, helped carry the fight for the school during a lengthy debate in the legislature.[6] Regardless of the obstacles, the Virginia Normal and Collegiate Institute (VNCI) (today Virginia State University) opened in October 1882.[7]

While unsuccessful at stopping the establishment of a state-supported college for Blacks, the Funders were not deterred. They morphed into the new and improved Democrats, promising honest government, sound financial management, and support of public education. They began a campaign of fear and intimidation warning white voters that radical rule would return to the state bringing mixed schools, social equality, and miscegenation.[8] This type of propaganda stirred up conservatives across the state, including Hanover County where, according to one historian, Black men were threatened and stoned to keep them from the polls during the 1883 elections.[9] In 1883 the Democrats took over the General Assembly and two years later, they won the governorship. While the Readjusters did not disappear from the scene for another twenty years, the 1883 election amounted to the party's death knell.[10]

Finally, back in power and afraid of losing it, the Democrats continually committed election fraud—by this time, a Virginia tradition. Widespread vote tampering, including cash and whiskey bribes at the polls and threats of physical harm—were common. These practices, which did not fit the genteel image that Virginians cultivated, discomfited some among the white elite who wanted to curb the Black vote, but they wanted to do so legally and "honorably." While the General Assembly devised ways to remove Black voters, including the 1884 Anderson-McCormick Bill,[11] nothing had the desired success—disfranchising the Black voter. The 1884 Anderson-McCormick Law failed to curtail the Black vote and election fraud continued. Some Conservatives believed that the only way to disfranchise Black men and end election fraud was through a constitutional convention. In May 1889, despite resistance from the Democratic leadership, the General Assembly voted to ask the electorate, "Shall there be a convention to revise the Constitution and amend the same?" The vote was a resounding NO!

Black people continued to believe self-help through organizing a key component for acceptance in America and for making better lives for themselves. When all else failed, self-help arose as the only answer.[12]

By the mid-1880s, Black men and women believed that political avenues were closing to them, so they augmented their efforts to gain citizenship through formal associations. Sometimes they organized into lodges or secret societies that pursued individual and group uplift; they defined this as improving their condition through learning and teaching acceptable modes of behavior and dress, saving money, establishing businesses, and hard work. Members of Black organizations maintained membership rosters, paid dues, and carried out their work. One society, the United Order of True Reformers, which was open to men and women, rose to prominence in Richmond and Hanover County, and soon across the United States.[13]

While many of the details of the founding of the Order are unclear, it appears that the True Reformers began in Kentucky under the auspices of the Right Worthy Grand Lodge, Independent Order of Good Templars, a white lodge.[14] There were True Reformers in Richmond as early as 1877, but the Order came into its own in the city under the guidance of William Washington Browne, who moved to the state's capital from Alabama in 1881. This order, like many of the organizations mentioned in chapter 2, was founded on the premise that Black uplift depended upon the Black community itself. Like other self-help organizations, the True Reformers offered death benefits to members to assist with "good Christian burials." However, Browne envisioned a broader mission than insurance. He believed that the Order would be "a great corporation by the Negro, not only for mutual aid, but also for mutual employment, by which thousands could obtain livelihood and the organization hold a commanding position in the mercantile world."[15]

To recruit members, Browne spent much time talking to Black people in shoe shops and barbershops. It might have been in one of these establishments that Browne met Clinton Winston and R.T. Quarles of Ashland in Hanover County. Eventually Browne spoke in Ashland, probably at Shiloh Baptist Church, where Winston was an active member and deacon. Impressed by Browne and the mission of the True Reformers, Winston and Quarles founded Fountain number four, the Mt. Zion Fountain of

Ashland. Fountains were the local chapters or lodges of the True Reformers. The Mt. Zion Fountain became the largest branch of the young order in Virginia, boasting some of the "leading Colored people of the community."[16]

By June 1881, fourteen Fountains encompassed one hundred and fifty members in Richmond and the surrounding communities. In October 1881, the first session of the Grand Fountain, the parent Fountain of the True Reformers, met in Richmond. R.T. Quarles and C.F. Tinsley represented Ashland's Mt. Zion Fountain. William W. Browne was elected the Grand Worthy Master, and R.T. Quarles of Ashland became the Grand Worthy Vice Master of the Grand Fountain, a position of national leadership. Black leaders, such as Browne and Ida B. Wells, a nationally known African American journalist and anti-lynching activist, promoted the goal of a unified front among African Americans. The difficulty of achieving that objective is evident in the problems that developed among the True Reformers.[17]

In its second year, the national order ran into problems often associated with growing pains. Reorganization led to change in leadership positions that did not sit well with the ousted leaders who became part of the Encampment.[18] The original Encampment consisted of past officers. Initially, Browne believed that the Encampment was good for the Order; he was pleased with the group's performance, and he offered its members the "right hand of fellowship and led them forward." The shift in the good feelings between Browne and the past officers occurred when the new rules made the Grand Fountain supreme. Previously, the Grand Fountain and the Encampment had been equals. This change meant that the Grand Fountain was the sole governing body, thus taking power away from past officers. The members of the Encampment decided that their group outranked the Grand Fountain and therefore did not have to follow the new rules.[19]

By the time of the second Grand Session, which took place in Richmond in October 1882, the internal conflict had turned into a full-fledged battle. Members of the Encampment took the floor to convince the members at-large that, even though they had belonged to the Order since the beginning, Browne was going to turn them all out. While the rebels were unsuccessful at the Grand Session, they continued meeting and eventually decided among themselves that Browne was no longer the leader of the True Reformers. A committee was appointed and asked to visit Browne to confiscate all documents related to the business of the True Reformers. Browne refused to turn the items over to the delegation. The Encampment sued Browne, but he successfully defended himself and the court ruled in favor of Browne.

Not long after his day in court, Browne called for an extra session of the Grand Fountain to take place in Ashland at Shiloh Baptist Church to discuss the actions of the rebel members. On March 26, 1883, representatives from both factions took the train from Richmond to Ashland. During the ride, supporters of the respective sides exchanged barbs, which provided a preview of the meeting to come.[20]

Once the assembly of Reformers and spectators gathered in the church sanctuary, the membership appointed a committee on grievances, which included R.T. Quarles of Ashland's Mt. Zion Fountain and five other men.[21] Browne read a statement outlining his charges, thirteen in all, against the Encampment and its supporters. According to Browne, the violations included calling a meeting of the Fountains; discussing Grand Fountain business; and falsely representing four Fountains (including the Ashland Fountain) without the consent of the membership. The ten violations that took place during the meetings included voiding a death payment and having the Grand Worthy Master arrested.[22]

At one point, the proceedings became so heated that a recess was called to avoid bloodshed. Once tempers calmed and the committee selected to review the charges was ready to report, the group reassembled. The Committee on Grievances found Browne innocent and found those members who had tried to unseat Browne guilty. The committee recommended that the guilty parties be dealt with as the order's constitution provided. Mayhem broke out in the sanctuary. Reportedly, a "three-hundred-pound" woman and Browne had a tug of war over one of the books. While Browne succeeded in obtaining the book, he narrowly escaped a lighted lamp that was thrown at his head. At this point, the meeting adjourned. Within a few months of this incident, William Washington Browne took steps to have the Grand Fountain of the United Order of True Reformers incorporated. The rebels incorporated under the name Grand United Order of True Reformers.[23]

Roses in December

The True Reformers of Hanover were intimately involved with the Grand Fountain in Richmond. Black men and women were serious about organizing and were willing to challenge each other when it appeared that members were involved in actions that would harm rather than help the race. African Americans practiced citizenship within the parameters they created for themselves; they perceived a problem, the members proceeded to find a solution, and the majority carried the day. The conflict within the True Reformers might suggest that there was as much disunity as unity within the post-Reconstruction African American community. The True Reformers' schism provides a vivid example of how intra-racial issues might have stymied racial uplift.[24] More importantly, it suggests that the African American community was not, and should not be expected to be, a monolith. The expectation that the Black community was of one mind is shortsighted and dangerous. It sets the community up for failure when differences of opinion in other cultures are a sign of growth. A dog whistle is harmful, unproductive, and untrue.

The True Reformers weathered this storm and continued to grow and added several new departments, including one focusing on attracting new members. By 1885, the True Reformers were an established presence in Hanover and expanding. The Rev. C. H. Phillips, a True Reformer and pastor of Union Baptist Church in Beaverdam, Hanover County, invited William Browne to speak at his church. This was the beginning of a major recruiting effort in the county. After Browne's appearance at the church, he and Phillips spent days going from house to house in the county telling farmers about the True Reformers and giving them tips on farm management. Neither man realized that they had already gained perhaps their most valuable recruit, William Lee Taylor, before they ever left Union Baptist Church.

After becoming a minister and joining Union Baptist Church, the hardworking Taylor was in the congregation when William Browne spoke at the church. Taylor might have seen his own commitment to bettering himself reflected in the goals of the True Reformers because he began working almost immediately on behalf of the order and organized the Beaverdam Fountain at Pin Hook. Soon Taylor, working with the Rev. R. F. Robinson of Hanover Junction, met with such success that he was authorized to organize Fountains wherever he found the opportunity. Taylor's

An Uneasy Citizenship

star was on the rise. His approach to building success for his family and later the True Reformers reflects his conviction, shared with the Black community at large, that education, spirituality, and financial stability were keys to the attainment of citizenship. Taylor's story is an example that the city was not always the source of innovation and vibrancy, but that sometimes the leadership flowed from the county to the city.[25]

While the state political scene remained discouraging, Black men and women never stopped looking for ways to establish themselves as citizens of the Commonwealth. The True Reformers, under the leadership of Browne and with the assistance of Taylor and Robinson, continued to make themselves a voice to be reckoned with in the state. In the late 1880s, Taylor quit his teaching position in Hanover to work full time for the order. By the end of the decade, he was a member of its board of directors.[26]

Outside of formal societies, Black people looked for other ways to establish themselves as citizens. One way they achieved some semblance of citizenship involved taking over public spaces for picnics, parades, speeches, and recitations. These events disturbed local white residents who understood that at these celebrations Black people taught and learned worldviews that ran counter to the Lost Cause narratives that glorified the Old South and the Confederacy. In this way, Black people conveyed their cultural memories to the younger generation despite the problem of illiteracy. Indeed, "postbellum Blacks, no less than Whites appreciated the power that flowed from the recalled past."[27]

This transference of historical knowledge was a goal of the organizers of the first National Emancipation Day 1890. Organizers, including executive committee member and True Reformer William Browne, pointed out that, while individual communities celebrated Emancipation, there was no national holiday recognizing the end of slavery. A national holiday would mean that whites would receive an annual reminder that Black people had not been content with enslavement. A committee of Black men from across the country came together and determined that the first national observance should take place in Richmond October 15–17, 1890.[28]

Notices went out about the big event, asking Black residents to bring items illuminating slavery and Emancipation, such as old clothes and other artifacts. They were promised fair compensation for these items,

Roses in December

which were to be used in exhibits during the three-day event and eventually housed in museums. Event organizers also promised to set up an information bureau to help Black people find relatives sold away during slavery. Black Union soldiers conducted reenactments, and the singing of old plantation songs and hymns was included on the agenda. Although women did not have leadership roles in this event, they did participate as presenters. For example, men and women presented poems, essays, orations, and addresses that demonstrated the intellectual progress of the race. Societies paraded in their formal regalia, and boys between the ages of ten and sixteen wore blue stockings and belts in Union colors. [29]

While celebration and thanksgiving were important goals of this event, organizers also planned to ensure that the national observance of Emancipation would become a regular event on the calendar, a national holiday. To this end, organizers asked for delegates from each city and county in the United States to participate in a meeting that would take place the second day of the festivities. The task of this group would be to determine a permanent date for Emancipation Day celebrations. Black residents in Hanover County met at Hanover Courthouse and selected eleven delegates and alternates to participate in this process. Once at the gathering, the delegates chose from several possible dates for a permanent holiday: September 22, 1862, when the Emancipation Proclamation had first been announced; January 1, 1863, the day that it took effect; April 3, 1865, the fall of Richmond; or April 9, 1865, the day Robert E. Lee surrendered. The debate was probably quite lively, since some delegates believed that the January 1 date was not relevant since so few were freed on that day. At least one practical businessperson wanted the celebration to take place on January 1, however, because he was already closed for business that day. While the rationale for the selection is unclear, the businessperson won out. January 1 became the annual date for national Emancipation Day celebrations.[30]

The *Richmond Planet,* an African American newspaper, declared the three-day event a great success. The white-owned Richmond *Dispatch* shared that only three hundred attended the first day, and that thousands attended on day two to enjoy the longest parade of Black women, men, and children in Richmond's history. The three-day celebration ended with a formal ball.[31]

The reporting of this event represents an example of the different shapes a story could take depending on who was relaying the information. The *Dispatch*, a conservative newspaper, might have genuinely considered the first day a failure because the number of actual participants did not live up to the predictions. The editors may have resented the men in the leadership roles: men such as William Washington Browne, True Reformer and bank president; the Honorable William Gray, former Mississippi State Senator; the Rev. E.A. Randolph, of the Richmond Theological Seminary; and Professor G. W. Hayes, of VNCI, who predicted that thousands would be in attendance.[32]

By contrast, the *Richmond Planet* reported that each day, including day one, had achieved success. Of course, John Mitchell and other African Americans wanted and needed this to be a successful occasion and might have continued to exaggerate as they had in the planning stages. Success illustrated their ability to organize—a key factor in the uplift of the race. One of the many speakers at Emancipation Day pointed out that Black people "would in no other way receive the respect and liberties which were rightly theirs" if they did not organize.[33] Success was also apparent in the sheer number of Black citizens who rallied, which might impress upon white people not to take Black men and women for granted. Success might simply be measured by the fact that communities like Hanover thought it important to take out time to meet and select delegates. In addition, taking over public spaces in Richmond was a sign that African Americans would not accept exclusion from "ceremonial citizenship."[34]

There is another reason to ponder this occasion. Five months before the National Emancipation Day gathering took place in Richmond, the Robert E. Lee monument was unveiled on May 29, 1890, in that city. Later that summer, the state of Mississippi called a constitutional convention that led to the disfranchisement of its Black citizens and paved the way for the remaining states of the former Confederacy, including Virginia, to disfranchise most Black men in the South. While it is difficult to say how these events affected the Black community, there is little doubt that the men who organized the national Emancipation Day celebration and many who attended knew about these two events. White citizens were clearly expressing their values and concerns. Black citizens responded with determination not to go unheard and unseen. The Emancipation

Day organizers responded to the perpetuation of white supremacy with a national event, signaling their determination to remind everyone that slavery was over. African Americans would not backtrack.

While the national Emancipation Day Celebration represents organizing on a grand scale, Black people just as often organized on a smaller scale and around local needs. One example of this is the group of concerned citizens who recruited a doctor to serve Black people in the eastern end of Hanover County. Those present selected a chairman, clerk, and someone to offer prayer. They placed an advertisement in the *Richmond Planet*. While the outcome of the group's efforts is unknown, a notice advertising the position ran at least four times.[35] Deciding to discontinue the ad after four weeks might mean that a physician was hired. It could also reflect the financial limitations of the group.

Throughout this period, William Taylor's star continued to rise in the True Reformers and in Hanover County. By 1891, he was the Grand Worthy Vice Master and worked closely with William Browne.[36] Meanwhile, he and his family bought a farm in Doswell in Hanover County. The following year, he became the pastor of Jerusalem Baptist Church, also in Doswell. According to his biography and church history, he was instrumental in erecting a new, modern church edifice during his tenure at Jerusalem.[37]

Ten years after the volatile meeting in Ashland led to the incorporation of two separate organizations—the Grand Fountain of the United Order of the Reformers (led by Browne) and the Grand United Order of True Reformers—the True Reformers continued to operate in the county.[38] As a major leader in the Grand Fountain, Taylor must also have been an influential figure for the Hanover Fountains. In 1893, the *Richmond Planet* reported that several men, some from Ashland and at least one from Hanover Courthouse, had paid their endorsements or membership dues to the Grand Fountain. Later that year, the True Reformers collected funds on behalf of residents in Clarksville, Virginia, the site of a major fire and home to many Reformers. The entire business district had been destroyed. Four lodges in Hanover donated a total of $10.95. That same year the lodges paid death benefits to the family of Waddy Dabney of Ashland.[39] While the scope of these activities was modest, they illustrate the commitment of Black Hanoverians to resist white supremacy with the tools at hand and self-help.

An Uneasy Citizenship

In the summer of 1894, William W. Browne, the Grand Worthy Master, visited Ashland to see the organization's new building. The Order had purchased 1¾ acres of land the previous February and erected a new two-story building with six rooms, including a storeroom and four tenant rooms on the first floor. Various Fountains used the large second-floor room with a vestibule and anteroom for public meetings. At the time of Browne's visit, the store and the tenant rooms had been rented.[40]

Throughout the early 1890s, William Browne remained busy with the True Reformers, but he was also involved with the National Emancipation Day Celebration movement. Indeed, in the early 1890s, he was president of the organization. The organizers hoped with the 1890 Emancipation Day celebration that Black Americans would pick up the banner and make the celebration an annual event in their own communities. It is not clear how consistent these national celebrations became, but the record does indicate that Black residents of Hanover County celebrated the occasion in January 1893. At that time, the celebration was *usual* in the county. This is an indication that celebrations had taken place in the intervening years since 1890. The commemoration in 1893 took place at the Sons and Daughters of Zion Hall near Peaks Station in the eastern section of the county. Over four hundred people gathered to pray, hear a reading of the Emancipation Proclamation, and sing songs such as "Come Kind Friends to Greet You," "Slavery Chain Was Broke at Last," and "Come, Come Away." Some of the county's "best young men and ladies" gave presentations. William Henry Winston, the boy who had walked off the North Wales Plantation and out of slavery with the Union Army in 1863, was now a grown man and the president of the Sons and Daughters of Zion.[41]

The following year, no report was given of the Hanover celebration, but in all likelihood, organizers saw the December 1894 letter from William W. Browne admonishing Black people to remember and plan a special event for January 1, 1895.[42] The efforts to establish an Emancipation Day celebration and the other work of Black people show that they were not waiting for anyone else to plan their future. As some, like Peter Storrs and Frances Coleman, had done even before the end of slavery, they continued to secure their economic futures and to educate their children; they built social lives; and they continued to work out their souls' salvation.

Throughout the 1880s and 1890s, Black Hanoverians continued to make a living in a variety of ways. According to the censuses of 1880 and 1900, some black men in Hanover worked as craftsmen—bricklayers, carpenters, stonemasons, wheelwrights, and plasterers. Others earned their living as preachers, teachers, ferrymen, cooks, and messengers. Those who lived close to the railroad found work as porters, trackwalkers, or brakemen. There was one Black jockey in 1900.[43] He might have ridden or trained horses that raced at the Ashland racecourse. Horseracing was not an unusual occupation for Black men. Indeed, Black men dominated horseracing from the end of the Civil War until the dawn of disfranchisement.[44] In contrast, Black men had difficulties finding work in urban areas such as Richmond, but their wives typically found work as domestics and laundresses.[45]

Married Black women in Hanover in the 1880s and 1890s present a contrast to their urban sisters, in that most did not work for white people. Most married African American women in the county, like most married white women there, were characterized in the census as "keeping house," which was differentiated from housekeeping. "Keeping house" meant that the woman was what today might be called a "homemaker" or "stay-at-home-mom." "Housekeeping" by contrast was work done outside the home. In most cases in Hanover, the husband was the breadwinner; whether he was a skilled craftsman or a laborer, only on rare occasions did wives work outside the home. This did not mean that they did not put in a full day of hard labor cooking, cleaning, taking care of children, and working their gardens. They may have also taken-in wash. It did mean that they did not have to worry about advances or the attacks that plagued many Black women who worked outside the home.

Some married Black women in Hanover County did work as laborers, cooks, and domestics, but they were rare. Exceptions included the wives of Frank Watkins and Richard Venable, who worked as cooks. Ellen Brackett, who was married, worked as a seamstress. The rarity of this occupation among Black women in Hanover might reflect the fact that the freed people's schools in the county never offered sewing classes,

An Uneasy Citizenship

even though sewing was part of the stated curriculum. According to Freedmen's Bureau agents, they were never able to find anyone to teach sewing.[46] Another explanation might be that most enslaved Black women worked in the fields and did not learn the skill of sewing. Typically passed down to girls from female relatives, it is quite possible that there were very few older Black women in the late nineteenth century who could teach their daughters, nieces, or neighbors the skill.

Daughters in Black Hanover, in contrast to their mothers but like so many urban, married Black women, typically worked outside the home. For instance, the teenage daughters of William and Polly Braxton worked as laborers, and nine-year-old Emily Spurlock lived with a white family and served as a nurse.[47] Young Black women of Hanover often found employment as cooks, laundresses, nurses in white families, domestics, milkmaids, and occasionally as laborers. It was not uncommon for these women to reach a level of economic success. Matilda Derricott, Lelia Wingfield, and Isabelle Jones were all listed as washerwomen, and they all owned their homes—an accomplishment replicated by Black female laundresses across the South.[48]

Most Black Americans in the latter 1800s lived in the South, and more than eight out of ten lived in rural areas.[49] The large majority of Black families supported themselves off the land; a relative few were owners, but most were tenants. There were two basic tenant systems in Hanover County. Under one arrangement, the landlord supplied land, housing, draft animals, food, and necessary tools. In return, the tenant received one-half of the crop yield. Some tenants made a deal with landowners who furnished land and paid for one-quarter of the fertilizer; at the end of the harvest, the landlord received one-quarter of the yield. Usually the tenant lived rent-free, often in a former slave cabin. Regardless of the agreement between the property owner and tenant, the tenant usually ended the year in debt—sometimes the result of bad weather and poor crop yields, but often because of trickery on the part of the property owner. Either way, tenants in the South frequently found themselves in a cycle of debt with no end in sight. Most sharecroppers were not as successful as William Taylor and his wife; most never acquired their own land or farm animals. Indeed, "for most rural Black southerners, the line between freedom and neo-slavery was an exceedingly narrow and fragile one."[50] Unfortunately, the census does not provide race-based statistics on tenancy in Hanover for this period.

In at least one instance, individuals banded together to overcome the financial obstacles to land ownership. In 1886, a group of fifteen Hanover County Black residents formed a partnership known as the Hickory Hill Club. The group purchased 85½ acres of land located between Ashland and Hanover Courthouse. The land was to be divided among the members based on the dollar amount each contributed.

Hickory Hill was the name of the Wickham plantation just east of the Ashland town limits. Hickory Hill Club members or their parents had been enslaved on that plantation. They pooled their money and bought land. Unfortunately, the sellers of the land, Charles Winston and David Hewlett, died intestate before the deeds were properly completed. In addition to the problems encountered when an individual dies without a will, the club members also had to deal with the fact that Winston's and Hewlett's wives had not yet signed on saying that they agreed to the sale. In the nineteenth century, when land transactions were recorded, the wives were taken aside, asked by the clerk or a notary public whether they knew of, and agreed to the sale of the property. The response was noted and certified in the deed book. Without the signatures of the wives, club members faced an additional legal challenge. The Hickory Hill Club took the heirs of Charles Winston and David Hewlett to court to try to obtain full rights to the land.[51] The case of *James Shelton, Jr. v. Ella D. Hewlett, etc.* was finally settled in 1891 when the wives finally acknowledged that the land belonged to the Hickory Hill Club.

It is intriguing that this group decided to name their club after the plantation where they or their ancestors were enslaved. They might have felt nostalgia—not in the sense that they longed for the days of old, but perhaps an acknowledgment of the idea that no matter what the circumstances, home was home. It might also be an oblique proclamation that the question was finally settled in 1891 when the wives acknowledged that the land belonged to the Hickory Hill Club. Perhaps it was evidence that they had transcended slavery and could have their own Hickory Hill. Finally, "Hickory Hill" may have evolved into an ordinary geographic term denoting the neighborhood surrounding the plantation of the same name.

An Uneasy Citizenship

Black women and men understood that land was wealth, and they wanted to build wealth. Charles Clarke was the married thirty-one-year-old son of William Clarke, who was mentioned in the previous chapter; he probably learned from his father's example. The elder Clarke began purchasing land not long after Emancipation. In February 1891, Charles Clarke became a landowner. He and his brother Garland bought just over 151 acres of foreclosed land for $682.62. Sadly, Charles's tenure as a landowner was short-lived. He died of a malarial fever on January 6, 1892. Since he died intestate, the land went to Clarke's father, thus expanding the older man's wealth. The record does not explain why Garland, who outlived Charles by several years, or Charles's wife did not get the land. The record does indicate that William Clarke sold the land to his youngest son, Alexander Clarke, who lived in Pennsylvania, for the greatly reduced price of $240.[52]

Land ownership provided a place to live and put down roots, and it represented a way to make a living, feed families, and pass on wealth. Hanover was largely rural until well into the twentieth century, and most African Americans who lived in the county worked the land, a challenging way to earn a living. Tools and draft animals were expensive, yet they were necessary for success. Black farmers in Virginia sometimes adapted by joining forces. The Colored Farmers Alliance of Virginia was part of a national movement of farmers at the end of the nineteenth century to improve conditions and opportunities in agriculture. In 1891, the Colored Alliance held its second annual national meeting in Richmond. Most Virginia counties, including Hanover, sent a delegate to the meeting.[53]

A few Black men ran their own businesses in Hanover. William Wright was listed as a merchant in the 1880 census, and T. Major Lightfoot was a merchant by 1900.[54] In the 1897–98 Virginia State Gazetteer and Business Directory, three African American individuals, J.C. Bagby & Company, and True Reformers R.T. Quarles and Clinton Winston, advertised as "general merchants" in the County. Winston was also listed as an undertaker.[55] It is not clear whether Winston was born enslaved or free. Family lore suggests that he was the son of a white doctor in the County, and his physical appearance clearly indicates that a very recent ancestor had been white. Winston was a successful blacksmith, and by 1887, he had purchased land on which to build a shop and his home on Hanover Avenue in the town of Ashland. He kept his caskets on the second floor of his shop. There he prepared bodies for burial and then returned them to their homes for viewing by family and friends. When indigent people or prisoners died, Winston was sometimes hired by the county to build their coffins at approximately $2.50 per unit. Between 1894 and 1896, he built at least seven coffins for the county government and was paid $17.50. Winston also rented a room to Charlie Long, a Black barber.[56] In 1896, Winston and his wife appeared in the *Richmond Planet.* In an article, two unnamed male visitors to Ashland noted that they had stopped by to see Mr. Winston, and that they were impressed to see "his wife is pulling along with him; while he is striking upon the anvil, she is just a few yards from him conducting a grocery."[57]

While Clinton Winston did not make his living as a farmer, he did understand the value of land, and he worked to acquire enough of it so that his descendants were able to build good lives for generations to come. During his lifetime, Winston owned at least twenty-five acres of land in Hanover, not including the six lots he held in the town of Ashland. Some of this land he purchased in the conventional way; he received other real estate in payment for burials when the families were cash-poor.[58]

Black Hanoverians continued to view education as a vital component in the advancement of African Americans. Throughout the 1880s and 1890s, the number of public schools and students expanded. By the 1881–82 school year, there were 726 Black students enrolled in twenty schools with an average aggregate monthly attendance of 576. The discrepancy between enrollment and attendance in rural areas was generally the result of family needs. Children, typically a labor source for rural families, remained at home during planting and harvesting times. Such large enrollments indicates that while not able to always keep their children in school, rural parents desired to educate their offspring.[59] The rural mode of life also led to erratic school terms. The state required that schools operate a minimum of three months per year, but beyond that period, it was up to local officials and often up to the parents to determine how long the school year lasted. At times, children spent so much time out of school that they had forgotten much of what they had learned by the next session. The average session in Hanover County was just under six months in 1880, up from just under five months in 1870.[60]

An Uneasy Citizenship

Staffing rural schools was not easy, and salaries were typically low. In Hanover County during the 1881–82 school year, there were seven Black teachers and forty-five white teachers, a much greater discrepancy than the modest difference in numbers of Black and white pupils would justify; the implications for teacher-pupil ratios and class sizes are obvious. Teacher salaries varied slightly from district to district, but white males consistently earned the most. During the 1882–83 school year, the Henry District paid the highest salaries at $27.93 per month for white men, $27.89 for Black men, $27.05 for white women, and $25.01 for Black women. Salaries were contingent upon numbers of pupils in attendance, so teachers also recruited.[61] During the 1883–84 school year, the number of students remained about the same, as did the number of white schools, but the number of Black schools increased from twenty-seven to thirty. The number of white teachers decreased from fifty to forty-four, but the number of Black teachers increased from twelve to twenty-one. The Henry District remained the highest-paying district—white men earned the most at $33 a month; white women earned $30.62; and Black men earned $32. Black women lagged far behind the other groups, earning a mere $22.50.[62]

Throughout the period studied here, there were obvious disparities between schools, but it is not always obvious whether these disparities were based on race. For example, during the 1884 school year, there were four graded schools in the county—two for white and two for Black residents. (Graded schools contrasted with schools in which multiple grades were taught in a single room.) Each of these four schools offered two grades, and all had the same number of teachers. The two schools in the Atlee community, one Black and one white, had a six-month term. The white school in the town of Ashland offered only a five-month term. The Black school listed as "near" Ashland offered the longest term of all: eight months. The available records do not indicate the reasons for these differences, but they do suggest that in Hanover, educational opportunities were not always skewed in favor of white students.[63]

By 1890, all the county's schools were still frame or log buildings, and the number of students housed within them had increased. There were slightly more Black pupils in the county (1,892) than there were white (1,713); yet the county provided far more teachers for the white pupils than for the Black pupils (57 versus 26), and significantly more classroom space as well (2,200 classroom seats for white students compared with 1,700 for Black students). During the five-month school term, Black students received more assistance from the school district in the form of textbooks than white students did.[64]

By the end of the century, the number of students attending school in Hanover had increased significantly. Of the 6,900 Black and white children eligible for school, 3,400 enrolled, and of that number, an average of 2,600 actually attended on a given day. Forty-seven percent (3,510) of school-age Black children enrolled in school, almost as high a rate of enrollment as among whites at fifty-one percent. The number of white schools and teachers continued to outnumber greatly those for Black children, however, yielding substantially greater class sizes for African American pupils; herein lay the clearest disadvantage Black students faced.[65] In the 1900–1901 school year, there were sixty-two white schools and thirty-seven Black schools, even though the Black and white pupil populations were almost identical. The county employed sixty-six white teachers and only thirty-three Black teachers. The average monthly salary for white men was $30.36; Black men, $20.00; white women, $23.55; and Black women, $20.46.[66] There was a substantial reduction in salary for Black men and white female teachers from just a few years before. The record does not account for the salary cuts, but they could be due, in part, to how the information was gathered and handled from year to year. For example, in the early 1880s, the salary reports were given for each district, but by the end of the century, the averages were based on the entire county. Therefore, while the salaries were lower for the 1900–1901 school year, some of the difference might have been simple arithmetic.

In his introduction to the 1900–1901 school report, the state superintendent of public instruction lamented the condition of the state's rural schools. He pointed out that many of the country schools were uninhabitable, and that the school terms were so short that students were not able to retain the information needed to build on for the next term. He also deplored the inadequacy of teacher pay and preparation, white and Black. [67] Moreover, the statistics show that from 1890 until the turn of the century, Black children and teachers in the Hanover County public schools continued to operate at a disadvantage. There were consistently

An Uneasy Citizenship

too few seats and teachers, but this did not stop Black parents, teachers, and students from making the most of the resources that were available.

Where the Virginia School Reports generally give a broad view of the county, the local newspapers often carried items of special interest from the schools. For example, every year the *Richmond Planet* announced commencement activities. These ceremonies not only recognized the graduating students but also the teachers. Parents prepared and served dinners.[68] Sometimes the school news focused on the teachers, such as the time a notice appeared announcing that Samuel B. Steward had passed the public-school exam and received a first-class certificate from the Hanover superintendent.[69]

Like education, religion played a key role in Black life. In the *Richmond Planet's* issue of June 7, 1890, John Mitchell wrote, "If the Negro had one half as much money as he has religion he'd control the financial centers of this country."[70] Much as they had during slavery and the early days of freedom, Black people continued to turn to God for help overcoming obstacles. Religion permeated almost every aspect of Black life. Gatherings, formal and informal—meetings, conventions, festivals—all began with prayers and often hymns. Of the sixteen Black churches in Hanover County between 1865 and 1890, fourteen were Baptist and valued at over $9,000, with a total seating capacity of 3,550. The two Methodist church buildings were valued at $500. There were approximately 2,319 Black Baptists and 99 African Methodist Episcopal congregants out of an all-county Black population of 8,211.[71] Pleasant Grove Baptist was established in 1876 by Ebenezer Baptist Church in Richmond, one of the largest and most influential Black churches in that city.[72] In 1881, the short-lived *American Guest*, an Ashland newspaper, reported that an association of Black residents had met in town. Its goals were to spread the Gospel, promote fellowship, exchange ideas, and encourage the intellectual and moral advancement of the members.[73]

Much of the news reported in the *Richmond Planet* was from or about churches or religious leaders. For example, in the issue of March 1, 1890, Robert Taylor of Beaverdam reported that he had been tried by his church and that the congregation had found nothing to hold against him. He implored the reader not to believe any of the rumors he or she might have heard about his conduct.[74] One year later, Mt. Salem Baptist Church, a Black congregation in the county, was crowded for the ordination service of two new deacons.[75]

Occasionally service organizations with a religious affiliation met at one of the Hanover churches. This was the case with the Working Sons of Hope. They held an "annual protracted" meeting at Jerusalem Baptist Church in 1893. Three well-known but unnamed ministers conducted the meeting. According to the newspaper account, this organization was known for its meetings and always provided a pleasant time.[76] Similar to the Reconstruction Era, the church was a house of worship and community center.

By the 1890s, many of the Black ministers in Hanover had been educated at the Richmond Theological Seminary, a privately funded Baptist institution. A letter appeared in the *Richmond Planet* on April 7, 1894, announcing an upcoming meeting of the school's alumni association. The letter, signed by the pastor of Shiloh Baptist Church in Ashland, invited the alumni to participate and show their love and appreciation for the school by sending their annual dues. Also, by the early 1890s, a greater Richmond area Ministers' Conference had been established. This group met at least once a month in Richmond. While details of the meetings are not available, a regular order of business was for each minister present to give an account of the Sunday services at his church, which included time and regularity of Sunday school and morning worship services. Shiloh Baptist of Ashland was an active member, even sending a substitute when their minister could not attend.[77]

By the end of the century, the Hanover churches founded soon after Emancipation were well established and able to mentor new churches. Rockhill Baptist Church, founded in 1866, participated with the group of churches that determined in 1894 that New Bridge Baptist Church, also in Hanover, was indeed "a regular Baptist church."[78] Church members did not confine their interests to worship experiences. The people of Shiloh Baptist threw a surprise party for their pastor in 1895. Reportedly, the table in the home of the Rev. T.M. Allen was "loaded down with towels, handkerchiefs, socks, cuffs, collars, shirts, neckties, pillowcases, and other useful articles."[79]

While earning a living, educating one's children, and worshipping God were all of paramount importance, so was social life. Often African

American community life centered on church or fraternal picnics, plays, and other forms of entertainment. Evening church services provided a chance to spend time with friends and neighbors. These took place inside the church building, outside on the grounds, or at a recreational venue. The church was not the only social outlet for the Black community. For example, in 1892 advertisements for Bothwell Park, located at a village of the same name near Doswell, began appearing in the *Richmond Planet*. Located twenty-four miles from Richmond, near the junction of the Chesapeake and Ohio and the Richmond, Fredericksburg and Potomac railroads, Bothwell was said to be the only Black-owned park in the area. The ads touted its good water and swings, which made it a wonderful place for excursions, picnic parties, and especially Sunday school outings. Black men, women, and children continued to take advantage of this park at least throughout the late 1890s.[80]

Black people maintained an active social life as the movement against their civil rights unfolded. They were not unmindful or unconcerned about what was happening in the political arena, but they did not allow the maneuvers of powerful white men to control every aspect of their existence. In 1896, an article appeared in the *Planet* titled, "Old Hanover Heard from Again." The story described a social event that took place in Bothwell, which started at 5 p.m. and lasted until the next morning. The available details are limited, but guests arrived in carriages and buggies.[81] The next year the *Planet* reported "An Evening of Pleasure" in Goodalls, Virginia. Described as a "grand social event," the gala began between 7:00 and 8:00 p.m., when "by the bright moonlight could be seen groups of fair young ladies and gentlemen, winding their way toward the residences of Matilda Green." As at Bothwell the previous year, the group socialized throughout the night.[82] All-night parties attracting well-behaved guests had become a staple of Black social life in Hanover County.

An organization known as the BPS Club organized regular socials for its members and friends. In March 1898, the *Planet* reported on a party that took place on the previous Friday night at the Bachelor's Headquarters at 7:30 p.m. The article does not elaborate on the exact mission or nature of the BPS Club, but the name of the headquarters suggests that it was probably some type of social club for men. According to the reporter,

"Vehicles could be heard and seen coming from different directions with the gentlemen bringing in their lady friends, while in spite of the inclemency of the weather many could be seen wandering their way on foot, and at 8:30 pm the Bachelor's Headquarters was packed from pit to dome and everyone was enjoying themselves to the full extent of their hearts desire."[83] The revelers partied until midnight and then ate; at 2 a.m., they played games and talked; at 4 a.m., they had dessert before going home at 6 a.m. The exact nature of the BPS is unclear, but the news item makes it clear that its activities were respectable: the story included a list of the names of those present. The respectability of the event is further supported by the presence of an out-of-town visitor, who attended the party and remained in the area long enough to offer a message at the Sabbath school on Sunday. The reporter concluded by complimenting the club saying, "Much credit is due to the B.P.S. Club for the manner in which they conducted such a grand entertainment."[84] These events suggest that there was a rather sizable Black middle class in Hanover, or at least that the county offered social events that attracted Black people of that class from surrounding areas. They also suggest a possible legacy to these Black men and women from their ancestors. Enslaved Black people typically worked from sunup to sundown and therefore had little free time. As a result, it has been well documented that enslaved persons on most plantations found time in the wee hours of the morning for socializing. Perhaps by the late nineteenth century, these types of gatherings represented a cultural heritage from slavery.[85]

While Black people were moving forward in many categories, they were still vulnerable to political attacks as the Democrats continued to look for ways to take the franchise. Like Anderson-McCormick, the Walton Election Law of 1894 with its special constables and complicated requirements for marking the ballots, had led to more fraud and failed to disfranchise a significant number of Black men. Corruption was still the order of the day where electoral politics was concerned.

In response, Black male Virginians formed the Negro Protective Association of Virginia. A notice appeared in the *Richmond Planet* on May 4, 1897, calling for a meeting of Black men to come together and organize against political attacks. The notice explained that "one reason why the Negro is so badly treated is because he has no organization. Organization will beget for us that consideration which nothing else can."[86] Black Virginians were turning inward in the cause of "self-preservation." The goal was not only to end white oppression, but also to help each other by clearing the streets and alleys of gambling boys, to protect Black women, and to curtail Black prostitution. To this end, the race needed more Black colleges, newspapers, businesses, and schools of literature.[87]

The meeting took place at the True Reformers Hall in Richmond on May 18, 1897, just a few days before the referendum on calling a constitutional convention took place. The proceedings of the meeting were printed for distribution. The back cover of the pamphlet featured a picture of the American flag and a smoking cannon. The caption read, "Our First Gun. We Mean Business."[88]

Once again, the Virginia electorate voted "no" to a constitutional convention—83,453 to 38,326—but the results clearly indicated a change in attitude among the voting public, or at least a change in thinking among some of the Democratic poll workers since 1889. The significantly increased number of affirmative votes meant that the matter of amending the constitution was not dead. Indeed, it soon rose again.[89]

On March 5, 1900, the General Assembly once again passed an act providing for a referendum that replicated the one in 1897.[90] Black male leaders spoke out against the idea of the convention that they understood would lead to disfranchisement. The vote on the referendum took place on the fourth Thursday in May 1900, and the final count was 77,362 in favor and 60,375 opposed to the convention.[91] On July 14, 1900, a notice appeared in the *Richmond Planet*. The headline read "Wake Up Colored People! Your Rights Are at Stake." It was an invitation to all Black people, men and women, to attend a meeting at the True Reformers Hall in Richmond. It said, "If you want liberty, peace, happiness and protection come to this meeting."[92] The gathering, called by the National Constitutional Rights Association, represents one of the few, if not the only, times that women were directly addressed as also having a stake in the outcome of the planned constitutional convention.

The constitutional convention began in Richmond on June 12, 1901, and ended on June 26, 1902. It took place in the hall of the House of Delegates and included one hundred delegates, all white and all male. Eighty-eight of the delegates were Democrats, including Hill Carter, who represented

Hanover, and Roger Gregory, who represented Hanover and King William.[93] The convention lasted for just over one year and reviewed the entire constitution, not simply the question of the franchise. In the end, the new constitution codified segregated schools, recognized the state's system of independent cities, and established the State Corporation Commission. Finally, the new constitution disfranchised most Black men and some poor white men by using poll taxes and empowering registrars to administer tests that required citizens to read and explain documents to the satisfaction of the examiner who was free to nullify the answer at will.[94]

During the period from 1880 to 1901, the leadership in the Black community championed, more loudly than ever, the need to organize and build from within. One effort toward this end was the campaign of Black men, including William Browne and William Taylor, to build up an organization that would serve not only as an insurance agency, but also as a foundation on which the Black community could stand. This struggle, which aimed to organize Black people throughout the South and even beyond, took shape largely in Richmond and in Hanover. Similarly, Black citizens in and beyond Hanover County planned an annual national celebration of Emancipation. On the local level, they invested energy in neighborhood-improvement efforts, such as the search for a doctor to serve the Hanover community. Black Hanoverians built homes and churches and fought for the best education they could give their children.

Building from within did not mean living in a cocoon. Black men and women worked hard to stave off racism, but they failed in preventing the ultimate loss—that of the franchise. While the threat that white people perceived when they contemplated Black voting had been quashed by 1902, the very real threat that Black people themselves faced took on an entirely new dimension. Black people were no longer enslaved, but neither were they full citizens.

This did not bode well for Black men and women, but their setbacks seem to have motivated them to a new level of resistance. Contrary to the *Richmond Planet* editor's fear that Black people would lose their will to participate in civic life if they lost the vote, Black men and women rallied. Even as many ordinary whites lost interest in politics, ironically, Black people awakened to the challenge. They took on oppression with the notion that success was the best revenge.

While Black Hanoverians did not protest in the streets, Black women and men steadily acquired land, built homes, churches, businesses, and schools. They did not cower or flee, but rather took full advantage of the rights and privileges that remained available to them. They built lives for themselves and their children that in many ways unfolded parallel to yet separately from those of their white neighbors. The old Christian admonition "to be in the world, but not of it" might help to characterize, and even to explain, the Black way of life during the first years of the twentieth century. Black people of that time were in the white-dominated world, but they were only partly of it. In short, they established a pattern of self-help that would hold for decades to come. As the old spiritual says, "They made a way out of no way."

4

Disfranchised

The First Generation

ALMOST A RACE RIOT
TROUBLE AT ASHLAND
THE TROUBLE AT ASHLAND

THE PRECEDING HEADLINES APPEARED, respectively, in the Richmond *Daily Dispatch,* on August 31, 1902, and September 2, 1902, and in the *Richmond Planet* on September 6, 1902.[1] There is no obvious connection between the Ashland riot and the disfranchisement of Black Virginians, but it might reflect the tension caused by the actions of the people John Mitchell referred to as the "negro-hating element."[2]

The Ashland Riot took place on August 30, 1902. At its center lay a well-worn motif underlying much early twentieth-century violence against African Americans—the alleged assault of a white person by a Black person. There are two accounts of what happened: In an interview conducted in the 1980s, Charles Stebbins Jr., who was fifteen in 1902, traced causation to the attack of a young white girl. A contemporary newspaper account reported that a white man had been badly beaten by a Black man in Ashland. The proximate account is probably accurate; however, in this instance, either version of the story would have been enough to raise the ire of southern white people and instigate talk of lynching.[3]

The details are this: An unnamed Black man was arrested sometime prior to August 30 and placed in the Ashland jail. White people in the town were outraged by the man's alleged crime, and soon rumors of a gathering lynch mob began to circulate among the townspeople. Word quickly reached the general store and tying lot (a "parking" lot for the customers' horses and wagons) owned by Charles Stebbins Sr., a white man, who was assisted by his son, Charles Jr. According to the younger Stebbins, white Ashlanders were "terribly upset," and talk of lynching was mentioned by the white customers in his father's store. Stebbins Jr. recalled that the Commonwealth's Attorney (prosecutor) for Hanover, George Haw, asked him what he thought about the rumors. Stebbins replied, "I've heard some talk, but I think it's mostly students. I don't believe anything is going to happen." Stebbins's reference here to students is unclear and ambiguous. He might have been referring to Randolph-Macon College students, or the fifteen-year-old Stebbins might have been referring to comments that he had heard among his classmates at school. He might also have recalled incorrectly.[4]

Stebbins changed his assessment of the situation the next day when he noticed more "country people" (he does not specify race) than usual coming to town and securing their horses in the tying lot. Once again, Haw conferred with the younger Stebbins, but this time, Stebbins recalled, he advised Haw to move the prisoner to Richmond. Accordingly, Haw arranged for the train to stop just before the Ashland depot, which was close to the jail, and the man was moved without incident.[5]

The tension did not abate with the removal of the prisoner, however, and the little town came to a boil on the night of August 30. There was a Black-owned saloon directly across the railroad tracks from the train depot. On the evening of the riot, a group of Black and white people, probably mostly male though the newspaper accounts do not specify, faced off from opposite sides of the tracks. A story in the white *Richmond Dispatch* reported that someone from in front of the saloon threw a rock toward the depot, hitting a white man in the head just as a train was coming into the station. Though heavily armed, the white men in front of the station did not retaliate because the train blocked their path.[6]

When the train left the station, the white men crossed the tracks, but the Black crowd in front of the saloon had dispersed. According to

Stebbins Jr., the white men crossed the tracks with guns pulled and ready for a fight. At the same time, James Morris, a Black man, walked out of an alley, apparently unaware of what had taken place just moments before. Stebbins believed that Morris, who he described as "one of the best colored fellows around here. Didn't have a thing in the world to do with anybody," was shot and killed by a town policeman, Bill Trevillian, who, according to Stebbins, was untrained and probably agitated because of the rock-throwing incident. At that time, the town had one policeman: the town sergeant. When additional assistance was needed, he hired temporary policemen. Bill Trevillian was temporary and untrained.[7] It is quite possible that Morris, who was reportedly walking home, happened on the scene after the rock-throwing, and was mistaken for one of the groups that had been in front of the saloon.[8]

This is not the end of the story of the Ashland Race Riot, but it is important to pause here to consider the root of the event. At the turn of the twentieth century, W. E. B. Du Bois observed that race remained the driving force in American society. That was certainly the case throughout the region, the state, and Hanover County was no different. On July 10, just a month prior to the riot, Virginia's new disfranchising constitution had become law. Based on much of the reasoning behind the need for the new document, the so-called "Negro problem" should have been solved, but race remained a concern for white Virginian's. Indeed, race and place were at the center of the "almost" riot. If the Black prisoner who was moved from Ashland to Richmond had indeed badly beaten a white man, he was guilty of stepping out of his place. Even if he acted in self-defense, the audacity to beat a white man outweighed any justification.

In 1896, the United States Supreme Court, in *Plessy v. Ferguson,* codified the *place* of Black Americans as separate from, but equal to that of white Americans. The effort to maintain separation was all consuming. Everything from water fountains to cemeteries to hospitals were segregated. The equality of these spaces and places was rarely attempted and never achieved.

The never-ending battle to maintain separation of the races was always futile. Separating Black and white people was not enough because they existed in the same spaces and more importantly, whites needed Black workers—domestics, farm laborers, trash collectors, etc. This chapter will explore the question of race and how Black people responded to this obsession.

For all intents and purposes, white people had succeeded in establishing a place for Black people, but Black people would not accept their placement. White people wanted to control Black people, but Black Hanoverians would not be controlled. The irrationality of racism forced whites to continue to think about race and how to gain control over a people who would not be controlled. Fear of loss of power controlled white people. Black people also wanted power and standing, but over their own lives and communities, not over white people.

While the actual riot lasted a relatively short while, the aftermath took place over several days. On August 31, the day after the shooting, the mayor and acting coroner of Ashland, Edward L. C. Scott, wrote to the Governor of Virginia, John Hoge Tyler, notifying him of the riot and of Morris's death and asking for help. As the mayor explained to the governor, "The killing was unjustifiable and as a consequence, his [the dead man's] people are greatly incensed and wrought up."[9] The mayor asked the Governor to dispatch the state militia to Ashland, because he believed that the police were unable to handle the challenge presented. Governor Tyler responded by sending one company, about 131 men of the 70th Infantry to Ashland.

When Captain C. G. Bossieux and the company arrived in the town, the mayor asked them to patrol the streets, disperse any crowds, and suppress any violence they came across. Bossieux and his troops toured the town and surrounding areas and reported that despite rumors among white people that the town was to be destroyed, they found no evidence that Black residents were plotting any such activities. The troops did come across what Bossieux described in his report as two camps of Black people, one above the town and one below, but he had no trouble dispersing those gathered.[10]

After receiving Bossieux's report, the mayor informed the captain that the troops were needed in the town until after the verdict of the coroner's jury. Scott feared that the verdict, if not to the liking of Black residents, might lead to a disturbance. The coroner's jury, which began the inquest on September 1, was described by the *Richmond Daily Dispatch* as consisting of "the best citizens of Ashland." The jury concluded that Morris died from two buckshot that entered the right side of his head about one inch from his ear. They interviewed twenty-one witnesses, and determined that the shooting was a random act, and therefore, they were unable to determine who pulled the trigger.[11]

Following the coroner's verdict, Morris's body was released to his family, and he was buried without incident. The troops left the town on September 5. The *Richmond Daily Dispatch* reported that "the colored people are very reticent, and refuse to discuss the affair at all or to express any opinion as to the killing of Morris."[12] The town's Black citizens were in a precarious position; whether they agreed with the verdict or not, they had already seen what could happen if they struck back openly against a system they believed to be unfair. Perhaps, like Stebbins, Black people in the town believed that Bill Trevillian killed Morris but thought better of crossing the police. They probably also believed that, even if the police had killed Morris, neither Trevillian's colleagues nor the white townspeople were going to testify against him for killing a Black man.

Finally, the reticence observed by the reporter might have arisen for two additional reasons: the reporter was a white man, and he was trying to interview Black Ashlanders who were not part of the crowd in front of the saloon. Possibly, he was trying to talk to individuals who would never have frequented the saloon or addressed issues of concern with a rock. John Mitchell asserted that those involved in the incident, both white and Black, were from the "lower elements of both races." He went on to point out that James Morris, a good man, which Mitchell defined as a Black person who handled himself in a way that elevated the race, was lost, while many who would not have been missed were still "alive and kicking."[13]

The Ashland riot presents a unique opportunity to take a closer look at the connections and misconnections between history and memory. As is often the case with these types of events, the details of the riot vary, in small and large ways, depending on the storyteller. William Chenery, who grew up in Ashland and went on to become the editor of *Colliers Magazine* in Chicago, wrote in his 1952 memoir, *So It Seemed,* that this riot took place in the 1890s. He maintained that when Black farm hands, mill hands, and lumber camp workers came to town on Saturday afternoons they were tired after working twelve-hour days and often became "very obstreperous" after a few drinks. According to Chenery, "Out of a few such incidences our race riot was born. One innocent Negro man was killed by a white man who shot into a crowd. State troops at once were called out and restored order." There is no evidence of any incident vaguely resembling a riot in Ashland or elsewhere in the county in the 1890s, but Chenery's account does sound like a flawed recollection of the events of August 30, 1902.[14] It is quite possible that, by the time he wrote his memoir, he could remember narrative details—not necessarily with accuracy—and had forgotten the timing.

The account of Charles Stebbins Jr. also warrants a closer look. First, there is a discrepancy between Stebbins's account of what instigated the riot and the contemporary report. Stebbins's recall of a young girl being attacked might simply have been the result of his remembering the most common reason given by white men at the time for the eruption of violence between Black and white people.[15]

Second, although militia reports support many of Stebbins's assertions, his memory regarding the Commonwealth's Attorney is suspect. Would the attorney really look to a fifteen-year-old boy for advice on how to deal with a potential lynch mob? It is more likely that Haw conferred with Charles Stebbins Sr. as the younger man listened. In the 1980s, when Stebbins told his story, he might have been recounting it for the first time in eighty years, or it might have been a regular part of his story-telling repertoire. If the former was the case, lack of retelling could have caused the younger Stebbins to forget certain details, and if the latter was true, he might have told his version so many times that it had become the truth as he knew it.[16]

There might be yet another factor playing itself out in Stebbins's memory of the riot. As times changed in the latter twentieth century, and racial dividing lines became less rigid, many white people were reluctant to share the truth about their attitudes and actions during the period of segregation. The Stebbins name was an old and revered one in the town. First Charles and his wife had moved to Ashland, the site of their summer home, from Richmond, during the Civil War. They opened Stebbins Store in the 1880s, and until the 1960s, it was a favorite gathering place for townspeople. Charles Sr. served on the Ashland Town Council from 1890 through 1908.[17] Stebbins Street, named for this family, is still home to his descendants. Indeed, if Charles Jr. found that his actions were not as honorable as he would have liked them to be in retrospect, or in comparison with attitudes in the 1980s, he might have wanted to defend his "good name"—to keep his image in the eyes of his neighbors and of society in general free of any public shame. In 1902, when most white people believed Black people to be inferior, there was no dishonor in sharing that opinion publicly, but for an esteemed public figure to harbor those same opinions and act on them publicly would have been perceived as inappropriate in the 1980s. If Stebbins did invent his role as consultant to the prosecutor, his version supports the idea that he who controls the narrative controls the memory. Perhaps, whether consciously or subconsciously, Stebbins did not want to acknowledge that he, his father, and white Ashlanders to be the people he remembered.

The differences between the accounts of Stebbins, of Chenery, and of the contemporaneous newspapers in no way lessen the importance of the event. Indeed, when considered together with contemporary accounts, they shed additional light and fill in a few holes. For example, Chenery's version lends insight into the background of the individuals who might have been hanging out in front of the saloon.

By September 5th, a week after the riot, the troops had left Ashland, the town reverted to its usual quiescence, and the state was preparing to pay the bill. In all, it cost $652.34 for the troops to guard Ashland. This amount covered long distance phone calls between Ashland and Richmond, train fare for the troops to and from Ashland, rent to Charles Stebbins Sr. for quarters, medicines from the Hanover Pharmacy, and payroll. Regardless of race, the attention of Hanoverians during the week of August 30 to September 6, 1902, was undoubtedly focused on the riot and its aftermath, but once the dust had cleared, the new reality of disfranchisement remained.[18]

The real impact of disfranchisement in Virginia—significantly fewer ballots being cast—would not be fully felt for a few years. In 1901, when Black men still voted freely in Hanover County, 1,821 Black men voted for governor. This number decreased to 782 votes cast in the 1905 gubernatorial election.[19] Even stronger evidence lies in the county voter registration records of 1903. Each locality in Virginia was required to submit an official count, by race, of all its registered voters in 1903. While comparable information for the pre-convention period is not available, the impact of the constitutional change is readily apparent throughout the state. For example, in Prince Edward, a Black belt county, there were 1,083 white registrants and 186 Black registrants. In Dinwiddie County, the disparity was similar: 1,327 white voters and 208 Black voters. In Hanover County, where white people slightly outnumbered Black people, only 327 African Americans were registered compared with 1,857 whites. In the town of Ashland, sixty Black men were registered compared with 477 white men. Similar declines occurred across the South. [20]

Despite the significantly smaller number of Black men registered to vote in the South, the complete elimination of the Black vote still required a bit of chicanery. This was certainly true in Hanover County, where some Black men could pay the poll tax and pass a literacy test when administered fairly. To deal with these individuals, voting officials continued to commit fraud. Years after his term of office that began in 1904, one former Ashland Clerk of Elections remembered how he dealt with Black voters. He recalled that he and his fellow functionaries "committed no overt sins, but [they were] were given an intimate and disquieting picture of how elections were conducted so that white supremacy was maintained."[21] An election judge would read a portion of the Constitution and ask Black potential voters attempting to register, "You don't understand that, do you?" The answer was generally no. White men, who heard the same or similar passage, were asked, "You understand that, don't you?" To this query, the answer was typically yes. As a result, "not more than three or four Negro voters were registered during [his] term of employment."[22] In this situation, white people held the power, no matter what they had to do to obtain it.[23]

There were several ways in which Black people and sympathetic white men and women could have responded to disfranchisement. The Negro Industrial and Agricultural Society of Virginia (NIAS) pursued judicial redress. Chartered in February 1900, this Society first met in August 1900 in Charlottesville. The NIAS decided to buy farmland, build an industrial school, and plan a fair. These plans were probably a diversion to hide the organization's real purpose, which was to fight disfranchisement. [24]

In May 1902, the NIAS operation began. First, the group distributed a circular on May 31 condemning the constitutional convention for disfranchising 140,000 Black male Virginians and announced its intention to challenge the new constitution. The circular went on to announce that the NIAS had organized the state, employed lawyers, Black and white, and was now trying to raise enough money so that it could take its case all the way to the United States Supreme Court if necessary.[25] Organizations and churches across the state held fundraisers.[26] Just as they had in the past, Black Virginians put their funds together to finance a court battle that indeed, did go to the Virginia Court of Appeals. Black people moved on after disfranchisement, but ironically, white Virginians could not or would not. Even with the franchise now safely under their control, white people continued to spend a good deal of time concerned with the "Negro problem."[27]

One of the most telling events in the town of Ashland's quest to maintain control over Black residents in the community happened in 1911 and involved residential segregation. Residential segregation became the main method of controlling the movement of Black people in the second decade of the twentieth century. In Baltimore, Atlanta, and Greenville, South Carolina blocks were designated as Black or white. A law was passed in Virginia empowering city councils to prohibit Black and white people from living in the same districts. The city of Richmond adopted a plan that the Town of Ashland copied.[28]

On September 11, 1911, the Ashland Town Council held a called meeting to discuss a new ordinance submitted by E.W. Newman, a member of the council. The proposal, titled, "An ordinance to secure for whites and colored people, respectively, the separate location of residence for each race," spelled out restrictions that forbade white and Black people from living in proximity to members of the other race. Two exceptions were made: servants who worked and lived where they were employed, and Black and white people who already lived in proximity to each other. The ordinance was immediately referred to the ordinance committee, which unanimously adopted the law on September 12.[29] Segregation was slowly becoming the law of the land—churches, schools, and now neighborhoods—were to reflect white supremacist ideals.

An ordinance of this type might have been enforceable in larger cities like Richmond, but it was quite difficult to apply in a small town like Ashland. Since the end of slavery, there had been Black enclaves, but there must have also been some integrated neighborhoods, which necessitated the provision "that nothing in this ordinance shall affect the location of residences made previous to the approval of this ordinance."[30]

In 1912, John Coleman, a local Black businessman challenged the segregation ordinance.[31] Town Council minutes indicate that Coleman lost his case in the mayor's court, and any appeal that he might have filed is not in the available record. Regardless of the outcome of the Coleman case, the US Supreme Court declared all residential segregation ordinances unconstitutional in 1917. However, this did not mean that residential segregation ended. On the contrary, residential covenants were included in deeds that restricted who homeowners could sell to. This effectively carried on in segregated neighborhoods, North and South, for many years. In 1948, the Supreme Court ruled that any enforcement of these covenants by the states was unconstitutional; however, segregated neighborhoods remained.[32] One way of maintaining segregated neighborhoods was to refrain from listing a property and instead share the news via word of mouth.

Clearly, race—or more specifically, the maintenance of white supremacy—was never far from the minds of white Hanoverians. By 1919, the local weekly, the *Herald Progress*, had begun to publish words of wisdom from a fictional Black man, "Dumb Buck" the Philosopher of the Slashes. Dumb Buck regaled readers with sayings like, "Some folks says thar ain't no heben nor no hell. 'Spects I don't know. Maybe 'tis, maybe taint. No one eber come back to tell but as far as for dis por ole nigger—ain't taken no chances a-tall. De strait and narrow path is good 'nough for me. Safty first my moter."[33] Buck's creator was just as sexist as he was racist. For instance, in one paper he wrote that "the difference twixt a umbrella and a 'oman is dat you kin shut up de umbrella." Dumb Buck, who appears to have been generated locally, at first consisted entirely of text, but by 1920 Buck was pictured as a hunched-over, elderly Black man dressed in an overcoat, top hat, and cane and accompanied by a little dog.[34]

Cartoons demeaning Black people and women were common in the early decades of the twentieth century. Cartoonists in the antebellum North often used their art to ridicule members of the free Black elite.[35] When northern white women began to take a stand for abolition and women's rights, cartoons connected abolition and miscegenation. With these techniques as models, cartoonists in the postwar South employed this method of control against Black people inclined to step out of their place.³⁶

The local paper was an indicator of what white people thought about Black people during this period. This was evident in cartoons, editorials, and local organizations. The weekly *Hanover Herald Progress* embraced the pre-Civil War practices of northern white newspapers with "Dumb Buck," whose formally attired but bedraggled appearance caricatured the Black elite, the people who might have been perceived as stepping out of the boundaries drawn around the Black community. A cartoon like Dumb Buck showed that no matter how much money, education, and status African Americans attained, they would always be Dumb Buck.³⁷ The reaction of Black people to Dumb Buck is not available. He might have been the object of scorn or neglect, or they might have found him humorous. Whatever the case, his presence did not stop Black people from acting.

During the 1910s and 1920s, Hanover's Black community was not dormant. The idea of self-help through organizational development continued to thrive. At the turn of the century, Hanoverian William L. Taylor was still the Grand Worthy Master of the True Reformers, and it appeared that the order was thriving, but the truth would soon become evident. A banking division was added to the State Corporation Commission in 1910. With a young reformer, Charles C. Barksdale, at the commission's helm, vigorous investigations into the health of banks across Virginia began. In less than a year, Barksdale determined that the Savings Bank of the True Reformers was financially unviable, and he closed the institution for good. Like the order, the True Reformer bank was a highly respected institution among Black people, and many African American businesses, churches, and individuals trusted that their funds were safe in its care. Sadly, many of the investors lost their savings in what was known in Richmond's African American community as the "downfall of Africa."³⁸ According to the receivers, the bank's questionable financial decisions in the 1890s, even before William Browne died, led to the downfall of the bank, but this fact was not known in September 1910, when the True Reformers held a Grand Session in Richmond. The financial outlook of the order was bleak. Death benefits were in arrears, and it was determined that funds that had been intended for the use of the order had been channeled to the bank, which was a separate entity. Members of the order and the state commissioner of insurance believed that mismanagement on the part of Taylor had led to this problem. Taylor did not agree, and he attended the session with the intent of fighting any attempt to remove him as Grand Worthy Master. In the end, he came to understand that, if he did not leave the position, he would be held responsible for all the bank's problems. In September 1910, Taylor retired.[39]

While the True Reformers might have been on a downward slide during the first decade of the twentieth century, the Independent Order of St. Luke (IOSL) was on the rise thanks largely to the leadership of Maggie Lena Walker, who was elected the Right Worthy Grand Secretary in 1899. Founded shortly after the Civil War, the IOSL was in dire financial straits in 1899. When Walker took over, the order's assets totaled $31.61, and its debt was $400. There were just over one thousand financial members—members who had paid their membership fees and fifty-seven councils or chapters. The juvenile division, which had been headed by Walker until she became the Grand Secretary, included 1,600 children.[40] One year later, at the order's national convention, Walker proudly reported that the membership had grown to 3,830 in 89 councils.[41] Maggie L. Walker was a force to be reckoned with at the turn of the twentieth century. She focused on the needs of African American women, and she was passionately devoted to their uplift. She believed in gathering strong, hardworking women around her to get any job done. At the same time, she understood, as Black women understand today, that "only a strong and unified community made up of both women and men [can] wield the power necessary to allow Black people to shape their own lives."[42]

Black Hanoverians embraced the IOSL. Records indicating the order's presence in the county prior to 1917 are not available, but from 1917 to 1927, there were nine adult councils operating in Hanover and eight juvenile circles. Based on death benefits paid during this time, it appears that many of these councils did exist prior to 1917.[43]

Like the True Reformers, Walker and the IOSL enlisted Black people from the "country" to take part in the leadership of the order. By 1917, James R. Ware, a literate railroad worker with no formal education and a resident of the Hewlett section of Hanover, had become an organizing deputy in the IOSL. The duration of Ware's tenure in the organization is unknown, but he served as an officer at the state level until at least 1927. Like the True Reformers and many other fraternal organizations of the time, the IOSL paid death benefits to the families of members. For instance, between 1918 and 1921, the order paid benefits to the families of five juveniles in Hanover.[44]

Walker and the IOSL also worked for the economic independence of the Black community. The leadership strove to communicate good money management skills to members. In 1903, the IOSL opened the St. Luke Penny Savings Bank. In 1917, the order's fiftieth anniversary bulletin included the following notice:

Dimes make Dollars!!!
Start an account with St. Luke Bank
$1.00 opens an account
The bank pays 3% on all savings accounts
Get the Bank Book Habit
Save! Save!! Save!!![45]

The leadership of the IOSL believed that investing strengthened the individual, the family, and the order. As a result, organization funds were invested in several entities, including the town of Ashland. As early as 1919 and as late as 1927, the IOSL reported owning bonds in the town and getting a 5 percent rate of return on their investment. Records indicate that the bonds were consistently worth over $3,000.[46] The relationship between the town of Ashland and the IOSL presents the kind of paradox that pervaded segregation. The town was willing to accept money from a Black fraternal organization, but the council members would not have eaten a meal with the order's leadership. This financial connection is also illustrative of the pragmatism of Walker. If the order was to maintain its economic grounding, it needed to have income in addition to the membership fees paid by members. A town was a more stable investment than a business, especially a Black-owned business in those times. In general, this relationship is a good example of the notion that money knows no color.[47]

Maggie Walker also sought expanded educational opportunities for Black children, and Black Hanoverians concurred, but they fought an uphill battle all the way. While the taxes to pay for education had not been segregated in the Virginia constitution of 1902, very little money was allocated to the Black schools in Hanover, even for essentials. Most of the Black schools were one-room; many were little more than shacks with a wood-burning stove that was maintained by the older children. As a result, parents and teachers were compelled to raise funds on their own to keep the schools open. According to Inez Winston Gray, the daughter and granddaughter of Johnny and Clinton Winston, the County-Wide League was organized by Black citizens for this purpose. The adult league worked to raise funds for the schools. There was also a junior league that included schoolchildren, which prepared them to take over when their generation's turn came.[48]

In the early 1920s, there was still no high school for Black children in the county. Unless their families could afford private education, most Black children had to leave school after the seventh grade or moved to other places for schooling, perhaps living with relatives. At a meeting of the school board in April 1923, the superintendent reported that Black families came together to raise money to match the county to get a training school, which would provide for education for Black residents beyond the elementary level.[49]

The John F. Slater Fund, established in 1882 by John Slater, founded the County Training School Movement in 1911 when a Black school principal from Mississippi requested funds to hire an industrial teacher for girls. From this request grew, the Fund's call for better secondary education opportunities for Black youth. The stated goal of the training schools was to prepare Black teachers for the elementary schools and offer education to rural Black youth beyond elementary school.[50]

Early in the summer of 1924, Virginia's State Supervisor of Negro Education sent a letter to the Hanover school board promising to contribute $500 for teacher salaries if a training school opened in the county. On July 31, 1924, the countywide Committee of Colored Citizens presented $400 to the board.[51] In 1924, the Hanover County Training School for Black students opened.[52] Students from across the county attended, and since transportation was not provided, students walked for up to five miles to and from school in all types of weather. Some came from Mechanicsville in the eastern section of the county, others from as far away as Doswell, which was at the northern end. Inez Gray recalled that some of the Doswell students rode the train to Ashland; sometimes in the afternoon, they were locked out of the waiting room, even the side designated for Black people. This meant that they had to stand on the platform in all kinds of weather waiting for the train home.[53]

While the school board did contribute financially to the establishment of the schools, racism still played a major part in the education of Black children. The County-Wide League continued to operate and every year raised $400 to pay for the operation of the school. There is no evidence that white parents had to take such steps; indeed, there were three accredited high schools in the county for white students. The training school was not accredited, and graduates received a certificate instead of a diploma.[54]

By 1925, the school year still had not been equalized. The white schools in Ashland were open for nine months a year. The Black school session lasted seven months. There was an allowance in the budget for "matching the colored people dollar for dollar for the three teachers for an eighth grade" but not for the principal, whose salary came from the Slater Fund and from money raised by Black parents.[55] The Black schools outside the town, Vontay, Rockville, Gilman, Greenwood, Wickham, Newton, Brown Grove, and Elmont, were open only five months of the year. There were eleven white schools in Beaverdam, a magisterial district: five were open for nine months and six were open for seven months. By contrast, the six Black schools in Doswell, Beaverdam, and Bethany were open for only six months. In the end, then, no matter how much or how little time the white children spent in school, the Black children spent less.[56]

Teachers actively participated in bringing in funds to maintain the Black schools. In 1923, for example, Black teachers pledged to raise $800 for the Colored Training School in Ashland. Around the same time, the supervisor of the Colored Training School reported that a fundraiser had been held at Shiloh Baptist Church. Shiloh Baptist Church members collected an offering and deposited it in the bank. This money was for adding a basement to the school.[57] Another site of fundraising was the Training School itself. The facility was sometimes used to show "moving pictures." On one occasion in 1925, Dr. F.L. Day (race unknown) presented a movie, after which Dr. R.E. Blackwell, president of Randolph-Macon, spoke. Once again, the organizers solicited contributions for the basement at the Training School.[58]

While fundraising was an important part of the Black teacher's life, preparation was also crucial. Many of the teachers were not formally educated beyond the public-school level, and what is now known as in-service, or on-the-job, training was important to their success. Throughout the 1920s, the local paper reported on the training opportunities at the Black school. In 1925, the Hanover County Colored Teachers' Institute was held at the Training School. The sessions included methods for teaching arithmetic, reading, English, and geography.[59]

A similar event took place the next year, but this time, Hampton Institute, the historically Black private college on the Virginia Peninsula, was in charge. The paper reported that the organizers expected a big turnout and hoped that residents would participate. The organizers also shared their belief that education was the only thing that would solve the racial problem, and that Hampton had been doing its share for fifty years.[60]

The public schools also served other functions. At times, they became health facilities. For example, the Code of Virginia required that all teachers and students for the 1923–24 session receive a smallpox vaccination.[61] As a result, nurses from the County Public Health Office and school nurses visited all the schools in the county. Jean Folly remembered the day in 1923 when the nurse arrived. She laughed as she recalled a pact that no one would cry but remembered that some did.[62]

By the middle of the nineteenth century, reformers had begun to introduce a new type of school to the educational landscape in the United States. Reformatories or industrial schools opened to provide an opportunity for youthful offenders to be treated less like hardened criminals and more like redeemable members of society. Prior to this time, juveniles were imprisoned with adult criminals. By the turn of the century, there were sixty-five reformatories in the United States committed to rehabilitating youthful offenders; remarkably, two of them were in Hanover—the Hanover Reformatory for Negro Boys and the Industrial Home School for Colored Girls.[63]

Near the end of the nineteenth century, the Virginia General Assembly established the Prison Association of Virginia and empowered it to assume custody of minors "charged with any crime or being vagrant or a disorderly person or incorrigible."[64] Initially, these minors were committed to adult prison for an indeterminate amount of time. The length of the sentence depended on the judge hearing the case. The constitution of 1902 addressed the matter of what to do with juvenile offenders and mandated that the state could "in its discretion, make appropriations to non-sectarian institutions for the reform of youthful offenders."[65] In this instance, "youthful offenders" translated as male because only two schools existed—the Laurel School for White Boys and the Hanover Reformatory for Negro Boys, which was maintained by the Negro Reformatory Association of Virginia—neither of which addressed the needs of female offenders.[66]

Two issues become immediately apparent—one involving gender and the other race. First, young girls who found themselves in trouble were housed with women. Second, the names of the two male institutions set the young men up for two possible, and contrasting, reactions from the public. The Laurel School gives the impression of a private institution located in a picturesque location; additionally, laurel garlands are associated in western culture with distinction and victory. The school for African American boys, alternately referred to as the Virginia Manual Labor School or the Hanover Reformatory for Negro Boys, says to the observer immediately that this is an institution for "bad" boys.

The school for African American boys opened in 1897, but the earliest available biennial report was written in 1912. It reported that the Hanover boys' school housed offenders found guilty of crimes ranging from stealing to rape. It also noted that in the two preceding years, a chapel had been completed, and a Blacksmith shop was added to the campus. In addition to various trades they could learn, the boys attended an eight-month public school session. Throughout the 1910s and 1920s, the facility continued to expand to include a schoolhouse, cottage, and hospital. By 1914, the school had formed a marching band that over the coming decades would participate in local parades held by Black Hanoverians.[67]

Religious training, to encourage "straight living," was typically included in the curricula of these schools. Some privately controlled schools had a denominational affiliation, and for them, establishing a program of religious studies was straightforward. In state-supported schools, the staff might not have any training to teach religion. To overcome this obstacle, "provision [was] always made for preaching, religious services, and religious teaching, usually by ministers and others not connected with the school."[68] This was the situation with the reform school in Hanover, where chapel services took place weekly under the leadership of a local white clergyman.[69]

By 1919, the school was well established, and community support was evident. The officers of the Negro Reformatory Association of Virginia selected a committee of local Black women to prepare a holiday dinner and gifts for the boys. A newspaper article explained that more than fifty dollars had been allotted for sandwiches, hot chocolate, and over 200 bags of nuts, oranges, and apples. The president of the school suggested that these types of gifts and the thoughtfulness of the association went a long way toward instilling a sense of belonging in the young men.[70]

William Layton grew up at the boys' school. His father, William Sr., taught blacksmithing, and he and his family lived on the grounds. The younger man recalled that Dr. John H. Smyth, an African American and former United States Minister to Liberia, founded the facility when he realized that young Black boys served time alongside hardened adult male prisoners. The elder Layton soon rose to the position of "disciplinarian," and by 1927, he was the superintendent.[71]

Hanover became the site of the Industrial Home School for Colored Girls, which was founded in 1914 under the auspices of the Federation of Colored Women's Clubs. The board of trustees consisted of prominent Black and white women and men from around the state, including Maggie Walker, a major supporter. She often contributed to fundraisers for the school, once giving funds for a "moving picture machine."[72]

The school for girls was part of a national movement initiated by women across the country to provide structure for young girls who had not lived up to societal expectations. In the late nineteenth and early twentieth centuries, white women's organizations took on the task of supporting and reforming unwed mothers. These segregated institutions did not accept Black females, so Black women took on the responsibility.[73]

Janie Porter Barrett, a native Georgian, moved to Virginia where she attended Hampton Institute and was the superintendent and the driving force behind the Hanover School for Black Girls for over two decades. According to *The History of the Virginia State Federation of Colored Women's*

Clubs, Inc., in the early 1900s, a young girl in Hampton, Virginia, committed a minor offense and was jailed with adult women. Barrett and the other women of the Federation decided to found a school. They raised funds and eventually bought a 147-acre farm in Peakes, Hanover County Virginia, sometimes referred to as Peakes Turnout.[74] When the school opened in 1914, it housed twenty-eight girls ages eleven to eighteen in an old farmhouse.[75] By 1916, the campus included a new modern brick building, which according to Barrett, boasted all the conveniences except lighting.

In her report to the board of trustees in 1916, Barrett explained the procedures that a girl went through as she was processed into the school. First, they cleaned her up and gave her a clean bed. Next, they wrote her name on a clean page in the record book, telling her that the blank page represented a new beginning, and it was up to her to keep a clean record. Third, the girl told Barrett her entire story as soon as she was able. Next, they admonished a new enrollee not to dwell in the past. Finally, each girl was "made to feel that it was in her power to be one of the best women in the world if she really wanted to be."[76]

When the girls were eligible for parole, some returned to their families, but most of them were placed in the homes of families not related to them, for whom they worked; this was sometimes problematic. Black domestic servants were often preyed upon by the white men in the households. Black girls and women had been at the mercy of white men since slavery, and emancipation had not fully alleviated the problem. Barrett understood the pitfalls of placing young Black girls as domestics in white homes and was very selective regarding the placements. She did not hesitate to remove a girl who she thought misused. Since she could not be with the parolees, she placed them under the informal guardianship of Federation members who lived in the respective areas where the girls were assigned. Also, Barrett solicited the promise of Black clergymen in the area to visit the girls and invite them to join their churches. She believed that this too provided a measure of protection.[77]

To prepare the girls to leave the school and to serve in private homes, the staff at the school stressed religious study, academics, domestic duties, and farming. There was no time for idleness; they learned that no work, done well, was beneath them. Throughout the early days, Barrett struggled to find a clergyman to conduct weekly services. She said, "We realize that if these girls are to be changed and made safe members of society it must be by developing Christian character, so all work and play are planned with that in mind and the aim is to put our religion into everything we do."[78] Eventually, the school conducted services every Sunday, a midweek Bible class, and Sunday school. The goal was that each girl would accept Christ before leaving the institution.[79]

Of all the things Janie Porter Barrett fought for, academic classes for her girls were perhaps the most important to her. While the girls learned basic homemaking skills to prepare them to work in private homes, Barrett also wanted them to be prepared to enter high school, if it was available in their new community, when they left her care. They would have to obtain schooling through the eighth grade and acquire the prerequisites for further study. To accomplish this, two teachers were needed, an industrial teacher and a literary teacher. For many years, the request for a literary teacher went unanswered while the industrial program advanced; the board of trustees might have felt that academic preparation for these young women was less important than training them in the arts of cooking, cleaning, sewing, and raising food.[80]

In her 1918 report, Barrett stated the importance of a year-round school, which would ensure that the girls who missed classes when working on farms would have the opportunity to make them up. Continuing, Barrett said "that we will soon have a well-equipped school occupying the important place in our institution that it should . . . because . . . education is opportunity."[81] Barrett wanted to educate the girls at the school, not simply warehouse them like prisoners. Yet she pointed out that she did not have the proper equipment to conduct a school; she even lacked blackboards. The books used at the school were hand-me-downs from Kilbourne Farm, the reformatory for white girls located in Bon Air, Virginia, southwest of Richmond. She also pointed out that her school had not had a teacher during the first part of the preceding school year. When teachers were not supplied, Barrett and the head matron, Mrs. Griffith, taught the classes in addition to carrying out their regular responsibilities. In 1919, the school was placed on the agenda of the State Board of Education and finally received a literary teacher and an industrial teacher at state expense.[82]

The white and Black neighbors of the school were not always happy with its presence, and according to Barrett, protested the school's presence. Barrett tried to allay people's fears by appearing useful to the community. She had the opportunity to do this during World War I. In 1918, when harvest time arrived, labor was scarce. Men were either overseas or in military training camps. Realizing what this shortage of labor meant to the farmers in the area, Barrett offered the assistance of her girls. Initially, the farmers declined the offer, afraid the girls would do more harm than good. In the end, Barrett was able to convince her neighbors that their fears were unfounded. She explained to the girls that this was their opportunity to prove that they were worthy and valuable citizens. They harvested for Black and white farmers that year, and there were no complaints. Some of the farmers shared their crops with the school, but Barrett was not concerned with those who did not. She explained that she was simply grateful for the chance to show what her girls could do.[83]

In 1920, the boys' and girls' schools were transferred to the state. At that time, the girls' school became the Virginia Industrial School for Colored Girls.[84] While Barrett does not mention this change in status in her report that year, the president of the board, Ann Schmelz, does. Schmelz indicated in her report to the board that "special mention should be made of the fine spirit of the colored women in the matter of this transfer. The farm that they had bought, all of their subsequent contributions of money, materials, and sacrifice—with joy and pride they made the gift of *their* State, to *our* State, to the State of the White and colored citizens."[85] The following year, Schmelz talked about the problems that came with the transfer to the state. According to Schmelz, the Black women who had formerly supported the school had stopped giving—no clothes, food, or general supplies. She says Barrett tried to explain to them that even though the state had taken over, the assistance of the Federation of Colored Women's Clubs was still crucial to the survival of the school.[86]

This is a curious turn of events, raising questions about the willingness of the Black women to turn over their land and the school to the state. There is no mention of any exchange of money for this land—a possible controversy. The Federation women might have resented the loss of control of the school to the all-white legislature. It is hard to believe that simple naiveté about the school's needs led these women to withdraw their support.

Whatever the impetus for the Federated Women's Clubs' withdrawal of support for the school, the organization soon resumed their commitment to the school. In 1925, Maggie Walker attended the graduation exercises at the school. She wrote in her diary that she convinced seven carloads of Richmonders to attend the event, which included a pageant on the lawn featuring cooking, sewing, laundry work, feeding and attending horses, chickens, and pigs, serving food and house cleaning.[87] The Federation often had executive board meetings at the school, such as the one in February 1928, during which the students served a seven-course dinner in the dining room.[88]

While the education of Black children in Hanover proceeded, their parents were trying to find ways to feed, house, and clothe their families. As Chenery explains "Few, very few in Ashland, were regarded as rich. The overwhelming majority were poor and poorer. The people I knew were absorbed in a daily struggle to secure some kind of respectable living from the uncertain jobs available."[89] While Chenery was talking about his white neighbors, Black people fit even more squarely into the category of poor and poorer, and most had precious few opportunities to improve their economic condition. This is apparent in Chenery's statement that "boys and Negroes" were happy to work for much less, presumably, than white men.[90] This meant that Black men did not earn much more than their young sons or white people much younger than themselves and moving out of the ranks of the poor was challenging to say the least. Occasionally, a notice appeared in the classified section of the paper like the one placed by Arthur [Green] of Ashland: "Situation wanted—by colored man as working manager for small farm or shares."[91] Other times the newspaper included notices welcoming either white or Black workers, but more often the ads specified the race of the person the advertiser wished to hire: "Wanted—a white man with small family as farm hand. Good wages and house."[92]

At the turn of the twentieth century, farming remained the major source of employment for Black families and individuals in the county. According to the 1900 census there were 929 Black and other nonwhite farmers. Of those 929, there were 457 owners, 135 part owners,

334 tenants, and 3 farm managers. A decade later those numbers rose to 677 Black owned farms and 151Black tenants. In 1920, 693 farms were owned and 163 were operated by tenants. The numbers increased until 1930 when the owners decreased to 528 owners and the tenants increased to 187. In the early decades of the twentieth century, following disfranchisement, people made inroads into the farming business until the onset of the Great Depression.[93]

By 1926, conferences aimed at teaching Black farmers how to improve their output were taking place. One such conference took place at Brown Grove Baptist Church in Hanover County. At this time, the Black people in the county did not have a farm extension agent, so J.C. Stiles, the white county agent and the nurse attended. In addition, L.C. White—a member of the Negro Organization Society—one Mr. Jeter of Hampton Institute and J.L. Charity, the district agent, were all scheduled speakers. They also planned culinary demonstrations by the Black 4-H cooking club of Ashland. Refreshments were sold, and "all colored farmers and tenants of the county were asked to attend this conference."[94]

Work opportunities in Ashland were limited. Many Black women had no choice but to work in the homes and offices of white people, cooking, cleaning, and taking care of the children. These women were often the primary caregivers to the young children. Because of this closeness, many young white children felt a very real love for these Black women. This love might translate into a lifetime connection, but the connection ordinarily did not in turn evolve into a real feeling of equality among the individuals. When those white children grew up, they often adopted a paternalistic attitude toward the women who raised them. As William Chenery recalled, "We absorbed with our mother's milk, or with that of our wet nurse if we had one, even though she might be a Negro, the Southern belief in the segregation of the races. Nobody questioned the desirability of keeping and defending impenetrable social barriers. The whites assumed that they were superior. I was long past boyhood before I realized that to everybody that assumption was not self-evident."[95]

A 1919 obituary in the *Herald Progress* offers an example of the worldview to which Chenery refers: "Aunt Marie Dead. Aunt Marie Lataney, one of the best known of our colored citizens, died at her residence on lower Railroad Street on Sunday morning. She was one of the oldest citizens in

Ashland and had been associated with the best families in Ashland ever since the Civil War. Her funeral took place from Shiloh Baptist Church of which she had been a member for many years."[96] The notice placed in the *Herald Progress* by the Latney family indicates that they did not accept the community's assumption of superiority and inferiority. The week after the obituary ran in the paper, the family of Maria Latney sent a general thank you note to all "colored and White" who offered sympathy at the passing of their mother. Rev. T.M. Allen and undertaker Winston received special thanks.[97]

The difference between these two notices is evident. In the first, "Aunt Marie" is not granted the dignity of her correct given name or her surname. She had been a "mammy" to some of the best white citizens, but these citizens did not know her correct name or how to spell her last name. The thank-you note expressed "special" appreciation to only two persons, and they were Black men, not members of the "best [White] families." The Latneys took the opportunity of the notice in the paper to assert their mother's dignity.

Taking control of one's own name had been a battle fought by Black people since slavery. White men and women rarely employed the title of Mr. or Mrs. before the name of a Black person. Indeed, when race is not attributed to individuals in the public records of the time, determination of race can often be made by how the person is referred to in the meeting minutes and other official records. In lieu of the accepted terms of address that indicated respect among whites, white people might add "Uncle" or "Aunt" in front of a Black man or woman's name. This can be seen in the obituaries of "Uncle Sam," Samuel Harris, the beloved janitor at the white high school or "Uncle Robert," Robert Lightfoot, the bell ringer at Randolph-Macon.[98] Black people did not use these terms unless addressing their family members, and they always used Mr. or Mrs. when talking about those called Uncle and Aunt by white people.

In the white world, Black people had little control over how they were addressed, but there were instances in which they were able to take charge. John Morris of Hanover County related a story about white people coming to his family's home when he was a young boy and referring to everyone as aunt and uncle. He laughed and said, "I'll never forget one day, one of them came to the house looking for my grandfather and asked

Roses in December

if Uncle Pic was there. Mama called out, 'Hey, Papa, your niece is out here.'" Clearly, the practice of white people calling Black men and women aunt and uncle sometimes irritated Morris's mother, and in her way, she made her point to the visitor. Margaret Washington remembered having to address white people as Mr. and Mrs. and address Black men and women by their first name unless they were very old, and then they were called aunt or uncle. She laughs and says, "my father had more white nephews and nieces than ever because he was old."[99]

Similarly, Beryl Thompson Carter recalled her grandmother's encounter with a white man who called her Aunt Edna. Carter's grandmother was a well-known midwife in the county and provided services to Black and white families. She also worked as a domestic on occasion for one of the wealthiest white families in the county. Thompson remembered that this white family "just *loved* my grandma. The sun didn't set on her because there was nobody like her," but they still called her grandmother by her first name and expected to be addressed as Mr. or Mrs.; "that never went away."[100]

Carter, who describes her grandmother as self-assured and feisty, found her grandmother's interactions with the white people she knew and worked for a little confusing. Her grandmother was always respectful to the white people she worked for but not those she did not know and who did not know her. Carter recalled the time an unknown white man stopped to ask for directions. He called her grandmother "Aunt Edna [and] she gave him where to go and get off this property kind of talk." Carter emphasized, "Didn't matter whether they had nothing, and you had something. You still were aunt somebody."[101]

Beryl Carter's father and grandfather also managed to exert some control over how white people addressed them. Both men used their first initial only. Carter always believed that this was because they did not like their first names, but as an adult, she learned the real reason. Since white people did not know their first name, they could not use it. In this way, Carter's father and grandfather refused to give white people the ammunition with which to insult them. White people did not like it when they used the initial. Carter remembers that whenever she was with her father and he had to sign something, he would sign J. Conroy Thompson; the white people always wanted to know his first name, and he always

Disfranchised

replied, J. Even during segregation, when white people thought they were in control, they were mistaken.[102]

Returning to the topic of viable employment, some Black men were lucky enough to find work on the railroad, which was considered a good job for a Black man, no matter what the position. This was the case with Beryl Carter's grandfather. "Grandpa had a little more status because he was a railroad man." His regular route took him from Hewlett to Clifton Forge, Virginia. He would stay there for as long as ten days and then return home. Carter's grandfather also farmed his own land, but he did not earn enough from farming to support his family.[103]

One "town" occupation, referring to Ashland that seems to have been limited to Black men was that of "scavenger." Today, referred to as garbage men/people or sanitation workers, but during this period in history they not only picked up trash but they also emptied privies or outdoor toilets. One man who worked as a scavenger was Henry Dabney. He is first mentioned in the town minutes in 1923, and by 1925, he was removing trash from residences for twenty-five cents per house.[104] Regardless of the nature of his business, the fact remains that Dabney was an entrepreneur who negotiated contracts with the town and operated his business his way.

There were other Black entrepreneurs in the town. One such person was Judson Coleman. He owned Coleman's Barbershop where he catered to a white clientele. His state-of-the-art shop included showers, which were a special treat at the time. His ads ran regularly in the *Herald Progress*.[105]

In 1925, Coleman's brother John built a hotel for Black tourists in the Black neighborhood of Berkleytown. John Coleman was described in the *Herald Progress* as a "popular tonsorial artist." His hotel, known as the "Community Inn," was said to have cost approximately $10,000, roughly $148,539 today and held five bedrooms on the second floor. Expecting many tourists during the summer season, Coleman explained, "we ain't much on travellin' in the cold weather."[106] By "we" Coleman meant Black people. His remark might be an indication of how comfortable he was talking to whites about race, but it is more likely that he was playing up to his white interviewer by stereotyping his own people.

In 1919, advertisements for William M. Sullivan's cleaning business appeared in the newspaper. As with Judson Coleman, most of Sullivan's clients were white. Sullivan not only ran a brisk business, he also devoted time to improving his community. He founded and directed a Black marching band, which the white community also appreciated. First mentioned in the local paper in 1919, the band was lauded for a fine performance on Easter Monday. They were in new uniforms and looked "spic and span." Later that summer Sullivan's Band, as it was known, participated in a parade of Black Hanoverians on July Fourth. In the section of the newspaper called "Our Colored Friends," the article explains that "the colored citizens of Ashland did themselves proud on the Fourth by a nice parade, headed by Sullivan's Band—twenty odd strong. Our colored citizens assembled at the high school, and with 'old Glory' flying high formed a most commendable parade and marched through the principal streets out to Shiloh Church where a most enjoyable day was spent."[107]

In December 1919, the *Herald Progress* praised Sullivan's Band with a front-page article, a rare tribute to a Black man during this time. The writer suggested that Ashland could be proud of Sullivan and the other "energetic young colored men of our town." This time they had marched through town on Thanksgiving Day. The writer ends by saying that "the best part of this band is that their uniforms and instruments are all paid for."[108] Sullivan's Band also led parades of fraternal orders through town. This was the case for a society of Black women known as the Sisters of Damon. While it is not clear what they were celebrating, the women were dressed in uniform and marched in 1921 to martial music from Berkleytown to Union Baptist Church.[109] As mentioned in the previous chapter, these types of displays represented one way that African Americans claimed civic existence and even citizenship. William Sullivan's community spirit did not end with his band. In 1921, he founded a Young Men's Christian Association for Black males in Ashland that was open to all young men in the county. He rented a house on James Street to use as headquarters. It is not certain how long the organization lasted, but in 1923 the group held something called a wide-awake meeting on Sunday afternoon in Sullivan's Auditorium. Mr. William Davenport of Richmond was the speaker. This was, in part, a recruitment event. Reportedly, a sizable number of new men joined, "but the club hopes to have every right-thinking man of the community on its roll before the New Year."[110]

Disfranchised

Clinton Winston, a blacksmith who opened his business in 1892, was still operating successfully in the early part of the twentieth century. In the three decades following the virtual loss of citizenship for Black people in the state, Winston worked actively at his trade. During this time, he repaired streetlamps and street tools for the town. He built coffins at the request of the county. In 1920, he sold several acres of land that would become the Woodland Cemetery, one of the county's white burial grounds.[111]

Winston passed on his entrepreneurial spirit to his son, Johnny Clinton Winston. The younger Winston took over his father's businesses in the 1920s. He continued to do business with the town and county for the next thirty years. Johnny Winston was also politically minded. In 1905, at the age of twenty-five, he registered to vote. He was one of very few Black men in Ashland who registered after the 1902 Constitution took effect. His daughter, Inez Winston Gray, recalled that her father was always interested in politics. She remembered that he and her aunt, Ethel Winston Hicks, spent a good deal of time discussing current events. While Gray did not recall her father's response to specific incidents, she believed that he voted.

Winston's registration record is not available. According to records, sixty Black men managed to register in Ashland. This brings up the question of why Winston and certain other Black men were allowed to register. He was well-known and respected in the community. Gray remembered that her father, like his father before him, was trusted and respected in the community by white as well as by Black people. Like his father, he performed work for the town and county. As a successful businessman, Winston could afford to pay his poll tax. He was also literate and could have passed a fairly administered literacy test, but as Chenery suggested, the test was not typically administered to Black men without prejudice.[112]

Winston was a religious man, and this could have added to his stature in the community. He was a leader in Shiloh Baptist Church, the oldest Black church in Ashland. As a church leader, he was instrumental in the institution's survival and growth during this era. His daughter, Inez Gray, remembered that church services lasted all day Sunday and usually her father and some of the other men stayed rather than making the walk back home between services. This was especially true in the winter when someone had to keep the wood stoves burning. As important, she also recalled her father and other men standing on the corner near the church discussing the issues of the day, even as they tried to find a way to pay all the bills.[113]

All the entrepreneurs mentioned above—Dabney, the Coleman brothers, Sullivan, and Winston—represent a small but interesting component of the Hanover business community. Except for Dabney and John Coleman, all had white customers and one, the barber Judson Coleman, dealt primarily with white men. There was something about these men that attracted and maintained a white clientele. It might simply have been that they provided a good service at a reasonable price. It might have happened because Ashland was a small town, and everyone knew each other and had a mutual history. There might also be an element of "place" involved in this scenario. These Black entrepreneurs, while they probably carried themselves with dignity, presumably understood their place and remained in it. Judson Coleman, Sullivan, and Winston each provided a service, and white people were accustomed to Black people providing a service. But this explanation is not absolute: in 1912, John Coleman stepped out of his "place" when he purchased a home on Henry Clay Road and subsequently, challenged the residential segregation ordinance.

There is at least one other example of white people in Hanover stepping out of the box of racism to embrace a Black man. In 1926, George Washington Carver visited Randolph-Macon College. Carver was lauded in the newspaper as a credit to his race—language that typically implies that one is an exception to the rule. The *Herald Progress* article that reported the visit said that Carver offered an interesting lecture on 202 products made from the peanut. The reporter ended his story by saying of Carver that "as a chemist, he has few equals possibly no superiors," high praise indeed from a white person for an African American man in 1926. At least publicly, Carver was welcome in the town. When he returned to Tuskegee, he sent a note to the college thanking his hosts for an enjoyable visit. Carver was accepted as a scientist and a scholar, and perhaps it was his genius that enabled white people to overlook his race. This largesse was not extended to Black Ashlanders: according to Dorothy Jones, who was a white high school senior in the audience for

Carver's talk, Black people in the county were not allowed to attend the RMC lecture.[114]

The lack of voting privileges and the indignity of being kept away from George Washington Carver's lecture did not deter Black people from speaking up. Indeed, they still expected elected officials to work for them. They were not shy about going to the town council or the county board of supervisors when they found it necessary. In 1918, Black people asked the county board to allocate funds for a Black farm demonstration agent. These agents were assigned to rural areas to teach the farmers how to get the most out of their land. They taught cultivation techniques, crop rotation, and business skills. There was already a white agent, but he did not readily work with Black people. Indeed, the agent, J. C. Stiles, had to be courted strongly by the white trustees of the girls' school before he agreed to act as a consultant for the agricultural program at the school.[115] In the end, the application for a Black farm agent was denied because the "County finances do not at this time justify an appropriation for this purpose."[116] This topic was not discussed again by the board of supervisors until the 1950s.

In 1926, Black county residents Judson Coleman, William Sullivan, and Willie Buckner petitioned county supervisor W. H. Davis for relief from the bad roads in Berkleytown, the Black community just north of Randolph-Macon College. The road out of Ashland, Henry Street, which led to the Black school, about one thousand yards in all, was typically impassable during the winter months. Berkleytown included $50,000 in taxable homes, stores, a hotel, and public school. The road needed grading, draining, and a topcoat of gravel. The property owners offered to pay for half the expenses in hopes of getting some relief from the county.[117] In 1928, Linwood Henderson, a deacon at Shiloh Baptist Church, went before the Ashland Town Council to request that a waterline be constructed to his property, which was in the rear of the Porter Estate.[118] The record does not include information on the outcome of these requests.

The county board of supervisors seemed reluctant to offer Black people assistance to better their lives, but they were at times quite generous when they could act out of paternalism. For example, they readily cared for the sick and indigent. In 1922, the board agreed to give Mary Johnson three dollars a month for three months in provisions, "it appearing that the said Mary Johnson is sick and incapable of earning a living and without any other means of support."[119] The board committed Tom Coleman to the poorhouse because he is "old and [infirm] and has no viable means of support."[120] In 1927, three years after Coleman was committed, the board authorized the overseer of the poor in the Henry District to buy food for Mary Wingfield, "an old colored [woman]." She was allotted two dollars a month.[121]

The first generation living without the franchise in the county did not back away from the spiritual fortifications that their ancestors had built. The Black church continued to grow. African Americans played a noteworthy role in the spiritual, social, political, and educational life of the county. Many of the churches opened schools; they also held fundraisers to help pay for extra teachers, they served as meeting places for betterment organizations, and they sponsored social events that were aimed at exposing their congregations and guests to the finer things in life.

The Black churches in the county also held annual revival services aimed at rejuvenating the community and re-awakening, if needed, their faith walk. These services rotated among all the churches in the community each fall, which was also known as revival season. These weeklong services began on Sunday with Homecoming, which Black citizens also called the Big Meeting, a time when current and past members came together to worship and pray and share a huge meal followed by an afternoon service. From Monday through Friday, an evangelist would preach each evening beginning at 8 p.m. It was his job to remind the congregation of the goodness of God—that the Lord had not left them alone before and would not leave them alone now. These services were typically packed and usually attracted new people to Christianity and to the respective congregations.[122]

The ministers were concerned for their parishioners' mortal souls, and this meant providing good clean entertainment that would not tempt them to sin. There were not many "Godly" places that Christians could go in the County that were outside the church arena. As a result, the churches themselves provided social opportunities. In June 1920, Shiloh Baptist presented a May Queen event. The *Herald Progress* reported that the event "was most creditable entertainment from all accounts."[123] These accounts apparently came from the large number of white people present, who spoke very highly of the organization of the event. Almost one year later, the pastor of Shiloh, the Rev. E.W. Murphy, invited the Municipal Band (race unknown) of Richmond to present a classical concert at his church. The notice in the paper informed white readers that seats would be reserved for them.[124] This last note let white men and women know that, if they attended this concert, their ideals of racial segregation and white supremacy would not be challenged. It also assured the African American organizers that they would be able to benefit from white attendees' contributions to the offering.

The first generation of Black people to live with the loss of the vote was far from helpless or hopeless. While in some ways they might have given the appearance of submissiveness, the Black citizenry of Hanover County continually sought and sometimes obtained redress for wrongs. Taking advantage of such opportunities as were offered, they made the best of a bad situation. And they maintained a rich social life. Hard work, an eye on the future, putting God first, organizing, and patience are the themes that continually come up in the sources. Black residents believed that a better day was coming, so they waited patiently, but not idly. While they waited, they acted: they built schools and churches, homes, and businesses. They interacted with white people, but they maintained lives that were separate from those of whites, both physically and emotionally. Through simultaneously waiting and actively living their lives, Black people made sure white people had to exert themselves in order to control them, all the while maintaining a little control for themselves.

5

The Great Depression, New Deal, War, and Ordinary Acts of Resistance

THE GREAT DEPRESSION presented many financial challenges to Black families, and survival often meant that even the youngest among them sought ways to bring resources to the family. Children sometimes worked odd jobs running errands, cleaning homes, doing yard work, or babysitting, as in the case of Ruth Winston Carter. Carter's job also allowed her to resist attempts by white people to demean her. Carter recalls that she got her first afterschool job when she was about ten years old. Many white families hired young Black girls to take care of their children after school. The babysitters left school at 3:00 p.m. and picked up their charges by 3:30 p.m. They would all meet at the white First Baptist Church, where they would run around and play, ride tricycles, and the like. Carter worked as a babysitter from ages ten to thirteen.

First Baptist, with its large grassy lawn, was the gathering place of all these young nannies and their charges. White mothers often gave the Black girls money to buy the children ice cream. Some mothers also gave the sitter a nickel to get ice cream for herself. The woman Ruth Carter worked for would give her a nickel for the child but not one for her. Carter remembers with a chuckle that, since the child could not talk, she could not tell the mother that she never got any ice cream.[1]

With economic depression, world war, and the promise of a new deal in the background, chapter 5 looks through the same lenses—education, religion, employment, and organizing—considered in previous chapters and finds Black Hanoverians continuing to expect their rights as citizens despite the continuing entrenchment of white supremacy. Specifically, this chapter considers the Great Depression, World War II, and resistance to the era of disfranchisement as seen in the young Ruth Winston Carter. Black residents endured financial downturns, took advantage of the New Deal, continued to seek the best education available for their children, and they fought for democracy overseas and on the home front, while living in an undemocratic society. The church remained a mainstay as the Black community continued to rise to the top evermore boldly agitating for their rights.

The decades of the 1930s and 1940s wrought major changes in American life. Economic depression, the New Deal, and finally World War II left an impact that continues to be felt today. By 1932, President Franklin Delano Roosevelt was elected with the promise of a New Deal, but even FDRs wide array of programs and agencies failed to fully alleviate the effects of the Great Depression. It would take a war with all the related industrial growth and development to put real if ironic meaning to the song, "Happy Days Are Here Again." Depression, New Deal, World War—Black residents in Hanover County experienced and reacted to this triumvirate of national and international chaos and hope. Black Hanoverians played their part—they shared what they had, they took advantage of the New Deal, and when the time came, they fought in Europe and the Pacific and served on the home front. They acted as citizens although their rights as citizens were severely limited.

While scholars suggest that the seeds of the Great Depression were planted earlier, October 29, 1929, is commonly acknowledged as the start of "one of the most transforming decades in the American chronicles."[2] Following World War I, *prosperity* was the buzzword. The gross national product rose to more than $51 billion between 1915 and 1920, the largest five-year increase in US history.[3] Delayed gratification went the way of the Pony Express as installment buying became the answer to limited funds—put a few dollars down, agree to weekly or monthly payments, and take your dream kitchen appliance home today—leading to major debt for families who had formerly paid as they bought.

The Great Depression was felt by all Americans, but relatively little has been written about its impact on African Americans. It was difficult to measure changes in the economic condition of most Black people, who already lived at or below the poverty line before the Depression hit. Even before October 29, most of the Black men and women who had jobs were barely surviving on their earnings.

In urban centers, the effect of the Depression was far more noticeable than in rural areas. Soup lines, shantytowns, and beggars were commonplace in cities. In rural areas, many people grew their own food, cut wood to keep warm, and shared with their neighbors. Carrie Burton of Hanover remembered that her father always had a garden, and that he would go through the neighborhood delivering bags of vegetables to neighbors. Whatever he had, he divided with family and friends.[4]

Sharing was a way of life in rural areas, so receiving extras from the garden of a neighbor was normal. Accepting help from an agency, however, was another matter. Dorothy Gardner Jones, a white Hanoverian and the director of the federal welfare office in the county during the Depression, recalled that many people, Black and white, were simply too proud to ask for help.[5] The owners of local general stores knew who was not able to pay their bills and told Jones who would load her truck with surplus food and supplies and deliver the food to the store or to private homes. The available provisions varied but might include cheese, beans, flour, and sometimes fruit.[6]

Robert Grimes began working at a boarding house when he was thirteen. Looking back, Grimes grasped just how poor his family was, but this realization did not hit him until he was a grown man and in the Marines. He remembered that while they had shoes for school, they took them off after 3 p.m., and when the soles of those shoes wore out, they stuffed them with paper. Grimes's family did not have bedspreads, so they slept under World War I overcoats, and "they were *heavy!*" While they slept in relative comfort, the house was very cold. Indeed, from November to March they had to break the ice to wash their faces. "It was hell," Grimes recalled. During the Depression, his father worked at the Henry Clay Inn, a hotel and restaurant in Ashland. He earned three dollars a week, and brought home leftovers, so while the job did not pay much, the family ate well as long as the senior Grimes worked at the inn.[7]

While some people managed to make a living during the Depression, many Black people sank to new levels of destitution. Poverty, like a whiff of smoke, snakes its way into every crack and crevice, and it affects people in ways that are not always clear at first glance. For example, few people, if any, in Hanover County starved to death during the Depression. As pointed out earlier, most people had something to eat, but there was often insufficient food to fill all the stomachs of the typically large rural family. Poor nutrition, along with lack of access to dental and medical care, led to major health problems. This was perhaps most evident in schoolchildren.[8]

Lack of knowledge, understanding, and money led to major dental problems for poor people, Black and white. As a result, the Hanover County Health Department and the Red Cross sponsored dental clinics in county schools.[9] At one clinic in 1932, of the 650 Black children examined, 616 needed dental work. Fifty received "corrections," leaving 566 children untreated.[10] Presumably, the untreated problems worsened leading to lifelong difficulties. For example, bad teeth led to issues related to appearance and self-esteem, and untreated gum disease can lead to heart problems, diabetes, blood infections, and a variety of illnesses linked to the digestive system.[11]

Living under the strictures of white supremacy, health care was always challenging for Black residents of the county, and the Depression brought little change.[12] Tuberculosis, or the White Plague, continued to menace the community. Not everyone died from TB, but patients could be removed from the community to sanatoriums, some for many years until they were well or died. The county provided segregated chest clinics—Black people went to Shiloh Baptist Church.[13]

In 1934, the State Department of Health sponsored a hot lunch campaign in the schools. Many children did not have breakfast before school and malnourished children often became ill, caused discipline problems, and had difficulty learning. The community was aware of this need and contributed to the hot lunch campaign. In May 1936, the two teachers at the Mt. Zion School in Hanover sent a thank-you note to the *Herald Progress* thanking members of the community for contributions of canned food for the students.[14] School supporters furnished and cooked the food, and the teachers served it with the assistance of a student committee.[15]

Adele Dabney, supervisor of the Black schools, reported that the Wickham School at Hickory Hill served hot lunches daily.[16] Six-year-old James

Edward Henry entered first grade in the fall of 1936. He attended Wickham School, also known as Providence Church School. Providence Baptist Church and the school were located on land that had formerly been part of Hickory Hill Plantation.[17] He was born in the community known as Wickham, but not on the former plantation where his grandfather had been enslaved. He attended the one-room school, leaving to attend the Hanover County Training School in Ashland after second grade. While Henry does not remember much about the first and second grade, he has vivid memories of the training school. Unlike his first two years, Henry walked several miles in all kinds of weather to the training school. He also remembers that the school did not have running water and was heated by a wood burning stove that the custodian started in the morning and the students kept going all day by going back and forth to the basement to get wood and coal.[18] According to Claudius (Mick) Dabney, on rainy days the basement flooded, the wood was wet, and students were cold.[19] There were two buildings—one for elementary students and the other for high school students and there was a water pump between the buildings.[20] He remembers Eunice Bundy, the principal who lived across the street from the school. According to Henry, she was a good principal. She was a caring but strict disciplinarian, and she did not play. Mrs. Bundy was also prepared to do what she needed to do to support her students. There was no cafeteria at the training school, so Mrs. Bundy prepared soup or beans in her kitchen and carried the food across the street so the students had lunch.

By February 1938, two other Black schools were receiving soup, vegetables, potatoes, cocoa, and other items from "interested patrons in the community."[21] Near the end of 1938, the faculty and students of the Training School thanked members of the community, including the Union Baptist Church Sunday School and the South Anna Elks Lodge, (both African American organizations) for contributing food to help feed the sixty-one underweight children at the school.[22]

Of course, the need for hot lunches was only the tip of the iceberg. For other health care concerns, a county nurse was available. For a while, Mae Mathers, the white county nurse, worked with white and Black citizens. Her job was multifaceted, but in general, she was responsible for carrying out the edicts of the state with regard to health care. She

The Great Depression and Ordinary Acts of Resistance

conducted workshops at the Black schools explaining the fundamental principles of health. She also aided the county teachers with the state-mandated five-point check-ups of children's hearing, vision, teeth, throat, and weight. Mathers was acting in this capacity when she visited the Pine Tree Colored School in Hanover in March 1932.[23] Typically, parents were encouraged to take their children to a family physician for the five-point check-ups, but most Black families did not have access to doctors, at least not for proactive health care measures. Teachers addressed such concerns in the Black schools.

Mathers also registered residents with the state Bureau of Vital Statistics. Most children born in rural areas were born at home, their mothers assisted by a midwife. For many years, registering births was not required, and even after it became obligatory, midwives were not always diligent in carrying out this part of their job. Sometimes it was simply a matter of getting the information into the proper hands, but some midwives did not read or write and could not fulfill this task. In 1932, Mathers took blank birth certificates to the Black schools and parents completed and returned 150. Fifty of the children were not registered.[24]

African Americans could not depend on the white-run health system. Black leaders on the local and national level believed that education was critical to overcoming the health-related concerns plaguing their communities. Established in 1914, National Negro Health Week responded to this concern. This week, sponsored by the National Negro Health Movement, part of Roosevelt's New Deal, in conjunction with the United States Public Health Service, state and local agencies and interested organizations, took place each spring. [25] When the Office of Negro Health Week was established during the New Deal Era, "it was the first time since the Freedman's Bureau" that the federal government prioritized healthcare for African Americans. This office was the headquarters of the National Negro Health Week campaign, which evolved into a year-round program known as the National Negro Health Movement. Churches, schools, organizations, and private citizens educated Black people about the importance of health care. These campaigns addressed mothers and children for the most part. There were lectures, demonstrations, and contests. Days were set aside to focus on personal hygiene, community sanitation, and communicable diseases.[26]

On December 12, 1934, the work of Mae Mathers, the white nurse, and Adele Dabney, the Black school supervisor, ended abruptly and poignantly when a train hit their car killing both women. The community's acceptance of Mathers and Dabney presents an interesting quandary. Accompanied by many restrictions, segregation dominated life in the county, but it appears that Dabney and Mathers worked together comfortably, and even more striking, county residents liked and respected both women. No one was surprised that the two women were in the same car. An article in the paper mentioned that Mathers had been in the county for three years, and Dabney, who had been working in Hanover for just under two years, was given the title of "Miss," a show of respect rarely bestowed on a Black person during this period.[27] Local churches, schools, and organizations contributed to the Mathers-Dabney Fund, in memory of both women with the funds earmarked to fight hunger and malnutrition.[28] Despite the efforts of parents, teachers, and the county, Grace Bushell, the supervisor of Negro schools, reported 100 undernourished Black children in 1935.[29] By 1937, the Mathers-Dabney Fund expanded the hot lunch program in the Black schools. In addition to helping students learn, hot meals reduced the number of children contracting tuberculosis.[30]

Black Hanoverians prioritized good health care. For many years, Black residents sought a public health care nurse to maintain the "tuberculosis work, maternal welfare program, child health program, colored school health education and examinations, smallpox, diphtheria, immunizations, and other activities among the colored people, which make up 42% of the County's population."[31] In 1937, the Works Progress Administration (WPA), a New Deal agency, agreed to pay a portion of the salary for a graduate nurse who had special training in public health. Members of the Black community raised funds, which were supplemented by other community organizations.[32]

Health care was a major concern during the Depression, and so were unemployment and vagrancy. In response, the Roosevelt administration developed the Civilian Conservation Corps (CCC). The most successful of the New Deal initiatives, the CCC put young men to work saving forests and creating national and state parks. The agency fell under the umbrella of the Department of Interior; the Departments of Agriculture,

Labor, and War also had major roles. Initially recruits were required to be male and between eighteen and twenty-five years old, but the minimum age was lowered to seventeen. Prospective enrollees had to be unemployed, healthy, 60–78 inches tall, weigh at least 107 pounds, and they had to have at least 6 teeth—three on top and three on the bottom. The Department of Labor recruited the men[33] who signed on for six-month terms, but could re-enlist like Robert Lee Johnson, a Black resident of Gum Tree in Hanover County. He served his six months in 1939, went home for a two-week vacation, and returned to camp for another term of service.[34]

The War Department clothed, housed, fed, and took care of the medical and dental needs of the participants. It also paid the workers—$30 for regular recruits; $36 for assistant leaders, $45 for local experienced men (LEMs), who were from the surrounding community, knew the area, and could help guide the young men. LEMs were especially important to young urban men placed in rural locales.[35] Additionally, the enrollees selected leaders and assistant leaders from among their ranks. These men earned a little more than general enrollees.[36] Recruits were expected to send money home. The Department of Interior provided vocational and academic training through the US Office of Education.[37]

In the planning stages and in the original legislation establishing the agency, the CCC did not discriminate by race, although it excluded women.[38] Undoubtedly, this gender bias represents adherence to traditional values of male breadwinners being in greater need of employment. In the West, this translated into integrated camps. Some of the white enrollees dealt well with the integrated facilities, but others resisted. Robert Fechner, director of the CCC, wrote, "Whether we like it or not, we cannot close our eyes to the fact that there are communities and States that do not want and will not accept a Negro Civilian Conservation Corps company. This is particularly true in localities that have a negligible Negro population."[39] Westerners believed the myth that Black men presented a danger to white women and children.[40]

While segregated, Georgia, Arkansas, and Alabama had African American camps and appreciated the work the men performed. Of course, these men performed hard labor, which was considered the place of Black people in the South. Additionally, policy prevented the assignment of Black enrollees outside their own state, and the governors determined the location of Black camps.[41]

Hanover County welcomed the African American camp for which the Ashland Kiwanis Club lobbied. Established in 1935, two years after the creation of the agency, Camp 1372 was Virginia's first CCC camp. Initially reported in the local paper in March 1935, this camp was to be the home of approximately 200 white men.[42] For unknown reasons, when the camp opened in May 1935, it housed 65 Black men to serve Hanover, Caroline, and possibly King William Counties.[43] Soon there were 212 enrollees, including sixteen county men. At first, the camp was not finished, so the men slept in tents. The group, divided in two with half the men working to set up the camp, which included building barracks and laying out roads. The remaining men worked cutting fire lanes for a Hanover landowner. By August, the men worked in Louisa and Chesterfield counties, constructing quarters for forestry camps, and in Caroline and Hanover, they did forestry conservation work. [44]

Bertha Parnell, an African American woman and a longtime resident of the Georgetown section of Hanover, recalled that the men at the CCC camp also put out fires. Watchers could see a good portion of the county from the fire tower that was several floors high. In the 1930s, the camp was about a half a mile from Parnell's childhood home. One day, when her mother was burning off a field to prepare it for planting, the fire got out of hand, and she ran to get the "CCC boys." When she returned the fire had surrounded Parnell and her siblings. Parnell remembers being very happy to see the CCC men come up the road with their wagon.[45]

As is evident from the Parnell story, the surrounding communities profited greatly from the presence of the camp, but the men also benefited. An educational component was added shortly after the establishment of the CCC, and newsletters became a teaching tool. Initially, the newsletter for Camp 1372 was called the *Bomb*, which was produced using a typewriter and mimeograph machine. A 1935 issue of the *Bomb* featured an editorial encouraging the men to take advantage of the opportunities offered by the CCC including learning to read and write. According to the editor, there was no excuse for a man in the CCC to be illiterate. The men also learned skills, including carpentry, landscaping, plumbing, and how to plan and build roads, bridges, and fire trails.[46]

The Great Depression and Ordinary Acts of Resistance

The newsletter itself was part of the educational process at the camp and most, if not all, of the staff and editorial department was African American.

The men thought of their campmates as family, and Camp 1372 like home. Camp beautification was an expectation of the program. Virginia fell in CCC District Four, and according to one brochure, "The beautification of their camp-sites has been set by the companies of District Four as their most important leisure time activity." By learning to landscape and maintain the camps, the men would appreciate well-kept lawns and shrubbery, and "their home[s] 10 and 20 years hence will show the results of this present plan."[47] By December 1935, Camp 1372 was well on its way to accomplishing the goal of beautification. According to a letter from Special Investigator Charles H. Kenlan, the camp showed remarkable development.[48]

The men of Camp 1372 worked hard and played hard. They formed a baseball team, and by summer 1936, they played the Ashland Tigers, a Black semi-pro team.[49] The men also played volleyball, quoits, and softball, and they even worked in a little boxing. There was no football equipment available.[50] Additional recreational activities included singing, dramatics, games, and movies. Occasionally, they took trips off the premises to attend social events at local churches. Camp 1372 formed a quartet, which sometimes sang at local church events.[51] The Camp glee club appeared on WRVA, a Richmond radio station. Camp members also took an active role in Hanover's bicentennial pageant honoring native son Patrick Henry in 1936.[52] The record does not share how the men felt about this opportunity or whether or not they knew that Henry had been an enslaver in the county.

By 1939, the name of the newsletter changed to *White Chimney Eagle* and had a more polished appearance.[53] It included articles about the history of the CCC and highlighted educational activities and the achievements of individual enrollees and was distributed in the community. The publication included news of enrollees who were about to graduate. The August 23, 1939, issue featured three first-class cooks, as well as chauffeurs, truck drivers, hospital attendants, laborers, and those prepared for domestic service. At the end of the list, potential employers learned of the high quality of all graduates. The note assured the reader that all the men were "government trained" and held certificates attesting to their "proficiency and leadership."⁵⁴

The camp newsletters informed readers and served to put local residents at ease. The success of the camp and the reliability and responsibility of the men associated with it were communicated clearly; moreover, the occupations the young men were trained for did not challenge the racial status quo. At the same time, however, African American staff seized the opportunity to challenge some of the traditional stereotypes held about Black people, especially men. In the column titled "Did you know that," the readers were asked several questions highlighting successes of the men from the camp, such as the fact that two White Chimney enrollees would soon matriculate at Virginia Union University. The column also included items such as the 1600 patents held by Black inventors and mentioned that Olympian Jesse Owens visited the camp. The column pointed out that the second wife of the Biblical Moses was an Ethiopian. Not surprisingly, the publication included signs of the gender norms of the day referring to the new wife of the camp surgeon as a "beautiful long-legged bird." The editors did mention Maggie Walker and her achievement as the only female bank president in the United States.⁵⁵

Another indication of the enrollees' esteem for their camp was expressed by assistant leader and editor-in-chief of the *White Chimney Eagle,* Leedom Jones, an African American, in his poem "The Thirteen Seventy-Two." The first stanza read:

> Of all the CCC under the blue,
> Give me Old Thirteen Seventy-two;
> Others are good and very fine,
> But none are like this one of mine.⁵⁶

Camp 1372 also had a spiritual side. In the 1935 report on the camp's progress, Kenlan wrote that there were usually at least 12 religious services per month and approximately fifty percent of all enrollees attended. This number did not include enrollees who attended churches in the community. The enrollees conducted a Bible class and regular Sunday school. Several of the newsletter items shared inspirational sayings and readings. "Lifted Above the Burdens" was one such article written by enrollee Leroy Sutton. He encouraged readers not to allow life's worries to get them down. "God will send aid," Sutton wrote, "because He knows our incapacity to function without His assistance. The daily loads that seem so heavy are really there to act as stairs to God."[57]

The men of Camp 1372 were not always serious. They also liked a good joke, even a corny one, at times. In the column "Bursting Bombs,"

> ROSS: I sat next to a swell looking dame in the movies last night and nearly talked her into having a date with me.
> NEWTON: What happened, did she change her mind?
> ROSS: No, she changed her seat.[58]

Some scholars have maintained that Black enrollees in the CCC typically did not receive the same treatment and opportunities as their white counterparts.[59] This does not seem to have been the case in Hanover. As discussed previously, Black enrollees were part of the newsletter writing staff and seemed to have had access to a good many opportunities. Some even took bricklaying classes at Armstrong High School in Richmond, and others attended college.[60]

The African American enrollees in Hanover did not face the same type of opposition as that encountered by their compatriots in the western part of the country. The community sought and appreciated their services. One explanation for this could be that white Hanoverians understood and could relate to Black people who labored on the land. The favorable response could also stem from a practical point of view. It was the middle of the Great Depression and, as the *Herald Progress* pointed out, construction of the camp employed local businesses, including carpenters, the Ashland Laundry, and local vendors supplying food. The men in the camp carried out local forestry projects. Two weeks later, the paper announced that a crew of sixty-five men from the camp was working on the land of a private owner to build fire lanes. There was also a camp baseball team and a quartet, along with the story about the litter of puppies adopted by the men. Finally, the article quoted the opinion of the white officers: that they had in their charge an "unusually fine bunch of boys."[61] The use of the term "boys" suggests that the presence of the

Black camp was acceptable because they were in their proper place or at least viewed as such.

Camp 1372, later camp 91, became an active participant in county life. The glee club's participation in the Patrick Henry celebration was but one example.[62] This means that they were probably not harassed or made to feel unwelcome. Also, the longevity of Camp 1372 is an indication that it found a comfortable place in local society. This was evident when the lease on the land was not renewed. The circumstances of the loss of the CCC camp in Hanover are murky. Prominent Hanoverians approached the owner of the land to no avail.[63] The camp moved six miles north into Caroline County in 1937. The Hanover Board of Supervisors voted to pay a portion of the lease, so the county retained access to the services of the enrollees. In an editorial in 1937, the *Hanover Herald Progress* lamented the loss of the camp but expressed happiness that it would remain nearby. The editorial went on to say that "the CCC camp is the one project of the New Deal that has come through its four or five years of service practically without criticism." When Ashland Kiwanis first proposed bringing a camp to the County, there was considerable fear expressed by many of the residents that the presence of so many Negro youths in the community might lead to trouble. These fears were ungrounded. "In the main, the boys have been well-disciplined, have conducted themselves admirably. We note their departure with regret."[64] The repeated use of "boy" to describe males from 17–25 indicates that many people in Hanover County appreciated the camp and the men for what they had to offer and because they remained in their place.

On December 1, 1938, the *Hanover Herald Progress* published an editorial titled, "What Will Hanover Be in the Year 1950?" This editorial followed a series of articles that began appearing in the weekly on November 24. That series, in turn, grew out of a two-year study conducted by the Rural Sociology Division of the Virginia Agricultural Experiment Station.[65] This study looked at issues of wealth, housing, living conditions, agricultural practices, and population in rural Virginia.[66]

The study and the editorial evoked President Roosevelt's contention that roughly one-third of the nation's citizens were "ill housed, ill clothed and underfed."[67] The situation in the South was much worse. The study revealed that in Virginia 57% of all agricultural families, and three-fourths of African American farm households were economically marginal—that is, they earned less than $600 a year.[68]

An introductory statement to a report on this study, which was prepared for the convention of the Virginia League of Counties in July 1939, lists some of the factors that fostered the development of this marginal society. This included topography, the original population, selective migration, and population increases beyond the "local optimum." Additionally, some issues stemmed from "the far-reaching consequences of slavery," Reconstruction, isolation of the poor, substandard educational and social opportunities, poorly conceived state and national use of land, soil deterioration, agricultural depressions, and shifting social and economic conditions. "We now face new conditions which demand new adjustments."[69]

According to the *Herald Progress* editorial, Hanover County was in a slightly better position than some of the other counties in the state, because "relief in Hanover is lower than the average, property values are higher here, living conditions are better." Yet, according to the editorial, "figures indicate problems in rural living that Hanover as well as the rest of Virginia and the rest of the South must solve if this section is to build for a future of success and content in rural areas."[70]

While the series of articles did not highlight racial differences in Hanover, the actual survey paints a picture of differences consistent with the era of disfranchisement. The study found that approximately one-third to one-half of the rural white population in Virginia was marginal or living below the poverty line. About three-fourths of rural Blacks were marginal.[71] During the 1936–37 school year, white teachers earned an average of $957 per year and Black teachers earned $413. Twenty-five percent of white students were in high school, compared with 6 percent of Black school-age children.[72] Forty-three percent of white farm workers earned marginal incomes compared with seventy-eight percent of Black farm workers.[73] These numbers suggest the impact of segregation and racism.

This survey inspired the Conference on Virginia Population Trends that took place in Roanoke, Virginia, in 1939. This conference was organized by the president of Virginia Tech, the chairman of the Virginia State Planning Board, the state superintendent of public instruction, the state commissioner of public welfare, the state administrator of the Works Projects (formerly Works Progress) Administration, and the president of the Virginia Welfare Council. A report titled "Virginia Does Care," which consisted of ten committee reports, including one from John M. Gandy, who chaired the committee on Special Negro Problems. Gandy, a Mississippian by birth and a well-known African American educator, focused on six key areas: economics, education, citizenship, negro land ownership, welfare agencies, and crime.[74] Gandy's committee identified low wages, lack of employment, and discrimination against Black people in the trades and industries as the biggest economic concerns of African Americans. Education, always important to the Black community, took up the most space in this report and issues related to transportation topped the list, followed by exclusion of Black men and women from participation in the operation of the schools, and poor or no facilities for vocational training on the elementary or secondary level.[75] Next, inadequate training for Black students seeking opportunities in health education in local and state agencies, and finally, the trend away from farming was also a concern.[76] The Division of Rural Sociology or the Virginia Agricultural Experiment Station conducted the study. It follows that this group would be interested in improving agricultural conditions and not sending rural residents to the cities. Since the majority of Black people in Hanover were considered marginal and manufacturing was almost non-existent, they needed to better utilize the land, the best resource available.

Citizenship was the third area addressed by Gandy's committee. The Fourteenth Amendment defined citizenship and that definition included Black people, but they did not have full access to the ballot. The group argued that the ballot was vital to active citizenship and that Black people needed to access the franchise without restriction. The report continued saying that the "Negro is handicapped because he does not have fair opportunities for participation in local and [S]tate government."[77]

Next the group found the decline in Black land ownership "regrettable." As discussed in chapter 4, landownership, as measured via Black farm owners, decreased between 1900 and 1930 and continued to decrease until 1950.[78] The study offered three reasons for the decline in the number of Black landowners. The first two were poor training in the methods of farming and the lack of support and leadership on the part of the "leading group [Whites]."⁷⁹ These concerns might have been alleviated in Hanover with the provision of a county agent to work with Black farmers. County farm agents were trained and hired in rural communities to work with farmers to help them remain up-to-date on changing agricultural techniques and technology. While there was a white farm agent in Hanover, there was not a Black agent, and the white agent did not readily work with Black farmers.⁸⁰ The third reason cited for the dip in Black farm ownership was the Depression, but economic downturn does not explain the full picture.⁸¹ The loss of land also stemmed from Black people moving to areas where they could find more consistent means of support for their families.

Mechanization was the fourth reason given by the committee for the difficulty faced by Black farmers. Without state-of-the-art equipment, Black farmers could not remain competitive. "Injustices frequently practiced by those who make the selling of land to Negroes prohibitive"⁸² was another factor leading to the decrease in Black landownership. In the collective memory of many Black people in Hanover County, Black landownership was affected by white trickery. Many Black men and women believe today that white people conspired to gain control of valuable property from uneducated and unworldly African Americans.⁸³

The fifth overall point made by the committee involved welfare agencies. Black people did not have equal access to job opportunities presented by, presumably, state agencies. While acknowledging that professional training was important, the committee suggested that practical training and experience should also be fundamental when considering an applicant for employment.⁸⁴

Finally, the committee addressed crime and found a correlation between low economic status and poor recreational facilities. The committee also touched on illegitimacy as a factor in the crime rate; the report quoted a finding by the Methodist Church Conference that the rate of illegitimate births in Virginia's larger cities was ten times higher among Black residents than white people. Poor housing and the lack of Black law enforcement officers rounded out the report's list of special problems facing the Black community.⁸⁵

While the New Deal made some headway in bringing the country out of the Depression, it did not complete the process. It would take a world war to get Americans back to work on a large scale and to improve the economy. Interestingly, the war on the home front began before the United States officially entered the fray. Indeed, on May 10, 1940, when the Germans barreled through French and British lines, the safety of isolation was replaced by the fear that the United States would not be able to stay out of the war, and that the country was not prepared.[86]

After Japan attacked Pearl Harbor, most citizens supported US involvement in World War II. Of course, this was not true for all, including some Black Americans. As in previous wars, some Black people questioned fighting for democracy in other parts of the world when democracy was not available to them at home. This argument had been heard among African Americans in response to every war since the American Revolution. Still there were African Americans who argued that taking up arms was a way to illustrate their commitment to the country. Most Black Hanoverians subscribed to this point of view.

Black Hanoverians worked hard at home and overseas to do their part to ensure Allied victory. On May 28, 1940, FDR appointed the seven-man National Advisory Commission on Defense, and the next day, Governor James Price of Virginia issued an executive order establishing the Virginia Defense Council, the first in the nation.[87] The order explained that the council would ensure Virginia's readiness in case of an attack. "In the accomplishment of this mission, the full and loyal assistance and cooperation of all Virginia citizens" was expected. The top tier of the council consisted of members of the white male elite, including representatives from the Newport News Shipbuilding and Dry Dock Company, the Virginia State Chamber of Commerce, the Virginia National Guard, and the *Richmond Times-Dispatch*. The second tier of council leaders included J. Alvin Russell, an African American and the president of the St. Paul Industrial School for Negroes.[88]

The Defense Council established the Aircraft Warning Service, including airplane watchers. Initially, Black Hanoverians were not included on the schedules, but they soon organized a meeting at the Elks Lodge in Berkleytown and invited the coordinator of the civil defense program and director of the air watchers. After that meeting, Black watchers were added to the schedule covering Friday from 4 p.m. until Saturday at 4 p.m.[89] Setting aside a day for Black people adhered to the segregation

The Great Depression and Ordinary Acts of Resistance

requirements. Although Black men and women demonstrated their commitment to the war effort, racism still reigned supreme.

Educating the public about the war was another major goal of the Defense Council and town meetings began in the summer of 1942.[90] National headquarters set the meeting agenda, which resembled religious gatherings. Beginning with singing, the first speaker fired up the crowd and paid tribute to all the local men serving in the military. The second speaker covered a specific topic such as rationing, salvaging, nutrition, or price ceilings. The African American community met on Labor Day 1942, at the playground in Berkleytown. Thelma Hewlett, the Chief of Mobilization for Black Hanoverians, planned the event. Women typically held these positions. According to Joseph H. Wyse, coordinator of the Virginia Office for Civilian Defense, women "had been most satisfactory because of experience along the necessary lines and available time to give to the work."[91] On the one hand, Wyse credited women with being able to coordinate large-scale events, while at the same time intimating that they had nothing else to do. Thelma Hewlett, the African American home demonstration agent, worked with Black women in the community setting up training sessions on all aspects of home and family care.[92]

While Hewlett wanted the town meeting to be fun, in a letter to J. F. Nicholas, the Negro Coordinator for Civilian Defense in Virginia, she explained that she also wanted to "get before our people the importance of taking an active part in the [war effort]. We want them to understand thoroughly what they can do and what is expected of them."[93] The meeting began with a parade, including the Virginia Manual Labor Training School Band, the Victory Club, the Volunteer Club, airplane watchers, and members of the nutrition, home nursing, and first aid classes. These classes were part of the community service initiative offered by the Civilian Mobilization Program.[94] "The object of the parade is to show what the people have done in defense," said the *Herald Progress*. Speakers included William Layton, the superintendent of the Virginia Industrial School for Boys, and Negro Coordinator for civilian defense, and other town leaders.[95]

In addition to being an aircraft watcher or educator for the councils, civilians could also purchase bonds, which was a new twist on an old idea. Bonds were a tangible way for citizens to support the war effort.[96]

By selling securities, or small-denomination bonds, the United States government sought the financial support of its citizens during the Revolutionary, Civil, and Spanish-American wars. During WWI, investment professionals handled selling bonds but were more successful among private corporations than with individual citizens. However, the groundwork for the very successful World War II bond campaigns was established.[97]

The United States Treasury instituted a Defense Savings Program on May 1, 1941. Ordinary Americans from across racial, class, and political lines took charge.[98] Great effort was expended to make African Americans feel a part of the process. The NAACP and Black celebrities such as musician Duke Ellington and Joe Lewis, the celebrated boxer, supported the bond drive. So did ordinary Black people who saw an opportunity to support the war effort, earn some money, and win a "double victory" against the Axis powers abroad and disfranchisement at home.

Defense bonds were sold in the Ashland post office, and residents from all walks of life participated by either buying or selling bonds. More bonds were sold in December 1941 than in any previous month, which was hardly surprising given the attack on Pearl Harbor. Black teachers led the way by committing to buying $1,000 worth. The headline in the local paper read: "Negroes Buy $1000 Bond—Teachers Aid U.S. Defense Effort."[99] Black people in Hanover County held at least two bond rallies. The February 1944 rally yielded $4,022. Held at the Elks Lodge, it was a major event. The speaker was the head of the State War Finance Committee for Negroes, and the band from the boys' school played. A German shell from WWI was auctioned and Lee Winston, an African American farmer from the Greenwood section of the county, won it with a $500 bid.[100] Five months later, on July 4, 1944, Black residents, gathered at the Berkleytown playground, and raised $3,000. Again, part of the profits came from auctioning donated items.[101]

If individuals did not have enough money to buy a bond outright, they purchased stamps; once buyers had accumulated a certain amount, they traded them for a bond. Teachers and students bought stamps at the Hanover County Training School. The school also had a Victory Garden, where food for home front consumption was raised so the produce of commercial growers could be used for soldiers. Victory Garden vegetables were canned and used in the school cafeteria.[102]

The Great Depression and Ordinary Acts of Resistance

Even the very young took up the challenge. Sammie Lee Jerry, an eight-year-old Black boy, had begun working at age five doing chores for a farmer. Most of the money he earned went to his mother, but the remainder he saved for three years to buy a bike; he decided to buy a bond instead, however, saying that the bike could wait, but the Nazis could not.[103] Patriotism aside, Jerry may have recognized a good investment.

War bonds present an interesting lens through which to view the efforts on the home front. The planners saw in the bond drives an opportunity to unite Black and white citizens in the war effort; many believed that in time of war, unity should be the watchword. Yet the planners did not fully understand that unity and segregation could not be reconciled. In the end, the bonds only unified their money.[104]

Wartime fundraisers were not limited to selling bonds. At least once, Black residents sold dinners to raise money for the Red Cross war fund. Held at the Elks Lodge in Berkleytown and advertised in the *Herald Progress*, organizers promised that "special attention [would] be given to orders from our White friends."[105] This meant that white customers who wanted to pick up their orders and eat elsewhere would not have to wait long for their orders, and that, if they chose to eat on-site, segregated seating would be available.[106]

Citizens' commitment to the war effort went beyond fundraising. Across the state individuals' rationed tires and gasoline, raised food, and prayed for a swift and victorious end to the war. As early as December 25, 1941, just a few weeks after the attack on Pearl Harbor, notices in the *Herald Progress* announced a county-wide sign up for citizens, "White and colored . . . to register for whatever service they may be able to perform" as part of the civil defense program.[107] While women in cities with manufacturing plants worked in non-traditional jobs, in Hanover, female volunteers sewed, cooked, worked in offices, nursed, and danced. Males covered auto mechanics, firefighting, map reading, and demolition. In a few instances the jobs for men and women overlapped, such as in the need for photographers and publicity.[108]

The record suggests that Hanoverians certainly did their part for the war effort at home, but they also contributed on the battlefront. Just over 2,000 men registered for the draft including 838 Black males. By the last year of the war, one African American Hanoverian family had four sons serving in the effort. At least five African American men from the county died during the war years. Four died from non-battle-related injuries, but Leroy Quarles died in action in the Pacific and is buried in the Military Cemetery in Honolulu, Hawaii.[109]

John Gordon, a Black Hanoverian, wanted to be a Marine, but was told that there were no vacancies. Gordon believed the rejection had racial undertones. Black men were barred from the Marines in 1798, and while Black men were once again accepted as of June 1, 1942, it is impossible to know whether or not a recruiter, set in the old ways, blocked Gordon. He joined the Navy instead, becoming a SeaBee, a construction battalion that supported the Navy.[110] This occupational choice first opened to African Americans in October 1942.[111] Since it was not a combat arm, the SeaBees did not engage the enemy directly, but Gordon recalled encountering difficult combat situations in the Pacific. This is entirely plausible since the enemy would have wanted to destroy structures erected by American military engineers. Indeed, the SeaBees did receive assault training as a supplement to their main duties.[112]

Gordon, a noted singer in his local Baptist church, recalled that he and some friends formed a gospel quartet. Sadly, one of the men from that group died in action. Gordon described another comrade as a risk taker, and he was also killed. Fifty years later, Gordon still regretted not being on the scene to save his friend.[113] Hanoverian Floyd Dabney Sr. had a very different experience from Gordon. Like Gordon, Dabney was born and raised in Hanover, in Ashland to be specific. His father, Henry W. Dabney, operated a funeral home in the area catering to African American clients, making the Dabneys members of the Black middle class. Upon graduation from the Hanover County Training School, Floyd left home for college, intending eventually to become a lawyer. He attended Howard University in Washington, DC, for one year, before being drafted into the Army. He ended up in the famous 761st Black tank battalion, the first African American armored unit.[114]

More than six hundred Black men representing thirty states served in the 761st tank battalion, and they represented the diversity of the African American community. Some of these tank corpsmen were from cities, while others, like Dabney, hailed from small towns. Many volunteered, while others were drafted. Several of these young men were from

The Great Depression and Ordinary Acts of Resistance

middle-class backgrounds, but most "were the sons of janitors, domestics, factory workers, and sharecroppers."[115]

Dabney was a member of the administrative staff. His specific duties included delivering mail. In conversation shortly before his death, Dabney explained that five days a week, he went to the local town to pick up the mail and returned to the office, where he sorted and distributed the mail for six companies. He was responsible for getting letters and packages to the men wherever they were—and sometimes they were on the battlefield. His son recalls his father telling him of instances when he was shot at in his jeep. Dabney was with the 761st when, according to some accounts, it moved into concentration camps in 1945.

At the end of the war, Dabney returned to Ashland. His older sister and his father approached him about going to mortuary school so he could join the family business. He eventually agreed and used the money he had saved and the GI Bill to go to school in Philadelphia.[116] By the time he graduated, Dabney and his sister and brother-in-law, who now ran the business, had parted ways, so he went to work for a funeral home in Richmond. In 1955, he opened his own business, F.E. Dabney Funeral Home, in Ashland, within walking distance of the establishment operated by his sister and her husband.

In 1992, in an interview for the *Richmond Times Dispatch*, Dabney described himself as a soldier and a morale booster, because getting mail meant a lot to soldiers. He had recently viewed the documentary *Liberators*, which is the story of the 761st. Dabney did not share his thoughts on the film except to say that he understood the bitterness of some of the men interviewed. Dabney attributed their attitudes to the fact that they fought for democracy but came home to the same racist and segregated society they had left. He added that, while things have improved since then, he believed that "there [was] still too much segregation."[117]

World War II represented several firsts for groups previously barred from certain kinds of involvement in the US military, including Black men serving in elite combat units and wearing officers' insignia. For the first time in the history of this country, women, Black and white, formally entered military service. Republican Congresswoman Edith Nourse Rogers of Massachusetts proposed the bill that established the Women's Army Auxiliary Corps so women who served in World War II had the same benefits as men. This had not happened for the women who worked as civilians during the First World War.[118]

Despite the best intentions of those involved in the establishment of the WAAC, and later WAC, women in the military was still controversial. While some people believed women should have access to opportunities afforded male citizens, others feared destruction of the natural order. Another challenge faced by the women in the WAAC was the perception of their sexuality. Many people believed that women interested in the military were "mannish" and as a result had "the potential to be lesbians."[119]

This was especially true in African American communities. Despite these concerns, in July 1942, Vashti Tonkins, a Black Hanoverian, joined the WAAC. A graduate of Hampton Institute, a historically Black college in Hampton, Virginia, Tonkins also earned a master's degree in education from the University of Chicago in 1939. Inducted into the WAAC in July 1942, she reported for training at Ft. Des Moines, Iowa, that September.[120] In 1943, Tonkins became an officer, and went on to serve as a recruiter in Salt Lake City, Utah in 1943. She eventually became the commanding officer at Ft. McClellan in Alabama.[121]

Family and friends gave Tonkins a party, which they shared in the *Herald Progress*.[122] Periodically, Tonkins visited Ashland while on her way to an assignment, such as the time she was en route from the West Coast, where she had spent three months recruiting, to Ft. Devens, Massachusetts, her next assignment.[123] Her family also happily notified the town in 1945 when she married overseas and honeymooned in Paris.[124]

As mentioned previously, the country did not fully come out of the Great Depression until World War II. The eventual economic recovery was largely due to the rapid growth of the defense industries. Men and women in every region of the country increased their incomes greatly as they moved into new and better jobs. As usual, African Americans fought to gain access to these opportunities, and Black people in Virginia had an interesting group of white male allies—white newspaper publishers. Indeed, Richmond, Lynchburg, Staunton, and Norfolk papers spoke out against discrimination in the defense industry. On January 30, 1941, the *Times-Dispatch* reprinted an article from the *Journal and Guide,* an African American newspaper based in Norfolk, commending the Richmond editor for taking a stand against discrimination in the defense industries. The writer asserted that lack of access to these jobs meant lack of access to a decent living wage and to the possibility of upward financial mobility.[125] Two days later, a letter from the Richmond chapter of the National Association for the Advancement of Colored People (NAACP) appeared in the "Voice of the People" section on the *Times-Dispatch*'s editorial page. J. M. Tinsley and Lawrence D. Bolling, Hanover president and secretary of the county's NAACP chapter, respectively, thanked the paper for its "intelligent efforts . . . to acquaint the people of Virginia with the economic blockade which has proven so disastrous to Negro skilled labor, so effectively barred from participation in the erection of the American defenses."[126]

By September 1941, J. Walton Hall, superintendent of the Hanover County public schools, announced that defense training classes would take place at night in seven of the county schools, including the Training School. At two of the schools, students would learn metalworking. The remaining schools, including the Training School, offered classes in truck, tractor, and auto mechanics.[127] The mechanic classes began at the Training School in November 1941.[128]

The support white editors offered for African American access to defense industries may seem odd, occurring as it did during the era of disfranchisement, but the behavior of these newspaper editors was in keeping with the activities of southern liberals at the time.[129] Vertical segregation opened doors for white southern liberals. They could join with Black people and speak out against the horrors of lynching or the unfairness of the defense industry without being guilty of favoring racial "amalgamation."

The New Deal and the war economy offered some encouragement to Black Hanoverians. Even during the Depression, they continued moving ahead with hope, as they always had. Spirituality, organizing, education, and employment remained the four key bases for progress in the Black community. Many Black Hanoverians looked at life through a spiritual lens, believing that everything would be better "by and by." Faith was the way to salvation, but faith without works was dead,[130] so Black people worked to provide a better life for the next generation. The main tool for achieving this was education. Organizing to pay teachers, provide food for poor children, and the like was the way to improve Black schools and to try to ensure that people's lives improved. Faith, community, organization, and education were so intertwined that it is almost as impossible to write about them as separate components as it was for Black people to separate them in their daily lives.

Sometimes cooperation evolved informally. As Carrie Burton recalled, when her father had food, he always shared, and others offered help to her family—a community working together to take care of its own. It was this type of sharing that may have lessened the impact of the Depression on rural Black people. This was certainly true of Walter Jackson and his wife Lelia or Lillian, who lived on a farm in the predominantly African American Brown Grove neighborhood, where their five children recalled being raised to believe in God, hard work, and education. The senior Jackson bought the twenty-five acres of land he farmed in 1908, and, while he quickly mortgaged it, he fully repaid the loan within two years.[131] The Depression presented challenges to the Jacksons, as it did to most families, and the entire family helped. The Jackson children awoke early every weekday morning to do their chores, went to school and returned home for their evening duties, and then homework by lamplight. [132]

On the weekends, the Jacksons' church activities interrupted chores. Brown Grove Baptist Church was down the road from their farm and across the road from the elementary school the children attended. As their son Benjamin Jackson says, "[he] got [his] ABCs from the school and [his] GODs from the church."[133] The Jacksons were not wealthy, but they had what they needed. Ben Sr., interviewed when he was seventy-seven years old, did not remember the Depression vividly. He recalled that things were tight; his lunch usually consisted of fatback and maybe a roll. Sometimes the fatback had a streak of lean meat running through the fat. It was then called "streak-o-lean." This was a treasure.[134]

Jackson retained all but two of his report cards and remembered his two-room school in detail. Like the other Black schools in the county, the Brown Grove School did not have many of the tools that one usually thinks of as needed for a good education. The children were split into two groups: grades 1 through 3 or 4, and grades 4 through 8. One teacher was responsible for each group. Every day began the same way: with a hymn, possibly "Church in the Valley by the Wildwoods," "The Lord's Prayer," and then another hymn. After the devotions, the day began, interrupted only by lunch. Students did not eat until they said the grace:

The Great Depression and Ordinary Acts of Resistance

Thou art great and thou art good
Father we thank you for this food
By your hands we'll all be fed
Give us Lord our daily bread.[135]

Before leaving for home, the children repeated the Mizpah,[136] which says, "Watch between me and thee. When we are absent one from another. Amen."

The junior league (the youth department of the countywide league) and the Negro Organization Society met on Friday afternoon.[137] On Fridays, all of the children came together to recite poetry, sing, or put on skits. It was their time to shine—a time for which young Ben learned many of the poems he could still recite decades later. Each May, the school held a May Day celebration. The girls danced around the May pole, and the boys participated in sack racing and other athletic events.

After the eighth grade, Jackson attended Hanover County Training School, the only school for Black children in the county that went beyond the seventh grade.[138] Unlike the experience of some of his older siblings, a bus was provided by the time he was going to the school in Ashland, so he was able to avoid the five-mile walk each morning. He hastened to explain, however, that the bus ride was hit-or-miss. Some mornings the vehicle got them to school, and some mornings it did not.

The fact that Jackson had a school bus at all was because of three Black families in the county. Before the mid-1930s, there was no transportation to the Black schools. Lucian Hunter and his family were the first to purchase a bus and brought students from Ellison, in the east end of the county, to Ashland. Later Contee Robinson ran a bus from Rockville, in the western side of the county to Ashland, and Henry Dabney, owner of Dabney's Funeral Home picked up riders from Beaverdam and brought them to Ashland. The Dabney bus, driven by Claudius Dabney met up with a man named Meredith who brought children to Beaverdam to join the Dabney bus. In every instance, these buses were a family affair, with the sons acting as the drivers. In 1935, the school board agreed to contribute financially to the cost of operating the buses.

Attending the training school was a successful experience for Jackson. He was active in organizations and often selected for leadership positions.

He took part in the traditional high school-level classes, but he also took advantage of the agricultural program, which had a permanent building on the campus. Jackson remembered that his teacher, John Fleming, a graduate of Virginia State College, taught his charges the "fundamentals of the purchase, maintenance and care of farm machinery including home building of sheds, stalls, pens, as well as complete care for poultry raising."[139] While the training school offered opportunities for Jackson and his classmates that had been missing just a few years earlier, it was still woefully short of the mark when compared with the county's white high schools. When Jackson entered the school in 1941, it had been designated a qualified school—the first step in becoming accredited by the state department of education. Maintaining minimum standards for at least one year led to accreditation. This was a monumental accomplishment for the training school. Though segregation still prevailed in society as in the schools, Black students at the training school would supposedly "receive the same consideration as shown the graduates of accredited high schools."[140]

By the time Jackson matriculated, the training school included a cafeteria so the principal no longer had to make soup and bring it to school to heat up for the students, as had happened in earlier years.[141] There was no gymnasium, however, and the only space resembling a recreational facility was an empty field out back where the pupils played, time permitting. There was no auditorium in the school, so when it was time for Jackson and his classmates to graduate, Shiloh Baptist Church hosted the baccalaureate and graduation ceremonies.

After graduation, Jackson found work as a bricklayer's assistant. This meant that he was responsible for making sure that materials were available when the white skilled workers needed them. He wanted to learn the trade of bricklaying, but recalls being denied instruction by white craftsmen. There was no law barring Black men from learning the trade. Indeed, Black men in the Hanover CC camp in the 1930s learned bricklaying, but because union and non-union employers practiced discrimination, Jackson did not have the opportunity to apprentice with a white craftsman.

Not to be defeated, he drew on the work ethic instilled by his parents. He located an old trowel, and every night, after working a full day, he would go home and practice laying bricks. He eventually taught himself the trade and proceeded to work in the field for the next thirty years. He laid the bricks on an addition to Shiloh Baptist Church, Scott's Funeral Home in Richmond, and his own home. He was selected to do the fancy brick work on the front of the funeral home. Initially barred from the profession, his skill and determination led to jobs in white-owned companies. Eventually attitudes softened and the field expanded to include Black men.[142]

In addition to being a brick mason, Jackson was also a Baptist minister. This vocation helps to explain his answer when asked how he managed to overcome all the obstacles placed before him. Like many Black people of his generation, he credited his success to the God he came to know in church and in his parents' home as a boy.[143] He explained that with faith and hard work, anything can be accomplished.

Faith and works regarding education during the era of disfranchisement usually involved organizing formally, raising money to resist the confines of racial segregation—and building the Black community within those confines. Some observers may be tempted to compare the organizations that operated in the 1930s and 1940s to the faith-based organizations of today. While there are similarities, there are more differences. One key difference is the belief system that fueled the Black individuals who came together during the mid-twentieth century. This was a time before the strictures of the Constitution had been so tightened that outward reflections of faith had to be separated from civic life. During this time, most organizations in the Black community, including public schools, were faith-based. For example, each of the Black schools was associated with a community league, and quite often these leagues were led by men and women who were devout church members. As a result, hymns and prayers were a standard part of the meetings as they were of the public school day.

As in earlier years, one key to the advancement of the Black community in Hanover was its ability and desire to organize for betterment. Black men and women had begun organizing both informally and formally from the time they were enslaved, and, as a result, hundreds if not thousands of Black organizations existed in the state of Virginia alone. Undoubtedly, the sheer numbers meant a duplication of efforts and may at times have lessened effectiveness. In answer to this problem, a group of what the *Hanover Herald Progress* described as the "highest type of Negro citizenship," including educators and professionals decided in 1912 to organize these different groups under one parent society. The Negro Organization Society (NOS) was founded at the state level. Its motto was: Better Schools, Better Health, Better Homes, Better Farms. Annual meetings were held in various cities and towns across the state. The NOS met throughout the Depression, and in 1934, the group convened in Ashland for a statewide convention. By this time, the Society included fraternal organizations, mutual benefit societies, churches, and the hundreds of countywide leagues working for better schools.[144]

The Hanover County-Wide League proved to be an invaluable asset to Black public schools during the Depression. Black Hanoverians raised hundreds of dollars each year to keep their schools running, and often to pay the salary of a sixth teacher at the Training School. J. Walton Hall, the superintendent of schools in Hanover, admitted that "Through the efforts of their own leaders, Negro citizens of Hanover County are doing much for the advancement of schools for Negro children." On September 24, 1931, in the early days of the Depression, the *Hanover Herald Progress* included an article with the headline "HANOVER COUNTY NEGRO CITIZENS HELP NEGRO SCHOOLS—Negro Citizens Contribute $400 Each Year Toward Support of Hanover County Training School in Ashland." [145]

The leagues sponsored rallies like the one held in 1933 for the training school. It took place at Shiloh Baptist Church where Major W. R. Brown, the keynote speaker and dean of men at Hampton Institute, stressed the importance of education. The training school glee clubs and an unnamed gospel quartet provided music.[146] The citizens—as Superintendent Hall, significantly, called them—raised $1,000 that year to move the old Henry Clay Spring School building to Berkleytown to be used as part of the Training School. The citizens of Rockhill raised $500 to make improvements to their school, including the provision of better sanitation. Neither school board minutes nor the county newspaper mentions any parallels to these types of activities in the white community—whose schools presumably received more generous public funding. Fundraising sometimes involved theatrical presentations. On one occasion, the Virginia Union University Dramatic Players performed. According to all reports, this was a real treat for the community. Not only did it give residents something different to do; it also allowed them to see Black college students in action.[147]

While Black people had been quietly speaking up for their rights all along, in the 1930s and 1940s in Hanover they began to speak louder. Perhaps the desperation of the Depression years led them to push harder against the tide of white supremacy. In the spring of 1933, the Rev. Eddie E. Moore of Hanover, pastor of Shiloh Baptist Church, issued a call in an article in the *Herald Progress* asking Black Hanoverians to hold a mass meeting. Moore, while addressing his own people, also spoke to white Hanoverians in a roundabout way. Referring to the "colored taxpayers," Moore argued that it was time for a political club to form so that Black people could make their concerns known. He continued, "it is now time and high time that the colored people of our county should put themselves in a position to be of some service to one or the other of the leading parties that in turn may be benefited thereby."[148] He admonished Black men to get up and fight and stop following the path of least resistance. He did not refer specifically to a struggle for Black equality, but rather to battles facing the entire country—economic challenges, but also the rising tide of nationalism, and political strife. He cried, "Let us go to the rescue."[149]

He then asked a series of questions aimed at encouraging Black men and women to pay their poll tax. First, Moore wanted to know if they even knew what was going on in the government at the local, state, and national levels. Second, he asked his readers whether they believed that the economic scales in the county, state or country were balanced. He then questioned whether they thought that Black children had the educational opportunities they deserved. He closed by charging Black Hanoverians to pay, register, subscribe to the *Herald Progress* so that they would know what was going on and then prepare to do battle at the polls.[150]

The first meeting of Moore's proposed political club took place on April 11, 1933, at Shiloh Baptist Church. According to the newspaper, Gordon Blaine Hancock, a sociology professor at Virginia Union University, addressed the meeting on the topic of "The Negro and the Ballot."[151] It is not clear that this group ever met again, but in January 1935, the Negro Citizen's League was organized by a group of concerned African

Americans who had attended the Negro Organization Society convention in Ashland the previous November. The initial meeting was held at the Black Elks Lodge in Ashland. Officers were elected, and the first Friday of every month was chosen as the regular meeting day. When announcing this new organization in the paper, the founders explained that they had decided to start the new league because of the "many inspiring messages they had heard at the convention of the Negro Organization Society."[152] The Negro Citizen's League met two or three times, but like Moore's political club, it disappears from the public record before the end of 1935.

The formation of this organization presents another interesting snapshot into Black-White relations in Hanover County. The article announcing the organization and Moore's comments ran under the headline "Negro Political Club to Be Formed: Moore will lead move urging Negroes to qualify for ballot in county."[153] Black leaders, and Moore specifically, felt that it was safe to run this article in the paper calling on Black people to "fight" and to "rescue" or, perhaps frustration made them brave. Presumably, they were called to fight white supremacy and rescue Black citizens. This group was not part of the public record for very long. Possibly it dissolved or went underground.

While Moore's group seems to have fizzled, the campaign to encourage Black men and women to pay their poll tax was taken up in the 1940s by the Negro Organization Society. Luther Porter Jackson, historian and professor at Virginia State College and Virginia's foremost proponent of Black voter registration, appears to have headed the campaign. African Americans, such as Contee Robinson from Hanover, were chosen from each county and charged with the task of getting Black people to pay their poll tax. Robinson, well-known and respected in the Black community in Hanover County, achieved less than dramatic results getting Black Hanoverians to pay their poll tax. Records indicate that in 1943, there were 325 Black voters in the county who were current with their poll tax. This number dropped to 258 the following year. The number went back up to 360 in 1945 but dropped to 250 in 1946. In 1947, Jackson wrote to Robinson to try to ascertain the problem and to urge him and his associates to "redeem [their] situation in Hanover."[154]

While Robinson's response is lost, James Woolfolk, an Elk, did respond to a request from Jackson in May 1948 regarding the voting preparedness of the Elks brothers. Woolfolk explained that lodge membership was small, and that many of the men lived some distance from the meeting hall. As a result, they were not able to meet as often as they would like. Woolfolk reported that ninety percent of the membership was qualified to vote. Continuing, he explained that when the group did meet, they discussed the importance of voting and encouraged all to register.

Woolfolk responded to a series of questions from Jackson: Many but not all lodge members belonged to the National Association for the Advancement of Colored People (NAACP). The lodge supported the NAACP membership drive then in progress. While the lodge had not sent a delegate to the state NAACP mass meeting in December 1947, it had sent a telegram to E. O. McCue, a member of the House of Delegates from Richmond City, asking for committee action on the anti-segregation bills that had been introduced by Walter H. C. Murray, a delegate representing Albemarle and Greene Counties and the city of Charlottesville. Woolfolk closed by saying that the lodge members regularly shared their views and supported President Harry Truman's civil rights proposals.[155] In February 1948, Truman presented a ten-point plan that outlined specific goals for extending full civil rights to every American.[156]

At the end of 1948, Luther P. Jackson was still trying to build a fire under Black leaders in Virginia's counties to motivate them to register people to vote. In a letter to county and home demonstration agents, he requested a list of five or six names of people in the county who were "thoroughly vote-conscious." He explained that "By this [he meant] they vote themselves and constantly persuade others as well. I mean the kind of persons who will take their fellow citizens to the county treasurer's office to pay their poll tax; who will take them in the same manner to the registrar; and finally, on Election Day, will take them to the polls to cast their ballots."[157] The Black home demonstration agent in Hanover, Thelma Hewlett, submitted eight names—two women and six men.[158]

Around the time that the state constitution was changing in 1901–2, Black people, especially those in positions of leadership, had been compelled to rethink their conviction that political action was the way to gain access to all that America had to offer. Economic equality became more of a focus, and education, hard work, spirituality, and organization became more central than ever as the main avenues toward African American uplift began to evaporate. After World War II, the focus began to shift once again as Black people, or at least some leading persons in the community, sought political power to gain civil rights. Historians have suggested that fighting for democracy overseas and returning home to segregation spurred Black people to re-focus their efforts on the vote. Luther P. Jackson and the NOS and NAACP certainly offer support for this conclusion as far as Virginia and Hanover County are concerned, but this is not the complete picture.

Hanoverians had never stopped pushing for their rights. They had indeed turned their attention away from the franchise toward other avenues. But they had never stopped organizing and making demands like other citizens in a democracy, and by doing that, they had never allowed white residents to ignore them or their needs. As a result, they held their own and even made progress during two of the most turbulent decades in US history—the 1930s and 1940s. The small and fluctuating number of Black Hanoverians paying their poll tax may have reflected their frustration with the system, but frustration on the part of some people was nothing new. It may also be a function of their financial situation. They may have had to choose between paying the poll tax and feeding their family. More important were the number of African Americans who were willing to keep working, keep pushing, keep pressing forward. These attitudes and this ethic, too, had deep roots in Black Hanover.

6

The Heat of Change

WHEN A TEENAGER or older adolescent began to show signs of readiness to accept Jesus as Savior, they were told pray: "Lord have mercy on me for I am a poor sinner serving for Jesus's sake."[1] They would then ask Jesus to forgive them for their sins. This could go on for days, but eventually the Lord would reveal to them that they were forgiven, and when this happened, the person was so overjoyed that they could not contain it inside. The convert would go house to house, knocking on neighbors' doors and telling of their conversion experience. The convert would knock on the door, shake the hand of the person who answered, and then repeat the saying given to them by God. One example was:

> I've been redeemed
> Washed in His blood
> God told me that the sun's gonna rise
> And the wind's gonna blow
> And nothing gonna frighten me from that shore.[2]

As the newly saved person went from house to house, the old saints, older followers of Jesus, left their homes and joined the singing. Eventually, the singing could be heard for miles around, and people would get up to await the knock on the door. This could happen at any time of the day or night.

Bertha Bernice Parnell's conversion came at midnight on a Saturday, and it was after 2 a.m. before she returned home.[3]

After notifying neighbors and before baptism occurred, the pastor and deacons questioned the convert: Do you believe He lives? How do you feel? When this phase of the process was over, baptism was scheduled. Baptists believe in immersing converts under water, and since most churches did not have indoor baptismal pools, several months might elapse before the baptism if the convert was "saved" during the winter. In Parnell's community, baptism took place at Allen's Pond.[4]

As is evident in the preceding story, Christianity continued to play a key role in the Black experience in Hanover County into the 1950s and 1960s. In this chapter, faith—along with organizing, employment, and education—continue to converge and to be the avenues through which Black Hanoverians exercised their rights as citizens. The Black churches founded following the Civil War continued to operate and flourish in the 1950s and 1960s. The buildings remained the meeting place for political, educational, and social events. As was true throughout this story, the secular and the divine overlapped. The leadership of secular organizations still consisted largely of churchmen and women, especially preachers. Women were often the secretaries in these organizations. They were also typically responsible for fundraising efforts, especially those involving cooking and selling dinners.[5]

The use of Allen Pond for baptizing is another example of the secular and religious coming together to share resources. The pond was located in the Liza and Andrew P. (A.P.) Allen Park in the eastern end of the county not far from where William Henry Winston and his family settled after the civil war. Liza and A.P. established this park as a recreational site for African Americans. People who grew up in the area recall that visitors came from as far away as New York, and that, during the 1930s, the men from the CCC visited. The Allen's sold food, and visitors played games and swam in the pond. A social scene during the week and Saturday, on the occasional Sunday morning during the warmer months, the pond was used for baptizing.[6]

When the time for baptizing came, the candidates went to Miss Liza, the proprietor of the property, dressed in white. At the appropriate time, saints, Christians, along with the pastor and family members processed

The Heat of Change

to the water. As the crowd sang a hymn, one by one the converts joined the pastor in the water. The preacher took the convert in his arms and dipped the individual under the water in the name of the "Father, the Son, and the Holy Ghost." The convert, quickly brought back to the surface, returned to the Allen house to change clothes. Before the end of the service, the new Christians received the right hand of fellowship, a ritual welcoming them into the church body.[7]

Sometimes this process began during the annual revival season, typically a week-long series of evening services in August or September that rotated around the Baptist churches in the county. Sinners—anyone who had not confessed Jesus to be their Lord and Savior—sat on the mourners' bench. People on these benches sat there, night after night, until they felt the "spirit" and confessed that they were sinners in need of salvation. Parents would not allow children to avoid the bench, whether they confessed anything while sitting there or not. The entire church prayed in hopes that the people on the bench would be saved. Those gathered might remain in church until midnight praying for someone on the bench. Dorothy Allen's conversion provides an example. She was a married woman who had never professed. She went up to the bench and the saints stayed in church until midnight praying and singing for her.[8]

For tough cases, the old saints would go to the sinner's house. They might encircle the sinner and pray and sing and tell them about the Lord. As odd as these activities may sound today, Black people who lived through the era of disfranchisement say that it was their belief in God that got them through. They helped each other, as Christian teaching directed them to do. Parnell, who grew up in this area of the county, says, "We are the church," and as such Black people helped one another to defeat adversity.[9] There is a practicality to Christianity that the uninitiated might miss.

As was the case with the preceding twenty years, the decades of the 1950s and 1960s included wars on foreign soil and domestic problems that engulfed the entire nation. Unlike the 1930s and 1940s, this time citizens questioned or even condemned the wars in Korea and Vietnam. On the domestic front, unlike the Depression, which in some respects united the country under an umbrella of despair, the fight for civil rights divided the country between Black people and their allies, and white supremacists and their silent supporters who wanted desperately to maintain the status quo. As was becoming apparent by the late 1940s, Black men and women in Virginia were changing their strategy and speaking out more forcefully. Like their counterparts throughout the South, during the decades of the 1950s and 1960s Black Hanoverians worked for civil rights.

Change rarely comes easily, and this was true in the South and in Virginia during this period. Many white Southerners believed that everything they considered important was being challenged, and indeed, values that had held sway longer than those alive in 1950 could remember were being called into question. White citizens were asked to consider a different social structure—one that might ultimately put them on equal footing with their Black employees and neighbors. This new structure would bring Black and white children together in the schoolroom. Many white parents believed that the next step would be social integration that could lead anywhere, including intermarriage and mixed-race or "mongrel" babies. Many white people were prepared to resist this scenario, as Black people prepared to fight just as hard to obtain their rights as citizens and as human beings.

The civic church, like the spiritual church, was at the center of the Black community. While Beryl Carter did not share a conversion experience, she remembered the church as key to the persistence of the Black community in Hanover. When she was a pre-teen, she recalled, civic groups often met at the church. Her parents were active in the County-Wide league and the NAACP. Carter's father encouraged people to register and vote and drove them to the polls. She also remembered the church as a gathering place for "Black folks away from White folks where you could talk about things and how you could deal with stuff." Here Carter was referring to the "stuff" of segregation[10] and this "stuff" included contradictions.

One of the items to consider under the "stuff" of segregation was the concerted effort to disfranchise Black voters. Indeed, the 1902 constitutional convention had been held for the sole purpose of taking, or at least limiting the Black vote, but this was not a hard and fast policy. Johnny Winston, the Ashland entrepreneur and Shiloh Baptist Church deacon mentioned previously, along with sixty other Black men registered to vote in 1904, two years after the adoption of the disfranchising constitution. Beryl Carter remembers that her father voted. There is no clear answer as to how and why this was true during the era of disfranchisement. It may have been due to familiarity. According to Carter, her father J. Conroy Thompson, was well-known in the community and participated in a type of cooperative, of Black and white farmers, which shared farming equipment. He also knew the registrar.[11] Johnny Clinton Winston, mentioned earlier, was also known and respected in the community, and voted, like his father before him. In Winston's case, family lore also suggests that he and his father were the son and grandson of a well-known white physician in the area. Johnny's daughter believed that this may have been the reason he was able to vote and carry on a successful business in Ashland.

Winston and Thompson were not anomalies. For whatever reason, across the South, there were always a few Black men who voted in spite of disfranchising state constitutions. Some may have been "properly" deferential to white people and dubbed "good negroes" and were, therefore, allowed to vote.[12] This characterization did not fit Winston and Thompson. The reason may have been numerical. The number of Black men who registered and voted was simply too small to make a difference in the outcome in any election. By allowing a limited number of Black men to vote, southern leaders could always point out that Black men were not barred from the franchise.

In 1963, Beryl Thompson Carter was excited to vote for John F. Kennedy. As mentioned previously, Carter's family knew the registrar. One of the men in the cooperative that her father belonged to was the father of the registrar, Barbara Johnson Boxley. When Carter arrived at the Boxley home, the registrar gave her a clean sheet of paper and told her to "write something." Carter recalls that she "puzzled over what to write," eventually settling on the preamble to the constitution. When she had finished, she handed the paper to Boxley and was registered. Carter chuckles saying, "I guess she could read."[13] Carter's experience may have been the experience of some African Americans in the county for generations. She was known to the registrar, and vice versa. If she had been a stranger, the woman might have denied her registration. However, Carter's experience also reminds us that, as at the turn of the twentieth century when William Chenery worked in the voter registration process in Ashland, white Hanoverians controlled the franchise.

In 1950, education was the arena in which change for Black citizens is most easily measured. Prior to 1950, Hanover County did not provide a high school for African American students, vocational training was almost nonexistent, Black parents provided transportation to and from school, and Black teachers and administrators received far less pay than their white counterparts.[14]

In 1950, however, one of the greatest wishes of African American parents in the county was fulfilled with the opening of the fully accredited John M. Gandy High School.[15] Construction of the new school began in 1949, and the finishing stages were reported on at a school board meeting in early 1950. On February 7, the architect appeared before the board to discuss the interior of the new high school.[16] The two-story structure had an auditorium, cafeteria, and for the first time, Black students in the county would have central heating. In the same minutes, the board discussed naming the school. While the minutes do not include the complete list of possibilities, they do report that the most popular suggestion was John M. Gandy High School, after the former president of Virginia State College.[17] It is not clear who nominated Gandy. He was not a Hanoverian and does not seem to have had a specific connection to the county, but several of the teachers were Virginia State College alumni, and they may have encouraged the naming in his honor. At the April meeting, the architect reported that the building was nearing completion, and the board voted unanimously to name the new school after Gandy.[18] The body had the luxury of granting a Black request without affecting white citizens in any way.

At the same meeting, the board discussed the needs of the auditorium, a space often left out of Black schools. The superintendent of schools was authorized to obtain bids "at the earliest possible time . . . in order that the auditorium and stage could be made available for commencement exercises in June 1950."[19] Finally, the board requested that the architect make sure that someone from the State Board of Education be present for the final inspection to certify that the school was up to state standards. The inspection took place on May 26, 1950, and, although the formal dedication would not take place until almost a year later, the school was certified ready for use.[20]

A group of seven John M. Gandy students who appear to be at the elementary level work on a display of the culture and art of early America.

When John M. Gandy High School, which served kindergarten through twelfth grade, opened in September 1950, it was the first and only high school for African Americans in Hanover, and it was the only state-of-the-art school in the county. The opening of Gandy was a high-water mark for Black Hanoverians. In October, a young African American student, Geraldine Winston, wrote an article about the new school for the *Herald Progress*. She reported on the indoor gymnasium and commented on the sight of the students in their gym uniforms. For the first time, Black children had the opportunity to participate in organized health and fitness activities at school. The boys learned tumbling, pyramid building, and stunts; both boys and girls learned square dancing. Ping Pong tables, to be used during gym class, were constructed by the shop teacher and his students.[21]

It is very interesting that the *Herald Progress* took this degree of interest in the new high school. Unfortunately, circulation records are not available, so there is no way to know the readership. Of course, the fact that the paper featured a section specifically dedicated to news from the Black community, suggests that the African American readership was significant and that white readers were interested in this news or at least not hostile to it.

Winston pointed out that, with all its amenities, the new school still had needs. Gandy, unlike many of the Black schools in Hanover, had a health clinic, and that facility needed supplies. While a mattress, sheets, and a bedspread were donated, to be completed the room still needed a hot water bottle, an ice bag, a basin, a clinical thermometer, a hot plate, and a screen. According to the reporter, library books were also donated.[22]

It is not clear exactly why the school board decided to provide this new school when it did, or why the building was so well appointed in some ways and lacking in others. Generosity toward Black students was not the school board's standard operating procedure. It is certainly possible that board members were simply acknowledging that it was past time for the Black children in the county to have an accredited high school and a facility that would motivate them and their teachers. The board may have also felt that, since a school was being built, it should embody the best. Given the times, the school board's decision was most likely a response to recent Supreme Court cases that were desegregating state colleges and universities across the country. Indeed, the University of Virginia law school admitted its first African American student in 1950.[23] Hanover County School Board members may have thought themselves proactive. Having ignored "separate but equal" for fifty-four years, by building a new, state of the art school, board members may have hoped to eliminate any desire, on the part of the county's Black citizens to push for school desegregation.[24] This arrangement also provided an opportunity for philanthropists to exercise their paternalistic tendencies. Regardless of why they built the school, Winston's story suggests that the county school board still believed that community members should partly pay for Black schools.

In 1939, the "Virginia Does Care" Conference pointed out the importance of Black citizens having a say in the running of the schools. In 1950, there were still no African Americans on the Hanover school board, or in any other leadership position in the county, but they continued to make their voices heard. They remained active in the organizations established in their community, and they continued to challenge the white establishment to respond to the needs of Black residents. The Black teachers and

The Student Participation Society, including Beryl Thompson and Na-Chay Jackson, also interviewed for this book, and Mr. Woodard in the John M. Gandy Library.

administrators must also be counted among those who played a major role in the success of Black students. These men and women were members of the Black elite. They were highly revered within the Black community for having attained an education and for their willingness to help others achieve. Even today, many of the teachers and principals from the period discussed here are still remembered as caring and inspiring individuals.[25]

Although 1950 was a red-letter year for the elementary and high school students housed at Gandy, the other Black schools in the county were not faring as well. This point was made by a committee, including Contee Robinson, E. E. Roane, and J. P. Giles from the Hanover County-Wide League, an organization established in the early 1920s by Black Hanoverians who wanted to expand educational opportunities for their children.[26] League members appeared before the school board on May 2, 1950, after having

The 1954–55 John M. Gandy junior class, including Frances Jackson, who inspired the title of this book, and John Morris, a descendant of William Henry Winston. Both Morris and Winston are featured in this book.

conducted a survey of the county's Black elementary schools and finding them in very poor condition. The group presented a resolution to the board asking for a plan of action including new consolidated elementary schools in the Beaverdam and Henry Districts and the completion of the consolidation of the elementary schools in the Ashland District.[27] Consolidation meant that the inadequate and dilapidated one- and two-room schools would be replaced by new, better-equipped buildings.

The board responded by promising that the needs of the Black schools would be considered when setting a plan for all the schools in the county. Also, the school board members pointed out to the committee that "it would take time to plan and still more time to carry out the general overall plans that might be projected with reference to the general school situation in Hanover County."[28] African Americans continued to ask for better schools, but met with excuses involving timing, money, or some other logistical block. There does appear to have been some progress in this area. The school construction program that took place between July 1949 and June 1954 produced, in addition to Gandy, two white high schools and two Black elementary schools. This covered the consolidation of Black elementary schools in the eastern and western sections of the county.

Contee Robinson and the League appeared before the board again two months later. This time, the representatives presented a petition asking the board to retain John Fleming as the agriculture teacher at Gandy for the 1950–51 school year. According to Robinson, the Black community was pleased with Fleming's job performance. He noted Fleming's "many years of service and the excellent work for the improvement of the agricultural interests of our entire County."[29] The board acknowledged that Fleming had served well in his position, but declared that "he had been reluctant in giving the proper cooperation to the principal and school board office and that the attitude Mr. Fleming appeared to have had was not conducive to the best interests of the general school situation of which he was supposed to have been a part."[30] Finally, the Board pointed out that the agriculture teachers had already been appointed for the 1950–51 school year.

The details of this story are missing from the school board minutes, so there is no concrete evidence as to why the board dismissed Fleming. As of the early 2000s, there were individuals in the community who remembered Fleming and could shed some light on the man and his personality. While it does not seem that he was the type who marched or picketed, he was a man who strove for the betterment of the race. He is remembered as having worked tirelessly to help young Black students obtain the funds to enter college. He also impressed people as one who, once he sank his teeth into something, would not let go. He had a reputation for standing up for the underdog, and sometimes this made him unpopular. Any of these actions could have landed him on the wrong side of the school board. What is known is that Fleming was brought back to the school the following year, and that he remained in the Hanover County school system for the next thirty years. [31]

A letter to the editor from Ozwell Robinson, the president of the Gandy PTA, appeared in the Hanover newspaper on March 29, 1951. The PTA had discussed the proposed budget for the upcoming school year and was concerned that the funds requested by the school board from the county

John M. Gandy Principal Eunice Bundy and Assistant Principal Mr. Booker at a celebratory dinner.

board of supervisors were inadequate. The organization pointed out that the schools needed more money "in order to afford better facilities for all the children of Hanover County."[32] In particular, they wanted enough money to add typing, bookkeeping, stenography, and business practice to the Gandy curriculum. According to the author of the letter, fewer than 10 percent of the students would go on to college, but most of the classes were college preparatory. He wanted students to get the training they needed to get good jobs after graduation. This letter is part of a recurring theme. Despite disfranchisement, Black citizens in Hanover freely approached the county leadership to request a service or complain about a problem. What is noteworthy is that the officials appear to have received them politely and listened to their concerns. Unfortunately, this attitude did not often translate into an immediate response—as apparently was the case with the request of March 1951, which the minutes do not suggest was granted.

The Heat of Change

In the 1930s, Black children walked to school, in rare cases were driven there by their parents, or took advantage of the school buses provided by private citizens. By the 1950s, the county provided buses to the Black schools, but transportation was still a major problem, as the PTA pointed out, the few buses assigned to Gandy were severely overcrowded. Bus seven from the western part of the county had a ridership of sixty-five students, but there were only seats for forty-eight. At least two other buses transported more than sixty pupils. The drivers had to make two trips in the morning and again in the afternoon; this meant that "children arrive at school as late as 9:15 in the morning and leave school as early as 2:30 in the afternoon." School began at 8:55 a.m. and the day ended at 3:00 p.m. "As a result, some high school students missed twenty minutes of class work each morning. Multiply this time lost by five days a week in a 180-day school year, and it is obvious that students are losing valuable school time."[33]

Nothing changed with the bus situation during the 1950–51 school year, and there was apparently no change at the beginning of the following school year, either, because in October, the Gandy PTA contacted the school board office again about severe overcrowding on the buses. The superintendent told the delegation that the board intended to address the bus situation at Gandy "as far as possible upon the arrival of the new buses."[34]

While the Gandy PTA was addressing the immediate needs of its constituents, a more dramatic event was taking place just a few counties away that would have far-reaching consequences for Hanover County, the state, and the country. On April 23, 1951, a group of high school students, led by sixteen-year-old Barbara Johns, went on strike in Farmville, Virginia, because of the poor condition of the Robert R. Moton High School in Prince Edward County. The strikers convinced Oliver Hill and Spotswood Robinson, civil rights attorneys affiliated with the NAACP Legal Defense Fund, to take their case, which when filed became known as *Davis v. County School Board of Prince Edward County, Virginia*. By this time, the NAACP had changed its strategy. Previously, the legal team had argued to make Black and white public schools equal. The attorneys for the plaintiffs in *Davis* and in four companion cases, which would become *Brown v. the Board of Education of Topeka, Kansas,* argued that "separate but equal" as a goal was unachievable and unconstitutional. They now wanted desegregation.[35] The Ashland paper responded to the Prince Edward situation with words of caution and chastisement for the Black attorneys and the state for not living up to "separate but equal."[36] While they may not have been calling for complete desegregation in 1951, it is clear from Ozwell Robinson's letter to the editor, that Black Hanoverians had not ceased their constant pursuit for better schools.

While the school desegregation cases were not mentioned again in the newspaper or the school board minutes until after the *Brown* decision in May 1954, Black parents continued to ask the school board for relief from overcrowding and dilapidated facilities. The prevailing issue for all the schools in Hanover County was overcrowding. The baby boomer generation had reached elementary school. Their sheer numbers overwhelmed school boards across the country. Hanover also faced the problem of deteriorating and outmoded facilities. This was especially true of the Black schools outside of Ashland. Most school board meetings in the early fifties included at least one request from an individual or organization asking the board to "please do something about the overcrowded schools."[37]

On February 12, 1953, the school board held a joint meeting with the Hanover County Board of Supervisors to review a proposed school building plan. There were several community members present. Most are named in the minutes, except for a "group of four Negro patrons from Hanover County."[38] Based on suggestions from those in attendance, the plan was revised and presented at the next school board meeting. The revised school plan included new construction and renovations to existing buildings. The new plan also included new schools for white students and two new Black elementary schools. The children from the one- and two-room schools would be consolidated into these newer and larger facilities.[39] The plan did not mention any upgrades to the Black high school. Gandy had not been open for very long, but it was already overcrowded; one high school for Black children was not enough. Also, students from outlying areas had to travel a great distance to school daily. The board may have been concerned with backlash from white people if the body voted to add another high school for Black students so soon after building Gandy. The five-year building plan seemed a major step forward, but in the meantime, the school situation worsened. The press announced that,

The Heat of Change

during the 1953–54 school year, students would experience double shifts and classes conducted in the hallways and cafeterias.[40] One wonders if it occurred to anyone, even in passing, that operating two separate systems was far more expensive than it would have been to operate one. Of course, anyone daring to voice this notion risked ostracization or possibly worse.

On May 17, 1954, the United States Supreme Court handed down a decision that rocked the very foundation of southern society. The Court overruled *Plessy v. Ferguson,* a judicial precedent since 1896. The court ruled that separate schools based on race were unconstitutional. Hanover County leaders made every effort to avoid desegregation. Prior to the *Brown* decision, the county had decided to sell bonds to raise funds to build new schools, and *Brown* led some people in the county to point out that the vote had been based on segregated schools. The board of supervisors offered a resolution declaring the body "opposed to the operation in Hanover County of integrated, or racially non-segregated public schools." "If it be unlawful to continue to operate segregated public schools," the board continued, "then, let the public schools of Hanover County be discontinued and closed, and the energy and substance of its people be devoted to the establishment of other facilities for the education of its children, both white and colored, alike."[41]

In the meantime, the school situation continued to deteriorate. In 1955, Martha Riis Moore, writer for the *Herald Progress,* produced a series of articles on county schools. The first school she visited was Bethany Elementary School for Black children. At the time of her visit, Bethany consisted of two identical buildings with four classrooms in each building. Each building was heated by a woodstove that was located by the only exit. Fire extinguishers were located near the doors. The heat was uneven, and on very cold days the partitions separating the classrooms were opened so students could gather around the stove.[42]

Moore pointed out that "some days there are 55 six- and seven-year-olds in the same space." The school lacked indoor toilets, running water, and coat closets. There was a basin where the children could wash their hands. For drinking, each child had to bring a glass from home. The principal, who also taught seventh grade, stopped accepting deliveries of milk because there was nowhere to store it. The Bethany School employed a janitor, who started the fires in the morning and cleaned the buildings after school.[43]

Moore also wrote about Pleasant Grove Elementary School for Black pupils in the east end of the county. There were ninety students in a three-room frame building taught by the principal and two teachers. This 30-to-1 ratio was actually better than in most of the Black schools. The classrooms were very small, and there was no room for the "instructional projects used in modern education." The toilets were located outside; there was no running water. According to Moore, there was a new well and the "water supply is adequate" so the Pleasant Grove students did at least have a good supply of drinking water. [44]

In the meantime, despite the activities to avoid desegregation, Black Hanoverians continued at their accustomed steady pace toward achieving their goals. While the *Herald Progress* carried the news of the segregationists, it also printed the news of the Black community. The Gandy PTA remained active, set goals, and continued to be a presence at school board meetings and in the community at large.

Despite the continuing issues of overcrowding, the Gandy PTA shared its positive outlook with *Herald Progress* readers in a report that ran on September 30, 1954. The organization announced that John Flemings' agriculture classes were going to beautify school grounds. The students planned to transplant evergreens, and this project was touted as presenting the opportunity to enhance the exterior of the schools and provide a teaching and learning experience for the participants. The PTA also hosted a chest clinic to check for TB.[45]

Gandy students continued to prepare for life after high school. Senior English students studying various occupations conducted a survey to find out their classmates' post-graduation plans. They interviewed 144 students and discovered that 108 had definite plans, while 32 of the students reported only a vague idea of what they would like to do. Four of the students interviewed admitted to having no plans at all. Of those with plans, 41 wanted to be physicians, nurses, teachers, engineers, or ministers. Twenty-five thought they would go into the service field, and 21 planned to obtain clerical positions. [46] The actions and aspirations of these young Black Hanoverians offer insight into their commitment to themselves and to the overall betterment of the race. Amid disfranchisement and resistance to desegregation, when it must have been easy to become discouraged, frustrated, and angry, they found time to hope and plan for a brighter future. By continuing to beautify the schools, the adults taught the children to work with what they had. In turn, the students learned to think beyond the limitations placed on them by a system beyond their control. This survey indicates that, while full citizenship might for the moment remain beyond the reach of these young African Americans, they still planned to attain their piece of the American dream.

Other Gandy students planned an all-French assembly, and the junior English students organized an assembly of their own to conclude the unit on assemblies they had been studying. These students had learned how to preside, introduce speakers, and make announcements. They planned to conduct a forum on a national topic. Regular morning devotions based on the Bible took place daily in the high school and were led by members of the senior class. Each morning a student gave a brief talk. Each month devotions were planned around the Bible. One month the theme was "The Bible, a Lamp and a Light." Using the intercom system, the students were heard all over the building. These activities reveal the continued role of Christianity in the schools; Black Hanoverians did not separate their spirituality from the rest of their lives.[47]

While the students were achieving and moving forward, the PTAs were busily working on their behalf. The Gandy PTA sent a letter proclaiming its stance on integration to the *Herald Progress* on February 17, 1955. The statement was addressed to David B. Webb, the superintendent of schools. The missive read, "We would hereby like to submit our stand on the integration of public schools issue. We are highly in favor of integration. We feel that such barriers as one's race, creed and other such minor differentiations should be entirely eliminated so as not to impede any man's progress." The letter continued, "We realize that this will be a somewhat radical change for we, the inhabitants of the south; but with sincere efforts of each citizen, we feel that any necessary adjustments can be made. It is not our intention to cause conflicts or disturbances between any persons or groups of people; we only think that each citizen should have an equal right to fully enjoy the many opportunities that are offered by our great country."[48] This letter was signed by Thomas Johnson, the president of the PTA, and Bessie Taliaferro, the secretary. Taking this very public stance and allowing their names to be published took courage on the part of Johnson and Taliaferro, who could reasonably worry that they were risking retribution, financial and possibly even physical, from members of the community who wanted to maintain segregated schools.

Also in February 1955, the Pole Green Elementary School PTA held a meeting at First Union Baptist Church. Delegates from other eastern Hanover County schools for Black residents were invited guests. The Rev. B. S. Giles, the pastor of First Union, started the meeting by emphasizing the importance of education. He went on to commend Black teachers for the work they had accomplished despite the poor facilities and few resources. He added that the times were changing; the scientific age demanded a different set of skills and abilities, and parents and teachers were going to have to make sure that their children had what they needed to succeed. He went on to say that all the schools needed good ventilation, heat, and cooling to bring out the best in the students. Black parents would have to make the school authorities recognize and fulfill these needs. At this juncture, Giles appears still to have been seeking equalization rather than desegregation; that he felt free to espouse that point of view, which differed from the position of the NAACP and other national groups, suggests that not all Black Hanoverians thought desegregation was attainable or desirable. Indeed, some may have preferred equalization of the schools.[49] Also, he may tacitly have been courting white public opinion; for some white people, equalization was preferable to desegregation. Lester A. Banks, the executive secretary of the state NAACP, was the guest speaker at the Pole Green meeting, and he seemed to take that sentiment into account even while standing up for his organization's goal of desegregation. He traced the role of the NAACP in putting legal pressure on localities when working for better salaries for teachers and better schools, and he reminded his audience that no change had occurred in the South without legal pressure. In closing, he said that the forthcoming decision by the Supreme Court on the implementation of *Brown* was pending, and he urged those PTAs represented at the meeting to move with caution—by which he seems to have meant they should avoid signaling acceptance of separate schools, no matter how good the facilities they might be offered. The PTAs represented at the meeting had been working for several years to obtain a consolidated

Black school for their area, but they voted to adopt a "wait and see" and "not fight for separate facilities."[50]

Indeed, while the *Brown* decision did not force any immediate changes in the school systems across the South, in Hanover at least, it spurred the school board into action. Suddenly, many of the obstacles that had previously prevented the board from improving the schools for Black children disappeared. In early 1956, the school board told the PTA members that they would get the consolidated school. The East End PTA turned it down and pointed out that, since the *Brown* decision, it was illegal to establish schools based on race.[51] The school board's offer was too little too late.

Shortly after the east end parents took their stand, a separate demand was unfolding in the western end of the county. School board minutes have regular notations regarding communications about poor conditions at the Bethany Elementary School for Black children. Like the parents in the east end, the Bethany parents had been told that the holdup was the acquisition of land. In response, the members of the Bethany Baptist Church, an African American congregation located across the road from the school, had agreed to sell land adjacent to the school so that the facility could be expanded. In March 1955, Robert Gwathmey, the school board attorney, wrote to J. P. Giles, a Bethany trustee, reminding him that Bethany Baptist Church had agreed to this transaction. Gwathmey said that it was his understanding and that of the school superintendent that the congregation had met in February to finalize the decision. He wrote, "Yesterday Mr. Webb [the school superintendent] called me and stated that the School Board is very anxious to get its program going in order to relieve the congested conditions at Bethany School."[52]

In response, Giles, Stephen Phillips, and Anderson Taylor, presumably all church trustees, sent a letter to Gwathmey and the school board informing them that the church members had decided not to sell the land after all.[53] In a letter to the board, the congregation noted that "we are aware of the congested conditions now existing at the Bethany School. But we also feel that it is unwise to make any definite plans for selling the church property, until the final decision has been made by the Supreme Court, regarding the law of segregation in the public schools."[54] This response provides another example of the awareness of the Black community of what was happening in the federal courts and of what it could mean for them and their children. Both cases, that of the East End PTA and the other involving Bethany Baptist Church, illustrate the exercise of a basic right of citizenship in this country—the right to change one's mind and then express that new viewpoint. These incidents also show the integrity of the Black men and women involved in this process. They could have taken the bribes as offered, in the form of new segregated schools.

August 1963 was a major time for Black people in the county. The March on Washington for Jobs and Freedom took place on August 28, and a bus left Hanover County carrying marchers and James Henry was one of the riders. Later that month, the two county high schools desegregated. In 1956, Virginia established a Pupil Placement Board (PPB) that theoretically gave all families the right to apply to transfer to the school of their choice. No students in the county, Black or white, turned to the PPB until 1963, when ten Black students applied to transfer from John M. Gandy High School to Lee-Davis or Patrick Henry High Schools. These first students were the sons and daughters of NAACP members in the county. The students' names, and their parents' names and their addresses, were listed in the *Herald Progress*. This was the standard procedure for the PPB, and it is quite possible that this practice was established as a deterrent.[55]

This first attempt at desegregating the schools did not go unnoticed by segregationists in the county. Yet despite the board of supervisors' resolution of 1956, and later reaffirmations by individual board members, resolving to close the schools rather than desegregate, when the time came to make the fateful decision, the board was unwilling to close the schools, and in this it reflected white public sentiment—not to mention Black opinion on that subject.[56] In the end, the PPB approved all ten applications, and county authorities opted for token integration in the schools rather than sacrifice public education altogether.[57] When schools opened that fall, two African American sisters entered Patrick Henry High School at the western end of the county, and six students entered Lee-Davis on the eastern side of the county. Two students decided to remain at Gandy. This transition happened without incident.[58]

While the schools began desegregating in 1963, in the nine years since the *Brown* decision had been handed down nothing had changed in the racial make-up of the schools in Hanover County. Another promise of racial change came along in 1964 in the form of the federal Civil Rights Act. Title VI of this act provided a new weapon to the NAACP legal team. School systems that did not take meaningful steps toward real integration ran the risk of losing federal funding.[59]

To ensure adherence, all school board members across the country were required to sign an "Assurance of Compliance" agreement with the Department of Health, Education, and Welfare. While some in Hanover, including the *Herald Progress*, felt this requirement was an insult to board members who had already pledged to uphold the Constitution, all representatives signed the agreement on February 18, 1965.[60] The Assurance of Compliance read in part: "no person in the United States shall, on the ground of race, color, or national origin, be excluded from participation in, be denied the benefits of, or be otherwise subjected to discrimination under any program or activity for which the Applicant [the Hanover County School Board] received Federal financial assistance from the Department."[61]

Ready to use its new weapon, the NAACP legal defense team for Virginia held a meeting in Richmond; representatives from counties and cities across the state attended. The lawyers informed the group of the power the Civil Rights Act had given them to force meaningful change in the state's schools. The team was looking for plaintiffs to step forward, and many of the attendees put their names on the list. The first step was to give local school boards a chance to make changes on their own. To this end, petitions were circulated in various Virginia counties.[62]

Harold Thompson, the education director for the Hanover NAACP chapter, coordinated the petition in that county. Thompson's daughters, Arlene and Stephanie, had transferred to Patrick Henry in 1963. On May 28, 1964, eleven days after the tenth anniversary of the decision in *Brown I*, a petition asking for the immediate desegregation of the county's schools was presented to the school board with a letter suggesting that failure to respond in the affirmative would result in court action. The petition asked the board to announce its intention to integrate the schools by its next regular meeting. A second step demanded by the NAACP-sponsored petition was that the board adopt and publish a plan "by which racial discrimination will be terminated with respect to administrative personnel, teachers, clerical, custodial and other employees" of the school system.[63]

The school board and the local paper responded to the letter by saying that the schools were already desegregated, and that they planned to maintain the plan already in place. Seventeen more Black students entered predominantly white schools for the 1964–65 school year, but the NAACP was not satisfied. Common practice in Virginia cities and counties in effect put all the responsibility for effecting desegregation on Black parents. State Senator Henry Marsh III, a civil rights attorney at that time, recalled that desegregation only took place when Black students were willing to "run the gauntlet" in white schools.[64] Because of the board's unsatisfactory response, Black parents in Hanover and seven other counties, along with the NAACP Legal Defense team, initiated action to sue their respective school boards on behalf of their children. Stephanie V. Thompson was listed as the lead plaintiff in the Hanover case.

In response to the lawsuit, the Hanover County school board began developing a freedom of choice plan to desegregate its schools. This plan allowed any student in the county to attend any school in the county "at which the grade for which the child is eligible is taught."[65] The numbers of African American students who enrolled at predominantly white schools increased, but no white students opted to attend the historically Black schools. Despite the lack of success of these plans, the Hanover County NAACP chapter opted to withdraw from the suit, but other complainants stayed in the fight, taking their case all the way to the US Supreme Court.

In May 1968, the Supreme Court handed down its decision in *Charles C. Green v. The County School Board of New Kent County, Virginia*. According to those involved, it was the simplest and clearest of all the cases. There were only two schools in New Kent County, one Black and one white, and both serving K-12 students. Unlike Hanover, New Kent did not have any students attending integrated schools at the time the petitions were circulated. In fact, the county did not make any move toward applying *Brown* until the lawsuit was filed. At that time, a freedom of choice plan was adopted, but the federal courts said it was too little, too late.

In May 1968, fourteen years after the *Brown* decision, the Supreme Court finally forced the matter of desegregation in the public schools in the South to a conclusion. The justices wrote that, where freedom of choice plans were not providing for real and meaningful integration, they were to be discontinued, and the local school board was to develop a plan that would integrate the schools immediately.[66]

Because of the *Green* decision, Samuel W. Tucker, a prominent civil rights attorney, asked Judge Robert R. Merhige Jr. of the United States Fourth District Court to review Hanover's freedom of choice plan, along with the plans in ten other Virginia counties. The school board in Hanover reportedly discussed its freedom of choice plan at length and determined that it was working. All members agreed that the attorneys should "defend the Freedom of Choice plan and its progress in the Hanover County schools and that if more rapid integration of the schools is required, as much time as possible should be sought for its implementation."[67] The board argued that the extra time was needed because "the complete reorganization" necessary to comply with the court ruling would be "virtually impossible administratively and would be disruptive to the educational program of the public this year." The board may have needed more time to reorganize, but they may also have wanted more time to bring the Black schools up to what they deemed an acceptable standard for white students. This was the rationale given by New Kent County when asking Judge Merhige for an additional year to comply.[68] While it was always clear that schools for Black children were substandard—overcrowded, outdated textbooks, often lacking auditoriums, athletic facilities, and equipment—the all-white school boards often ignored this reality until forced to desegregate.

On July 10, 1968, Judge Merhige directed the Hanover school board to "determine whether its system was being operated in compliance with the plan of desegregation as enunciated by the United States Supreme Court in its decision of May 27, 1968, in the case of *Green v. County School Board of New Kent County, Virginia;* and, if not, to file a plan of desegregation of the public school system to bring it in compliance with the principles of the said decision." Thus, the Hanover County school board was forced to take a close and realistic look at its plan of desegregation; it admitted that the freedom of choice plan in operation "may not result in a 'unitary' school system within the meaning of the New Kent decision as quickly as will be required by the principles of said decision."[69]

The board submitted a plan for the desegregation of the county's schools which Judge Merhige rejected. He found the plan to integrate the faculty inadequate. While Merhige had determined to give the schools an extra year to fully integrate the students, he required that the faculties be significantly integrated for the 1968–69 school term. This communication came to the school board in August 1968, after teacher assignments had already been set for the school year. Superintendent J. K Samples sent a letter to all the county's teachers explaining that "indications are that all the Hanover County Public Schools will be totally integrated beginning with the school session 1969–70. The school board, however, is currently under Federal Court order to substantially further desegregate the various school faculties for the session 1968–69. It is hoped that enough teachers will volunteer to be transferred to faculties on which their race is in the minority to satisfy the court order." There was a form at the bottom of the letter on which teachers could indicate whether they were already in the minority, would be willing to transfer, or were not willing to transfer. In the end, fourteen white teachers and thirty-one Black teachers indicated a willingness to transfer.[70]

In its attempt to formulate a plan acceptable to Judge Merhige, the Hanover school board ultimately proposed a complete reorganization based on geographic zoning, pairing of grades, or both to accomplish integration for the 1969–70 school year. The plan also included a promise to make every attempt possible to further integrate the faculties for the current term. Finally, the board agreed to study and consider programs to be conducted during the 1968–69 school year that would help with a smooth transition for the following school year. Examples provided included the formation of a county-wide bi-racial faculty committee and a bi-racial student committee to work together on transitional problems. Merhige approved this plan.[71]

During this tumultuous time in the county and in the country, the Black people of Hanover found themselves with an unexpected ally in their fight for civil rights: Randolph-Macon College students and faculty. In the spring of 1963, a group of 102 Randolph-Macon students signed a letter to the president of the college. The letter requested that the college prepare a statement disavowing discrimination and agreeing to accept students based solely on qualifications and not race or color. This letter was presented to the Board of Trustees. The board appointed a committee to examine the student proposal, which also asked for a policy on desegregation to be established by the school.⁷² The following spring, the trustees released a statement reaffirming their current policy, which they said did not discriminate based on race. The board also stated that, to its knowledge, no Black person had ever applied to the college.⁷³

In the midst of everything happening in the county, the nation was also dealing with a series of assassinations that rocked the country. John Kennedy, Robert Kennedy, Martin Luther King Jr., and Malcolm X, all seen as figures of hope for the Black community, were killed before the job was done. Perhaps the death of Dr. King had the greatest impact on Black people in this country. In life he had preached non-violence, but his violent death triggered a series of urban riots, some of the most violent events outside of war in this country's history. Oddly, the *Herald Progress* did not publish anything about Dr. King's death other than the fact that a memorial service was held at Randolph-Macon. The paper did print a picture of the sheriff and his deputies in their new riot gear, which had been purchased in case of problems arising because of the civil rights leader's demise.⁷⁴

In 1959, Deborah Dabney Joseph entered first grade at John M. Gandy. Joseph was born and raised in Berkleytown, an historically Black community located outside of the Ashland town limits that was founded after the 1911 residential segregation ordinance was passed in the town.⁷⁵ Berkleytown was her world, her family, friends, and her teachers lived within walking distance. All of the neighbors had gardens and they all shared their produce. Her extended family was in the mortuary business and her dad, Claudius Dabney, worked in that business with his brother and he also had a custard stand near Route 1 where he sold hot dogs, hamburgers, and soft serve ice cream. One uncle had a barbershop. Her first job was at Lightfoot's Bakery where she worked before and after school.

Regardless of all the turmoil in the world and stressors in the county, the schools in Hanover opened for the 1969–70 school year on a totally integrated basis. The public record is quiet about the desegregation of the schools during the first two years after desegregation. Deborah Dabney Joseph was one of the students to desegregate Patrick Henry High School in 1969. For the first time, she had to leave her neighborhood to go to school. In hindsight, she realizes that the process went more smoothly in Hanover than in other locales she has heard about, but that does not mean that it was without its thorny times. She remembers a school play when some white parents did not want their children to be on stage with Black students. She also remembers that some white students made rude comments like "you need to go back where you came from," but in the end, students became adjusted to desegregated schools faster than their parents.[76]

A year after Joseph graduated, Patrick Henry High School drew the attention of the local press. In February 1972, a group of students planned an assembly to celebrate Black History Month. Initially, the principal granted them permission to sing "Life Every Voice and Sing" also known as the Black National Anthem, but on Friday before the assembly he revoked permission saying that white students would be offended.[77] He likened it to white students singing "Dixie."[78] The African American students sang "Lift Every and Sing" anyway, and they were suspended for five days. The parents of the students met on Saturday and Sunday and decided to approach the superintendent asking for a reduced suspension. Seven parents and two students met with the school official on Monday and were denied their request to shorten the penalty.

On Tuesday morning, approximately 150 African American students walked out of school in support of their classmates. They gathered on the grassy area in front of the school and refused to leave until their classmates were readmitted. According to the paper, the Hanover County Sheriff's office contacted the Virginia state police saying that the protest was "out of hand."[79] Around 12 p.m., ten members of the state police arrived to join the three county sheriffs already at the school. About an hour later, the students were given three choices: return to class; leave the premises; be taken to Hanover Courthouse to be charged with trespassing. Thirty-seven students were taken to Hanover Courthouse, charged with trespassing, processed and jailed, or released to the custody of their parents. Bail was set at $300 cash or real estate. Of the 37 processed, 14 were jailed until bail was posted. The following day, the superintendent met with the parents and the students were allowed to return to class. A trial was set for March 2, 1972, but postponed until June 21 with no explanation.

Hanover County was like many other localities in the state and across the South between 1950 and 1970. It experienced continual growth and development. The Depression was over, and the economic situation had improved. The county was in a prime location. While still mostly rural, it also offered town living and it was just twenty minutes north of Richmond, a major urban area and the state capital, and just two hours south of Washington DC.

Brown Grove, the farming community and home of Walter Jackson and his family, written about in chapter 5, was greatly impacted by outside forces during this period. Interstate 95, which made travel from Florida to Maine easier, played havoc with many communities, especially Black areas. Indeed, using eminent domain, farmlands and homes were lost in favor of the highway which split Brown Grove. Despite this fact, many of the descendants of the community's original settlers remain.

Issues surrounding the provision of health care loomed large on the county's collective mind. While tuberculosis and polio were under control, cancer was taking their place as the most dreaded disease. Frequent articles related to fundraising for new medical research were found in the *Herald Progress*. Education was important to virtually all the residents of Hanover; having long since ceased to be regarded as a privilege, schooling was now universally understood as a right of citizenship. Citizens, Black and white alike, now expected that the school board would live up to their expectations. This meant good facilities, good teachers, and good administration.

What the county's leadership had not anticipated in 1950 was a many-pronged attack on the very structure of southern society, which had been in place, informally and formally since the end of slavery. During the period covered in this chapter, separate but equal was determined unconstitutional, the Civil Rights Act of 1964 provided a new weapon in the fight for desegregated schools, and section 2 of the Voting Rights Act of 1965 promised, among other things, that "No voting qualification or prerequisite to voting, or standard, practice, or procedure shall be imposed or applied by any State or political subdivision to deny or abridge the right of any citizen of the United States to vote on account of race or color." While it is difficult to determine the increase in number of Black voters in Hanover County during this period, according to the National Archives, "the Voting Rights Act had an immediate impact. By the end of 1965, a quarter of a million new Black voters had been registered, one-third by federal examiners. By the end of 1966, only four out of 13 southern states had fewer than 50 percent of African Americans registered to vote."[80]

Often forgotten today, however, is that white people in the county had always had to deal with Black residents who made demands of a system that did not respect their place as citizens. White Hanoverians believed, since they had made certain concessions to African Americans, that they were relatively happy. As had been the case down through the decades, white Hanoverians severely misread their Black neighbors.

In the years between 1950 and 1972, Black Hanoverians continued to study and address the needs of their community. They understood how the system worked—and failed to work for them—and they were determined to use it and even change it. This they had always attempted to do. After 1950, however, they had the added support and leadership of a national movement with the same goal of full citizenship for Black Americans.

True, Hanover did not experience the violence in these times that both white vigilantes and officers of the law sometimes perpetrated in the Deep South. And the actions of African Americans in Hanover were neither flamboyant nor sensational. They did not even picket or boycott in the county. Some people, therefore, might not regard what Black Hanoverians accomplished as significant. The change that occurred in Hanover County was the result of a slow and steady hammer, wielded by Black hands, knocking against a structure whose foundation had been made during slavery and the cornerstone laid in 1902 at the constitutional convention. The hammering was ultimately reinforced by federal courts and by a federal government responding to a national civil rights movement.

A blow was struck every time a group of Black citizens attended a school board or board of supervisors meeting. Another blow landed each time a letter was sent to the newspaper. Still another blow found its mark with every Sunday morning sermon calling for Black Hanoverians to stand firm. Countless blows hit home when local Black leaders stepped forward to organize and when Black citizens worked to improve the schooling or the healthcare their community received. They did not cower. They did not hide. Their demands were constant and unrelenting, and in the end, Black Hanoverians contributed to the overall betterment of their families, friends, and fellow Virginians. They helped change the South just surely as did their more broadly publicized brethren and sisters in Birmingham, Selma, or Mississippi. They built lives worth living, and ultimately, they did their part in reshaping the nation.

Epilogue
Black Life in Hanover County, Virginia, Today

IT HAS BEEN 160 YEARS since fifteen-year-old William Henry Winston and George Fields, along with his mother, Martha Ann Fields, and his siblings walked away from bondage, choosing freedom over fealty to their enslavers. Returning to the county after the Civil War, Winston worked hard, provided for his family, became a Deacon in his church and a community leader. He lived to the age of seventy-five and knew a time when Black men voted and saw that promised right of citizenship taken away. Many of Winston's descendants still live in Hanover County, and they have witnessed changes at the local, state, and national level that their ancestor prayed for and some that would have disturbed him greatly. Some of Winston's great-grandchildren live in or near the Brown Grove community where he first set down his roots. The land he purchased and left to his wife was sold in 1942, but his great-grandson John Morris bought land nearby and lived on it until his death in 2018.

George and Martha Ann made their way to Fortress Monroe near Hampton, Virginia. George and his older brother James attended what was then called the Hampton Normal and Agricultural Institute. Both of them went on to study law—James at Howard University and George at Cornell University, where he was the first Black person to graduate from the law school. George then returned to Virginia to practice law alongside James. These two remarkable men were the sons of Martha Ann Fields, who led them to freedom in 1863. Clearly, she impressed upon her children the importance of education.

Unlike Winston, Morris lived long enough to experience both the humiliation of segregation and the hope of integration. As a young man, he worked afterschool jobs to help take care of his mother, who worked at Virginia Products picking the eyes out of potatoes. While still in school, Morris decided to get a job so that his mother could quit hers. He worked at Kelly's Truck Shop just a couple of miles outside of Ashland. The white owner told Morris that, if he got off the school bus at the shop every day, he would make sure the boy got home, which may be an indication that the owner had some positive regard for the young man. According to Morris, it was a good job. He earned more money than many of his teachers. While it was profitable, his time at Kelly's was not easy: he was often called racist names, but he believed that this atmosphere prepared him for things that would happen later.[1]

After he graduated from John M. Gandy High School, John Morris worked at several jobs, but eventually landed at Reynolds Metals in Richmond. A self-described "finished product of Martin Luther King Jr.," Morris was the first Black person to work in the can division of Reynolds Metals. The manager told him that his hiring would probably cost the company nine white employees, but in the end, none of the white employees left, Morris recalled, because "they needed the job as much as I did."[2]

After five years, the company relocated workers to places all over the country, but Morris could not leave Richmond because his wife was very ill. By this time, he had proven his value, and the company did not want to lose him. Instead, he retrained as a machinist and joined the foil factory in Richmond. There were a lot of diehard racists in this division, "a lot of Confederates," according to Morris. For a while he was repeatedly called "nigger," "coon," and "darky."[3] Words did not bother him, explains Morris. He had heard them ever since he had worked at Kelly's. There was at least one older white worker who warned the younger white men that they had better be good to Morris because "he might be your boss one day." Indeed, Morris eventually became their boss's boss.[4]

Like his great-grandfather William Henry Winston, John Morris was a deacon in his church and deeply spiritual. This is evident as he credited his success at Reynolds to the fact that he walked what he preached. Morris asserted that leaders must "let your walking match your talking."[5] He began all his staff meetings with prayer, and no matter what other workers said to him, he responded as he believed a Christian should. He noted that, before he retired, most of the men in the shop had Bibles in their desks, and that, when he did retire, they gave him a beautiful Bible. Someone asked him how the people in his shop could keep the good feelings going that had been established in his time, and he pointed to the Bible. He treated his workers with respect, and he listened to every idea. In short, he respected his men, and they came to respect him.[6]

During his lifetime, Morris saw Interstate 95 come through the county splitting the Brown Grove community in two. He also experienced the addition of the county municipal airport which continues to disrupt life in the county.

Today, another outside entity, the Wegmans Supermarket chain, has once again infiltrated the historic community with the addition of a distribution center. While years of resistance have worn down some people in the community, others fought this latest incursion with some success. While the facility has been built, the resistance of Brown Grove residents garnered the attention of the national press, and the Board of Supervisors is finally listening. Until recently, the Hanover County comprehensive plan included two new economic districts—Sliding Hill and Lewistown Road—which would have brought more industry to Brown Grove. These districts are no longer part of the plan, and the descendant community claims this victory.[7] Also, as part of this most recent fight, residents and friends worked together, and the historic community is now on the state and national registries.[8]

It is 2024 and many things have changed in Hanover County since the end of slavery. The population has increased from 16,965 with a Black majority at the start of the Civil War to a total population of 109,979 according to the 2020 census. There are now 106,041 "non-Hispanic White alone" and 9,808 Black people.[9] While no longer a Black majority, today the county website features a story about five generations of the Brooks, a Black family who served in the US military in Vietnam, Iraq, Bosnia, and Herzegovina. This family still lives near the land where their ancestor,

Andrew Brooks, was enslaved. Indeed, the Brooks family and other Black people in the county have come a long way since the end of slavery, but there are still challenges and victories to pursue.

Where once the Fields family could be considered thieves, having stolen themselves from their enslavers, they are now honored. In October 2020, Hanover County named a building in the county's government complex after Martha Ann Fields. This building, located on land that was formerly the Nutshell Plantation where Mrs. Fields was enslaved, houses the departments of human resources, general services, the assessor's office and parks and recreation. As of March 2024, Martha's son George Washington Fields is now being portrayed in Hanover Tavern by local actor Anthony Keitt, for area fourth-grade students. While the ancestors of the Winstons and the Fields hoped for great things for their descendants, one wonders what they would have thought of the seeds they planted.

Another change in the community began in 2014 with the inaugural Untold Stories: Growing Up in Ashland/Hanover-Black and White Experiences. For over a decade now, the Center, the Ashland Museum, The Hanover County Black Heritage Society, and the Downtown Ashland Main Street Association have sponsored this annual Black History Month event which brings together a variety of panelists including three Black and three white residents to tell packed audiences their stories about life in the county. These oral histories, covering the 1940s to the early 1970s, cover the differing perspectives of the times, where experiences overlap, and provide a model for how talking about the past expands our understanding of the present.

During the summer of 2020, 155 years after the end of the Civil War, localities across the country experienced upheaval over Confederate memorials. Hanover was no different. In particular, two schools in the county were targeted: Lee-Davis High School and Stonewall Jackson Middle School, named after three Confederate generals, traitors to the United States, who took up arms against their former country. The county chapter of the NAACP had been trying to get the schools renamed since the 1960s to no avail, but finally some people in the county came to understand what those names represented to the Black community and as a result, Lee-Davis is now Mechanicsville High School and Stonewall

Jackson is Bell Creek Middle School. But many Black people in the community believe that this victory came at a heavy cost.

A new elementary school, consolidating John M. Gandy and Henry Clay elementary schools, is being built in the town of Ashland, and initially, it was slated to keep the name John M. Gandy.[10] Indeed, community members believe that county leaders promised that the consolidated school would be named John M. Gandy but as of May 9, 2023, the school board, ostensibly abiding by a decision made in 2007 to stop naming schools after people, decided to name the new school Ashland Elementary.[11] This decision also ignored the suggestion to name the school Berkleytown Elementary, after the historically Black community where the school is located. Indeed, the policy was changed in 2007, but as Peggy Lavinder of Mechanicsville, reminded the meeting participants, "the School Board changes policies whenever they want; therefore, John M. Gandy's name should remain the same."[12] Regardless of why, many people in the community believe that the name was removed as payback for the removal of the names of the Civil War generals from the Mechanicsville schools.

Today, Hanover County is part of a growing trend in Virginia and the United States to reconsider how and what history should be taught. For Hanover, this includes book banning, which harkens back to 1966 when the county banned Harper Lee's *To Kill A Mockingbird* from the schools. In 2023 the county banned 90 books from school libraries due their perceived inappropriateness, and while the motivation does not appear to be solely based on race, the chosen books all seem to deal with themes of difference supporting the belief that differences among human beings is not to be tolerated.

Indeed, Black people have always navigated life in this county with differing levels of success, but always with a commitment to stand up for what they believe is right. Black Hanoverians, through the hundred-year period written about here, have consistently spoken out against mistreatment and for what they need. In 1950, when John M. Gandy's name was suggested for the new, state of the art, segregated school, there was no opposition. In 2024, when students from all backgrounds will attend the school, the name Gandy is no longer acceptable.

Indeed, while strides toward acceptance of all, including the Black community, have been made, unfortunately in today's Hanover County, intolerance persists. But there is some good news. There is now a more inclusive generation of foot soldiers standing by and ready to make sure that, despite the thorns, all Hanoverians can have their roses in December. The nagging question remains: Will the necessity for soldiers ever go away?

NOTES

Introduction

1. Robert and NaChay Grimes interview, April 23, 2004.
2. William Chafe, *Civilities and Civil Rights: Greensboro, North Carolina, and the Black Struggle for Freedom* (Oxford University Press, 1980); and Matthew Lassiter and Andrew Lewis, *The Moderates Dilemma: The Rise and Fall of Massive Resistance* (University of Virginia Press, 1998).
3. Charity Adams Earley, *One Woman's Army: A Black Officer Remembers the WAC* (College Station: Texas A&M University Press, 1989), 5.
4. Deborah Dabney Joseph interview, December 19, 2022.
5. Social Explorer, "U.S. Decennial Census," https://www.socialexplorer.com/explore-tables.
6. Wythe Holt, *Virginia's Constitutional Convention of 1901–1902* (New York: Garland Publishers, 1990), 1.
7. W.E.B. Du Bois, *The Souls of Black Folk* (New York: Barnes & Noble Classics 2003) and *Black Reconstruction in America* (New York: Simon & Schuster 1995); Luther Porter Jackson, *Negro Office-Holders in Virginia, 1865–1895* (Norfolk, VA 1945); Carter G. Woodson, *The Miseducation of the Negro* (Las Vegas, NV: IAP 2010).
8. John T. Kneebone, *Southern Liberal Journalists and the Issue of Race, 1920–1944* (Chapel Hill: University of North Carolina Press, 1985).
9. Hilary Green, *Educational Reconstruction: African American Schools in the Urban South, 1865–1890* (Fordham University Press, 2016).
10. Nicole Myers Turner, *The Evolution of Black Religious Politics in Postemancipation Virginia* (The University of North Carolina Press, 2020), p. 143.
11. William Sturkey, *Hattiesburg: An American City in Black and White* (Belknap Press: An Imprint of Harvard University Press, 2019).
12. USDA Census of Agriculture Historical Archive, 1870, p. 332. https://agcensus.library.cornell.edu/census_year/1870-census/.

13. Shiloh Baptist Church History, Shiloh Baptist Church, Ashland, VA.
14. Letter from Phillis Wheatley to the Rev. Samuel Occom, 1774. This letter is in the public domain. Retrieved from https://www.amrevmuseum.org/news/in-the-news-1774-newspaper-printing-of-phillis-wheatley-s-letter-rebuking-slavery#:~:text=Wheatley's%20letter%20appeared%20shortly%20after,Lane.

1. Seeking and Embracing Freedom

1. Ebenezer Baptist Church History, Beaverdam includes the story of Negrofoot. There was a U.S. Post Office located in this community.
2. Clermont, p. 15.
3. Clermont, p. 15.
4. Henry T. Wickham, Address Delivered Before the Joint Session of The General Assembly of Virginia (Richmond, VA February 23, 1940).
5. Wickham Address.
6. Roseanne Groat Shalf, *Ashland, Ashland:* the story of a turn-of-the-century town (Lawrenceville, VA: Brunswick Publishing Corporation, 1994), 62.
7. Charles Perdue, et al., *Weevils in the Wheat* (Charlottesville: University of Virginia Press, 1976), 121.
8. Perdue, 121.
9. Perdue, 121. Mildred Graves was interviewed in 1937, by Faith Morris, an African American woman. The gold earrings were a gift from one of the children she had helped to deliver.
10. W.E.B. Du Bois, *Black Reconstruction in America 1860–1880* (New York: The Free Press, 1998), 55. According to Du Bois, "not one-tenth of the Northern white population would have fought for any such purpose."
11. Although writing about enslaved women in the colonial era, Jennifer Morgan's *Reckoning with Slavery: Gender, Kinship, and Capitalism in the Early Black Atlantic* gives insight into the vulnerability of Black women and girls to the enslaver over time and place. Leon Litwack, *Been in the Storm So Long*, 129. "to debauch black women, some Yankees apparently concluded, was to partake of a widely practiced and well-accepted southern pastime."
12. Peter Storrs Deposition, Southern Claims (SCC) approved claims, 1871–1880, Washington, DC: National Park Service, Virginia Genealogical Society (Reel 48186).
13. Storrs Deposition.
14. Jacqueline Jones, *Labor of Love, Labor of Sorrow* (New York: Vintage Books, 1995), 52.
15. There are several reasons for the decrease in the number of Black people in the county: enslaved people who ran away during the war did not return, Black people who died during the war, an incomplete/inaccurate census count due to movement around the county.
16. W. E. B. Du Bois, *Black Reconstruction in America* (New York: Oxford University Press, 2007), p. 53. Eric Foner, *Reconstruction: America's Unfinished Revolution 1863–1877* (New York: Harper & Row, 1988), p. 153.
17. Hanover County Freedmen's Marriage Register, https://www.hanovercounty.gov/DocumentCenter/View/1342/Freedmens-Marriage-Register-PDF.
18. Agricultural Census 1860, https://www2.census.gov/library/publications/decennial/1860/agriculture/1860b-07.pdf.

19. Agricultural Census 1880, https://agcensus.library.cornell.edu/wp-content/uploads/1880a_v3-05.pdf.
20. The Bureau of Refugees, Freedmen, and Abandoned Lands (Freedmen's Bureau) was charged with providing rations and other types of relief to former slaves and white refugees; it was supposed to help smooth the transition from slave labor to free labor and protect the rights of the freedmen and women.
21. Freedmen's Bureau (Reel 44,) 89.
22. Ed Murphy served in Ashland from 1865–66 and Ira Ayers served from 1867–68. Records of the Field Offices for the State of Virginia, Bureau of Refugees, Freedmen, and Abandoned Lands, 1865–72, Pamphlet Describing M1913, National Archives Microfilm Publications, 2006.
23. Lawyer and owner of Hickory Hill Plantation in Hanover.
24. There is a Charles Morris listed in the 1860 and 1880 Hanover County census. He was born in 1827 and lived in Ashland in 1880. He was white and a professor of ancient literatures.
25. FB (Reel 62), 491; FB (Reel 41), 89. The Freedmen's Bureau Circular establishing the Freedman's Court does not mandate how the men were selected, and Murphy's report simply mentions the names of those chosen.
26. Jacqueline Jones, *Labor of Love, Labor of Sorrow*, 54.
27. Jacqueline Jones, *Labor of Love, Labor of Sorrow*, 47 and 53. Jones writes about a Tennessee woman who remained saying, "I was given my choice of staying on the same plantation, working on shares, or taking my family away, letting them out [to work in return] for their food and clothes. I decided to stay on that way; I could have my children with me." Jones goes on to explain that "freedwomen with children found that economic necessity bred its own kind of slavery" forcing women to take any work they could find.
28. America Denton and the other women had been enslaved by William Lyme.
29. Freedmen's Bureau (Reel 62), 1.
30. Sharon Romeo's *Gender and the Jubilee: Black Freedom and the Reconstruction of Citizenship in Civil War Missouri*, like the women that Romeo writes about, America Denton boldly took advantage of the existing legal system.
31. Referred to as Dick in the Freedmen's Court record, Denton is listed as Richard in the Freedmen's marriage registry.
32. Freedmen's Bureau (Reel 62), 1.
33. Freedmen's Bureau (Reel 62), 2.
34. Jane Turner Censer, *The Reconstruction of Southern Womanhood, 1865–1895* (Baton Rouge: Louisiana State University Press, 2003), 99. While coverture may have been the law, the limitations of coverture were "neither complete nor permanent," according to historian Jane Turner Censer.
35. Suzanne Lebsock, *The Free Women of Petersburg* (New York: Norton, 1984), 84–86.
36. Freedmen's Bureau (Reel 62), 7.
37. Jacqueline Jones, *Labor of Love, Labor of Sorrow*, 62.
38. Freedmen's Bureau (Reel 46), 811.
39. Deborah Gray White, *Ar'n't I A Woman?* (New York: W.W. Norton & Company, 1999), 91–118. Historian Leslie Schwalm, writing about women in South Carolina, found that many white men who hired African American women to work for them wanted the same type of output that those women had produced while enslaved. Anything short of this kind of labor was considered a sign of laziness. Many men

found trivial the work that women, black and white, did in the home and family. Schwalm suggests that the notion of female laziness was "as concerned with the kind of work freedwomen were choosing to perform as with their rejection of field work for the planter." So America Denton's desire to feed her child was the problem, not her work when in the field—a desire that was seen as "natural" for white women, but not, by many white people, for black women.

40. Slaughter B. Bullock, "Agreement, 1865," Accession 22133, Personal papers collection, The Library of Virginia, Richmond, VA 23219.
41. Hewlett Family Papers.
42. Richmond *Daily Dispatch*, August 27, 1866. The term "church," as used in this context refers to the membership and not the building.
43. Litwack, *Been in the Storm So Long*, 24. Litwack asserts that the white preacher was perceived as a puppet of the master and capable of twisting God's word into a justification for slavery.
44. Although the names used in the newspaper for the gathering of Black Baptists in Richmond were reported differently between 1866 and 1867, it is likely that they refer to the same organization.
45. Richmond *Daily Dispatch*, August 9, 1867.
46. Richmond *Daily Dispatch*, August 9, 1867.
47. Richmond *Daily Dispatch*, August 12, 1867.
48. Richmond Daily Dispatch, August 12, 1867.
49. Richmond *Daily Dispatch*, December 25, 1867.
50. Richmond *Daily Dispatch*, August 9, 1867.
51. Richmond *Daily Dispatch*, December 25, 1867.
52. Richmond *Daily Dispatch*, August 9, 1867.
53. Melinda D. Gales, "African American Churches in Hanover County, Virginia 1865–1900" (master's thesis, Virginia Commonwealth University, 1999), 2. Melinda D. Gales in her 1999 M.A. thesis, argues that "church building is one of the first tangible signs of freedom in rural areas."
54. Evans C. & Rose B. White, *Eastern Hanover County Churches, Schools & Organizations: A Brief History "from a Black Perspective"* (Hanover: White Brook Printing, undated), 2.
55. A brush arbor was a structure made of branches that might only provide shelter to the preacher. According to the Shiloh Baptist Church history, founding members worshipped under a brush arbor.
56. Freedmen's Bureau (Reel 45), 251.
57. Glenn Feldman, *Reading Southern History* (Tuscaloosa: The University of Alabama Press, 2001), 221. Historian Susan Youngblood Ashmore quotes one white South Carolinian who believed that "to educate a Negro is to spoil a laborer and train up a candidate for the Penitentiary."
58. Freedmen's Bureau (Reel 46), 221. In Bureau records and in the church history, Shiloh Baptist Church is sometimes referred to as the Shiloh Freedmen's Church.
59. Freedmen's Bureau (Reel 45), 251.
60. Freedmen's Bureau (Reel 45), 251.
61. Richmond *Daily Dispatch*, October 12, 1867.
62. Freedmen's Bureau (Reel 46), 423.
63. Freedmen's Bureau (Reel 47)52.

2. The Politics of Reconstruction and the *Entente Cordiale* That Never Was

1. Storrs Deposition.
2. Storrs Deposition.
3. Storrs Deposition.
4. Funders, who in the 1870s and 1880s, could be found throughout the state's political parties, believed that Virginia's pre-war debt had to be paid in full or with only a small decrease in the interest rate. It was considered a matter of honor. For more on this topic see Encyclopedia Virginia's *Funders* at Tarter, Brent. "Funders" *Encyclopedia Virginia*. Virginia Humanities, (07 Dec. 2020). Web. 07 Jun. 2024 *Last updated: 2020, December 07;* and at Brent Tarter. A Saga of the New South: Race, Law, and Public Debt in Virginia. Charlottesville: University of Virginia Press, 2016.
5. Richmond *Daily Dispatch*, July 18, 1867
6. Richmond *Daily Dispatch*, August 12, 1867.
7. Andrew Johnson became president after the assassination of Abraham Lincoln.
8. Eric Foner, *Reconstruction: America's unfinished revolution*, (New York: Harper & Row) 1988, 198.
9. Foner, 198–216.
10. *New York Tribune*, November 15, 1865. Harrison B. Wilson Archives, Marvin Schlegel Collection, Norfolk State University.
11. The Bureau of Refugees, Freedmen, and Abandoned Lands (Freedmen's Bureau) was charged with providing rations and other types of relief to former slaves and White refugees; it was supposed to help smooth the transition from slave labor to free labor, and protect the rights of the freedmen and women.
12. Foner, 243.
13. Eric Foner, 250.
14. Foner, 268.
15. Foner, 276.
16. Tennessee rejoined the Union in 1866 during Presidential Reconstruction.
17. Richmond *Dispatch*, July 27, 1867.
18. Delegate selection was based on population, which meant that a county would get one delegate per a selected number of residents. If adjoining counties had more than enough residents for one delegate, but not enough for two, they could be combined to elect one additional delegate (a "floater") between them. This was the case with Hanover and Henrico counties.
19. Records of the Field Offices for the State of Virginia, Bureau of Refugees, Freedmen, and Abandoned Lands, 1865–1872, Accession 44121, Federal Government Records Collection, Library of Virginia, Richmond, VA (Reel 48), 1.
20. Society of Friends. Philadelphia Yearly Meeting Book Committee (Quaker Biographies, Series II, Philadelphia, 1926), 167–208.
21. Richmond *Daily Dispatch*, August 13, 1867. John C. Underwood Papers, Brock Collection, Misc reel 4596, LVA.
22. Society of Friends. Philadelphia Yearly Meeting Book Committee (Quaker Biographies, Series II, Philadelphia, 1926), 167–208. Freedmen's Bureau (Reel 48), 1.
23. Burrell Toler, who attended the Baptist association meeting in 1867, is not listed in the federal census of 1850 and 1860.

24. Richmond *Daily Whig,* October 12, 1867.
25. U.S. Census Hanover County 1870; Hanover County Marriage Registry, 1899; James Douglas Smith, "Virginia During Reconstruction, 1865–1870: A Political, Economic and Social Study" (master's thesis, University of Virginia, 1984); Richard Lee Morton, "The Negro in Virginia Politics, 1865–1902" (master's thesis University of Virginia, 1918.)
26. Freedmen's Bureau (Reel 67).
27. Richmond *Daily Dispatch,* October 25, 1867; and Election of Delegates to the Underwood Constitutional Convention, Ms Election Records, No. 427, Library of Virginia.
28. Freedmen's Bureau (Reel 48), 50.
29. Richmond *Daily Enquirer and Examiner,* October 30, 1867.
30. Richmond *Daily Enquirer and Examiner,* October 30, 1867.
31. Ancestry.com. *1870 United States Federal Census* [database on-line]. Lehi, UT, USA.
32. Freedmen's Bureau (Reel 48), 368.
33. James Weatherless had also been enslaved on the Carter plantation and knew the young William Henry Winston. He offered a deposition in support of Winston's request for a pension. Weatherless was also a Baptist minister. See Weatherless Deposition in William Henry Winston Pension file, NARA.
34. Freedmen's Bureau (Reel 48), 368.
35. Richmond *Daily Dispatch,* October 25, 1867.
36. The Debates & Proceedings of the Constitutional Convention (1867–1868) (Richmond, VA: Printed at the Office of the New Nation), 30.
37. Debates of the Convention, (1867–1868), 103.
38. Debates of the Convention, (1867–1868), 60.
39. Debates of the Convention, (1867–1868), 1.
40. Historian Eric Foner suggests that, for the most part, the backgrounds of most of the Black delegates left them poorly prepared for the complicated matters put before them. "They had 'little to say' during debates, and sometimes allowed White delegates to take advantage of their inexperience." While some, perhaps many, of the Black delegates may have been lost in the complexities of the process, Foner notes, they rallied around the issues of civil rights and education, both fundamental to the advancement of their constituents.
41. Smith thesis; This document was named for Judge John Curtis Underwood, one of the delegates from the city of Richmond, was elected president of the convention. Underwood was somewhat notorious among southern Democrats—a northerner by birth, and southerners might add, also by sentiment. He settled in Virginia in 1832 after college, but soon returned to the North where his antislavery sentiments were more acceptable. After the war, Underwood served as a federal judge in Virginia, and it was in his court that Jefferson Davis, former president of the Confederacy, was indicted and refused bail. According to Lyon Gardiner Tyler, a historian representing the conservative white southern point of view, Underwood was "bitterly denounced in the South on account of his violent and unbecoming partisanship." Tyler, vol. III, 291. Cynthia Miller Leonard, ed., *The General Assembly of Virginia* (General Assembly of Virginia), 1978, 504.
42. Wythe Holt, *Virginia's Constitutional Convention of 1901–1902* (New York: Garland Publishers, 1990), 1.

43. Freedmen's Bureau (Reel 59), 35.
44. Freedmen's Bureau (Reel 59), 58.
45. Freedmen's Bureau (Reel 59), 58.
46. Freedmen's Bureau (Reel 59), 65.
47. Jacob Neff Brenaman, (Richmond, VA. J.L. Hill Printing Co., 1902), 1.
48. James Tice Moore, *Two Paths to the New South* (Lexington: University Press of Kentucky, 1974), 14.
49. This did not impact federal forts, such as Ft. Monroe, that had been in Virginia since before the Civil War.
50. The Freedmen's Bureau was dissolved in 1872. National Archives of the United States, Washington, DC ttp://www.archives.gov/northeast/education/slavery/post-civil-war.html.
51. Southern Claims Commission Reports and Depositions, SCC (Reel 48186), Library of Virginia.
52. Frances Coleman Deposition, Southern Claims Commission (SCC) approved claims, 1871–1880, Washington, DC, National Park Service, Virginia Genealogical Society (Reel 48186); hereafter cited as SCC.
53. Storrs Deposition.
54. Richard Dandridge Deposition, SCC.
55. Taylor White Deposition, SCC.
56. B.C. Burnett Deposition, SCC.
57. Storrs Deposition.
58. The John Crenshaw who inherited this land from Nathaniel Crenshaw was the same man who sought the floater position during election of constitutional convention delegates.
59. No explanation for how "deserving" was measured.
60. Frances Coleman Deposition.
61. George Coleman Deposition, SCC.
62. Coleman, Hanover County File-General, SCC.
63. Storrs, Hanover County File-General, SCC.
64. Hanover County File-General, SCC.
65. Investigator's report on Peter Storrs, SCC.
66. Hanover County Land Deed Book 1, 360.
67. Hanover County Land Deed Book 15, 563.
68. Hanover County Land Deed Book 3, 192. Winston's will was contested by a white couple who owned land adjoining hers. The deed had been destroyed, and the couple argued that the land had never belonged to Winston. Anne Snead, white, was still alive and she informed the authorities that Winston had purchased the property from her for $800. The land was awarded to Winston's heirs.
69. Richmond *Dispatch*, October 2, 1867.
70. Hanover County Land Deed Book 6, 316.
71. Although several Hoggs appear on the list of free Black people of pre-war tax records, neither Elizabeth Hogg nor Elizabeth Tinsley is listed.
72. Known today as Shiloh Baptist Church, the 1874 deed refers to the church as Shiloe Freedsman Church and Shiloe Freedsman Baptist Church Hanover County Deed Book 8, 1874–1875, Reel 27, LVA.
73. Hanover County Land Deed Book 13, 81 Reel 30.

74. Inez Winston Gray interview, April 23, 2004.
75. For more on pre-and post-war landownership by Black people, see: Loren Schweninger, *Black Property Owners in the South, 1790–1915* (Urbana: University of Illinois Press, 1990) and Melvin Patrick Ely, *Israel on the Appomattox* (New York: Alfred Knopf, 2005).
76. Social Explorer Census Browser, https://www.socialexplorer.com/explore-maps.
77. For more on African American organizing see: Peter Rachleff, *Black Labor in Richmond, 1865–1890* (Urbana: University of Illinois Press, 1989); Tera Hunter, *To 'Joy My Freedom: Southern Black Women's Lives and Labors After the Civil War*.
78. Hunter, 70. Historian Tera W. Hunter asserts that mutual aid organizations "with antebellum roots in many Southern cities, rivaled churches in their popularity."
79. *Freedmen's Bank Records*, The Church of Jesus Christ of Latter-Day Saints, CD-ROM.
80. *Freedmen's Bank Records*.
81. Evelyn Brooks Higginbotham, *Righteous Discontent* (Cambridge: Harvard University Press, 1993), 185–229. A phenomenon that historian Evelyn Brooks Higginbotham has dubbed the "politics of respectability" took shape.
82. Deborah Gray White, *Ar'n't I a Woman?: Female Slaves in the Plantation South* (W.W. Norton & Company), 29. They were victims of what historian Deborah Gray White has called the Jezebel image—the woman "governed almost entirely by her libido"—which had its roots in slavery and represented the exact opposite of the white Victorian lady.
83. Virginia School Report of the Superintendent of Public Instruction, 1870–1871 (Richmond: Superintendent of Public Printing), LVA. Nothing in the record explains this unusual pay scale.
84. Virginia School Report of the Superintendent of Public Instruction, 1870–1871 (Richmond: Superintendent of Public Printing), LVA.
85. School Reports 1874/1875–1877/1878.
86. Brent Tarter, "Funders," *Encyclopedia Virginia*, Virginia Humanities (7 Dec. 2020) 11 June 2024; Brent Tarter, *A Saga of the New South: Race, Law, and Public Debt in Virginia* (Charlottesville: University of Virginia Press, 2016), 22–34.
87. Moore, 25.

3. An Uneasy Citizenship

1. Gertrude Woodruff Marlowe, *A Right Worthy Grand Mission: Maggie Lena Walker and the Quest for Black Economic Empowerment* (Washington, DC: Howard University Press, 2003), xxxii; Alexander, 121. The evolution of the name of the theological schools in Richmond is somewhat murky. At least one source suggests that the Richmond Theological Seminary began at Lumpkin's Jail, a former slave holding area, in 1865 under the auspices of the American Baptist Home Mission. This school evolved into the Richmond Institute, which later combined with Wayland Seminary to form Virginia Union University. A second source refers to the Richmond Theological Seminary as the name of the institution that would later merge with Wayland Seminary in Washington and Hartshorn Memorial College (for women) to become Virginia Union University. For information on Taylor's marriage, see Burrell and Johnson, 377.

2. Richmond Theological Seminary Registrars Book Volume 39, 21.
3. Burrell and Johnson, 379–80.
4. Richard Lee Morton, *The Negro in Virginia Politics, 1865–1902* (Charlottesville: University of Virginia Press, 1919) 234.
5. Moore, 109.
6. Luther Porter Jackson, *Negro Office-Holders in Virginia 1865–1895* (Norfolk, VA: Guide Quality Press 1945), 20.
7. The year that Virginia State University was founded is sometimes noted as 1883 and at others as 1882. The official college website marks the year as 1882. http://www.vsu.edu/pages/3881.asp.
8. Moore, 25.
9. Shibley, 113.
10. Moore, 109–18.
11. Anderson-McCormick was a set of amendments to the franchise clause of the state constitution which granted the General Assembly the power to appoint a state electoral board, which had complete control over all election personnel.
12. Alexander, 143.
13. D. Webster Davis, *The Life and Public Experiences of William Washington Browne* (Richmond: Mrs. M.A. Browne-Smith, 1910); Field, 143–56.
14. Alexander, 144.
15. Davis, 60.
16. Davis, 65.
17. W. P. Burrell and D.E. Johnson, *Twenty-Five Years History of the Grand Fountain of the United Order of True Reformers, 1881–1905* (Richmond, 1909), 48.
18. Burrell and Johnson, 48.
19. Burrell and Johnson, 54.
20. Davis, 75. In his book, Davis includes a picture of the church where this meeting took place. It is labeled Mt. Zion Baptist Church, but the church pictured is Shiloh Baptist Church.
21. Burrell and Johnson, 57. Information on how this committee was selected is not provided.
22. Burrell and Johnson, 60.
23. Burrell and Johnson, 67–68.
24. More negatively, the conflict within the True Reformers fits in with post-Foner work such as that of Reidy and Schwalm
25. Burrell and Johnson, 375–86.
26. Burrell and Johnson, 382.
27. W. Fitzhugh Brundage, *The Southern Past* (Cambridge: The Belknap Press of Harvard University Press, 2005), 59.
28. *Richmond Planet*, August 16, 23, 30, 1890.
29. *Richmond Planet*, August 16, 1890.
30. *Richmond Dispatch*, October 18, 1890.
31. *Richmond Dispatch*, October 18, 1890.
32. *Richmond Planet*, August 30, 1890; Richmond *Dispatch*, October 15, 1890, October 16, 1890.
33. *Richmond Planet*, October 18, 1890.
34. Brundage, 60.
35. *Richmond Planet*, June 13, 1891.

36. Burrell and Johnson, 382.
37. Burrell and Johnson, p. 380.
38. Burrell and Johnson, 67–68.
39. *Richmond Planet,* August 26, 1893.
40. *Richmond Planet,* June 30, 1894.
41. *Richmond Planet,* January 14, 1893.
42. *Richmond Planet,* December 15, 1894.
43. Ancestry.com U.S. Census Records, Hanover County 1900.
44. Jones, *American Work* (New York: W.W. Norton, 1999), 303.
45. Jones, *American Work,* 111.
46. United States Bureau of Refugees, Freedmen, and Abandoned Lands, Records of the Superintendent of Education for the State of Virginia, 1865–1870, accession 32073, federal government records collection, Library of Virginia, Richmond (reel 13).
47. Ancestry.com U.S. Census Records, Hanover County 1900.
48. Ancestry.com, U.S. Census Records, Hanover County 1900; see Loren Schweninger, *Black Property Owners in the South 1970–1915* (Chicago: University of Illinois, 1990), 78, for a discussion of the number of unskilled free Black people who purchased land in the South during the antebellum period.
49. Jones, *American Worker,* 316.
50. Jones, *American Worker,* 316.
51. Hanover County Chancery Court Records (EF 88 1891–015).
52. Hanover County Land Deed (Book 11) 603; (Book 3) 190; Hanover County Death Registry, Library of Virginia. Unfortunately, little information about the Hickory Hill Club remains.
53. *Richmond Planet,* August 15, 1891. F.G. Stokes represented Hanover County at the meeting.
54. William Wright, 1880 Hanover County Census; T. Major Lightfoot, 1900 Hanover County Census.
55. *Virginia State Gazetteer and Business Directory, 1897–98,* Volume 1 (Richmond, VA: J.L. Hill Printing Company), 538–39.
56. Gray interview; Shalf, 102.
57. *Richmond Planet,* October 3, 1896.
58. Gray interview. Family copies of deeds show that Winston began buying land in 1882.
59. School Reports 1881–1882.
60. School Report 1880; According to historian William Link, sometimes parents requested that a session begin during the growing season if the children were mostly female or very young. William Link, *A Hard Country and A Lonely Place* (Chapel Hill: University of North Carolina Press, 1986).
61. School Reports 1881–1882.
62. School Reports 1883–1884.
63. School Report 1883–1884.
64. Race-based data for teacher salaries are not available, but for men the average salary was $25.19, and for women the average salary was $24.19.
65. Social Explorer Census Browser; School Report 1900–1901.
66. School Report 1900–1901.
67. School Report 1899–1901.
68. *Richmond Planet,* April 28, 1894.

69. *Richmond Planet,* September 2, 1893.
70. *Richmond Planet,* June 7, 1890.
71. U.S. Census 1890.
72. "70th Anniversary of Ebenezer Baptist Church Richmond Program" The Maggie L. Walker Papers, National Historic Site Richmond, VA; Evans and Rose White, 16.
73. Ashland *American Guest,* August 15, 1881.
74. *Richmond Planet,* March 1, 1890; Taylor never explained why he was tried.
75. *Richmond Planet,* November 28, 1891.
76. *Richmond Planet,* September 2, 1893.
77. *Richmond Planet,* June 7, 1890; June 24, 1893.
78. *Richmond Planet,* September 8, 1894.
79. *Richmond Planet,* February 23, 1895.
80. *Richmond Planet,* July 2, 1892.
81. *Richmond Planet,* April 25, 1896.
82. *Richmond Planet,* February 20, 1897.
83. *Richmond Planet,* March 19, 1898.
84. *Richmond Planet,* March 19, 1898.
85. John Blassingame, *The Slave Community* (New York: Oxford University Press, 1979).
86. *Richmond Planet,* May 4, 1897.
87. "Proceedings of the Negro Protective Association of Virginia Pamphlet," Library of Virginia (Richmond: The Association, 1897).
88. Negro Protective Association Pamphlet.
89. Brenaman, 83.
90. Virginia Acts of the Assembly, Library of Virginia (1899–1900), 835.
91. Brenaman, 83.
92. *Richmond Planet,* July 14, 1890.
93. Brenaman, 83.
94. Virginia Constitution of 1902. The new constitution was put into effect by proclamation of the convention, so no Virginian white or Black, outside those attending the convention, had the opportunity to cast his vote in favor of or against the new document.

4. Disfranchised

1. Richmond *Daily Dispatch,* August 31, 1902, and September 2, 1902; *Richmond Planet,* September 6, 1902.
2. *Richmond Planet,* September 6, 1902, p. 4.
3. Nancy Hugo, a local white woman, interviewed Charles Stebbins Jr. but no date is given on the transcript. The interview probably took place in the 1980s. See also Shalf, 171.
4. Stebbins interview (Hugo).
5. Stebbins interview (Hugo).
6. Richmond *Daily Dispatch,* August 31, 1902; Stebbins interview (Hugo).
7. Shalf, 121–22.
8. Stebbins interview (Hugo).
9. Report of the Adjutant-General of the State of Virginia, 1901–1902 (Richmond: Rush U. Derr, Superintendent of Public Printing), 43.

10. Report of the Adjutant General, 45.
11. Report of the Adjutant-General, 45; Richmond *Daily Dispatch,* September 2, 1902.
12. Report of the Adjutant-General, 45; Richmond *Daily Dispatch,* September 2, 1902.
13. *Richmond Planet,* September 6, 1902.
14. William Chenery, *So It Seemed* (NY: Harcourt, Brace and Company, 1952), 11–12
15. Nancy Hugo, a white woman, interviewed Charles Stebbins Jr., but the date is not given on the transcript. The interview probably took place in the 1980s. See also Shalf, 171.
16. Hugo interview.
17. Shalf, 272–73.
18. Report of the Adjutant-General, (1901–1902), 50; (1902–1903), 61.
19. Commonwealth Election Records, LVA.
20. Leon Litwack, *Trouble in Mind, Trouble in Mind: Black Southerners in the Age of Jim Crow* (New York: Knopf, 1998), 224–26.
21. Chenery, 21.
22. Chenery, 22.
23. Litwack, *Trouble in Mind,* 224.
24. *Richmond Planet,* August 23, 1902; Richmond *Dispatch,* August 19, 1902, .3.
25. Negro Industrial and Agricultural Society of Virginia. Circular, April 15, 1902. Accession 31776. Organization records collection, Library of Virginia.
26. *Richmond Dispatch,* August 31, 1902.
27. Hanover *Weekly Herald,* October 28, 1904.
28. C. Vann Woodward, *Strange Career of Jim Crow* (New York: Oxford University Press, 1974), 100; Ashland Town Council Minutes, (ATCM) September 11, 1911.
29. ATCM September 12, 1911.
30. ATCM September 12, 1911.
31. ATCM November 16, 1912. Records of John Coleman's case have been lost.
32. Woodward, *Strange Career of Jim Crow,* 141.
33. Hanover *Herald Progress,* April 25, 1919; August 8, 1919; March 6, 1925.
34. Hanover *Herald Progress* after September 1920.
35. Eric Foner and Joshua Brown, *Forever Free* (New York: Knopf, 2005), 69.
36. Foner and Brown, 69.
37. Litwack, *Trouble in Mind,* 241–331.
38. Field, 177.
39. *Richmond Planet,* September 17, 1910.
40. Marlowe, 46.
41. Marlowe, 81.
42. Elsa Barkley Brown, "Womanist Consciousness: Maggie Lena Walker and the Independent Order of St. Luke," *Signs* 14, no. 3, (1989), 629.
43. Maggie Lena Walker Papers, Maggie L. Walker Historical Site, National Park Service.
44. Walker Papers. See also Shennette Garrett-Scott, *Banking on Freedom: Black Women in U.S. Finance Before the New Deal* (Columbia University Press, 2019).
45. Walker Papers.
46. Walker Papers.
47. Walker Papers. Alice Walker, an African American novelist, is credited with coining the term "womanist" to help explain the different ideas expressed by Black and

White women when discussing the aims of the women's rights movement. In her article on "Womanist Consciousness" published in 1989, historian Elsa Barkley Brown applies the term womanist to the study and understanding of the life of Maggie Walker. She asserts that the "concepts, perspectives, methods, and pedagogies of women's history and women's studies have been developed without consideration of the experiences of Black women." She argues that race plays a role in defining the opportunities Black and White women encounter.

48. Gray interview.
49. HCSB July 31, 1924.
50. Edward E. Redcay, "Pioneering Negro Education," *Journal of Negro Education*, 6, no. 1, January 1937, 38–53.
51. Donald Makosky, Carolyn Hemphill, and Kate Neckerman *One and Two Room Schools;* HCSB July 31, 1924; I have seen this organization referred to as the County-Wide League and the County-Wide Committee.
52. Makosky, et al.
53. Gray interview.
54. Gray interview.
55. HCSB March 23, 1925; February 29, 1927.
56. HCBS April 1, 1925; School Reports 1924–1925.
57. Hanover *Herald Progress*, January 23, 1925.
58. Hanover *Herald Progress*, January 23, 1925.
59. Hanover *Herald Progress*, February 13, 1925.
60. Hanover *Herald Progress*, February 10, 1926.
61. Makosky, et al., *School Reports* 1923–1924.
62. Makosky, et al., Jean Folly interview, November 9, 2001.
63. Bureau of Public Administration, "Report on An Administrative Survey of Virginia's Training Schools," (Charlottesville: University of Virginia, 1957), 2.
64. Virginia Acts of the Assembly, Library of Virginia (1889–1890), 131.
65. Virginia Constitution of 1902, section 67.
66. Report on an Administrative Survey of Virginia's Training Schools (Beaumont, Bon Air, Hanover, and Janie Porter Barrett), 4. The Negro Reformatory Association was founded at the turn of the century by John Henry Smyth, an African American man who served as the U.S. Counsel General to Liberia from 1878–85. Through this Association, Smyth opened the boys' school in Hanover County.
67. Virginia Manual Labor School of the Negro Reformatory Association of Virginia, Biennial Report (1914–1915), LVA.
68. David S. Snedden, *Administration and Educational Work of American Juvenile Reform Schools,* New York: Teachers College Columbia University, 1907), 66.
69. Boys School Report (1914–1915).
70. *Richmond Planet,* January 10, 1920.
71. William Layton, *Layton Looks at Life* (Washington, DC: W.W. Layton, 1996), 6.
72. Maggie Walker Papers, Diary entry, January 4, 1918.
73. Regina Kunzel, *Fallen Women, Problem Girls: Unmarried Mothers and the Professionalization of Social Work* (New Haven, CT: Yale University Press) 1993, 13.
74. Virginia State Federation of Colored Women's Clubs *The History of Virginia State Federation of Colored Women's Clubs Inc.* (Eastville, VA: Hickory House, 1996).
75. Hanover County Industrial Home School for Colored Girls, pamphlet, 1914, LVA.

76. Girls School Report (1916), 8.
77. Girls School Report (1916). Hunter, 51–52. Black women were especially vulnerable to sexual assault when working in private homes.
78. Girls School Report, (1916).
79. Girls School Report, (1916).
80. Girls School Report, (1916).
81. Girls School Report (1918).
82. Girls School Report (1919).
83. Girls School Report (1919).
84. Girls School Report (1920 and 1921).
85. Girls School Report (1920).
86. Girls School Report (1921).
87. Walker Diary, June 18, 1925.
88. Walker Diary, February 11, 1928. The Federation Board consisted of Black women, but the board for the school was mixed by race and gender.
89. Chenery, 4.
90. Chenery, 5.
91. Hanover *Herald Progress*, February 14, 1919.
92. Hanover *Herald Progress*, February 21, 1919.
93. Steven Manson, Jonathan Schroeder, David Van Riper, Katherine Knowles, Tracy Kugler, Finn Roberts, and Steven Ruggles, IPUMS National Historical Geographic Information System: Version 18 (Minneapolis, MN: IPUMS, 2023), http://doi.org/10.18128/D050.V18.0.
94. Hanover *Herald Progress*, April 21, 1926.
95. Chenery, 8.
96. Hanover *Herald Progress*, June 27, 1919.
97. Hanover *Herald Progress*, July 4, 1919.
98. Hanover *Herald Progress*, December 30, 1925; August 1, 1928.
99. Margaret Washington
100. Beryl Thompson Carter interview, June 6, 2006.
101. Carter interview.
102. Carter interview.
103. Carter interview.
104. ATCM July 2, 1925.
105. Hanover *Herald Progress*. Coleman advertised in the Hanover paper steadily throughout the early 1920s and then they taper off, until the late 1930s, when a much smaller ad appears.
106. Hanover Herald *Progress* May 7, 1925.
107. Hanover *Herald Progress* April 25, 1919, July 11, 1919.
108. Hanover *Herald Progress*, December 5, 1919.
109. Hanover *Herald Progress* May 20, 1921.
110. Hanover *Herald Progress*, November 8, 1923.
111. Gray interview. The Gray family holds paperwork for this transaction.
112. Chenery, 22; Gray interview.
113. Gray interview.
114. Dorothy Gardner Jones interview, October 26, 2005.
115. CBS (January 17, 1918), 85.
116. HCBS (January 17, 1918), 85.

117. Hanover *Herald Progress,* July 14, 1926.
118. ATCM June 7, 1928.
119. HCBS December 22, 1922.
120. HCBS November 1, 1924.
121. HCBS May 2, 1927.
122. Gray interview.
123. Hanover *Herald Progress* June 4, 1920.
124. Hanover *Herald Progress* July 1, 1921.

5. The Great Depression, New Deal, War, and Ordinary Acts of Resistance

1. Ruth Carter Winston interview, April 4, 2004.
2. T.H. Watkins, *The Hungry Years* (New York: A Marian Wood Book, Henry Holt and Company, 1999), xii.
3. Watkins, 8.
4. Carrie Burton interview, April 29, 2004.
5. Dorothy Gardner Jones interview, October 25, 2005.
6. Jones interview.
7. Grimes interview.
8. Discussion with Graham Rose, DDS, May 11, 2006.
9. Hanover *Herald Progress,* April 28, 1932, June 23, 1932.
10. Hanover *Herald Progress,* June 23, 1932.
11. Rose Discussion.
12. Litwack, *Trouble in Mind,* 336.
13. Hanover *Herald Progress,* August 7, 1930, December 4, 1930.
14. Hanover *Herald Progress,* May 7, 1936.
15. Hanover *Herald Progress,* December 6, 1934.
16. Hanover *Herald Progress,* December 6, 1934.
17. This land was donated by the Wickham family.
18. Claudius Wilson Dabney, April 4, 2004
19. Dabney interview, April 4, 2004
20. James Edward Henry interview December 15, 2003.
21. Hanover *Herald Progress,* February 24, 1938.
22. Hanover *Herald Progress,* November 17, 1938.
23. Hanover *Herald Progress,* March 3, 1932.
24. Hanover *Herald Progress,* February 25, 1932.
25. Susan Lynn Smith, *Sick and Tired of Being Sick and Tired: Black Women's Health Activism in America, 1890–1950* (Philadelphia: University of Pennsylvania Press, 1995), 58; Cherise Jones-Branch, *Better Living By Their Bootstraps: Black Women's Activism in Rural Arkansas, 1914–1965* (Fayetteville: The University of Arkansas Press, 2021).
26. Hanover *Herald Progress,* April 5, 1934.
27. Hanover *Herald Progress,* December 13, 1934.
28. Hanover *Herald Progress,* January 24, 1935.
29. Hanover *Herald Progress,* February 7, 1935.
30. Hanover *Herald Progress,* January 21, 1937.

31. Hanover *Herald Progress,* August 5, 1937.
32. Hanover *Herald Progress,* August 5, 1937. The sources do not provide the amount raised by the Black community. White organizations, including the Hanover Woman's Club, the Pamunkey Woman's Club, the Doswell men's and women's clubs, and the Hanover Tuberculosis Association that contributed $180 to hire a Black nurse.
33. Stan Cohen, *The Tree Army* (Missoula, MT: Pictorial Histories Publishing Company, 1980), 156; Jones interview.
34. Hanover, *Herald Progress,* July 13, 1939.
35. John A. Salmond, *The Civilian Conservation Corps, 1933–1942* (Durham, NC: Duke University Press, 1967), 34–35.
36. Salmond, 41.
37. Salmond, 50.
38. Robert Fechner to Robert J. Buckley, 4 June 1936, "CCC Negro Selection" file, Box 700, General Correspondence of the Director, Record Group 35, National Archives, College Park, Maryland. Fechner was the director of the CCC; Salmond, 30. The CCC camps remained all male, but She-She-She camps were established for women in 1934. Joseph M. Speakman, "Into the Woods: The First Year of the Civilian Conservation Corps" Prologue Magazine Fall 2006, Vol. 38, No. 36 National Archives https://www.archives.gov/publications/prologue/2006/fall/ccc.html#:~:text=Although%20the%20Federal%20Emergency%20Relief,at%20work%20in%20some%20camps.
39. Fechner to Buckley.
40. Salmond, 92.
41. Salmond, 92.
42. Hanover, *Herald Progress,* March 7, 1935.
43. Hanover, *Herald Progress,* March 7, 1935; Records of the Civilian Conservation Corps, Record Group 35, Entry 115, Division of Investigations, Camp Inspection Reports, Box 224, Folder P-78, NARA.
44. Hanover, *Herald Progress,* August 1, 1935.
45. Doris and John Morris, Doris Wingfield, Bertha Berniece Parnell interview March 3, 2006
46. Civilian Conservation Corps Newsletter, "The Bomb" (Hanover County, Virginia December 1935).
47. William H. Kiblinger, "Papers," Personal Papers Collection, 1855–2000. Acc. 39455, LVA.
48. National Archives, Records Group 35.
49. CCC, Record Group 35.
50. CCC, Record Group 35.
51. CCC, Record Group 35. It is not known if the churches were black or White or both. Given the group's inclusion in the Patrick Henry celebration, they may have also been invited to White churches.
52. Souvenir Program, "Liberty or death"; pageant drama of the life of Patrick Henry presented on the occasion of the bicentennial of his birth (Hanover Courthouse, Virginia: Richmond, Whittet & Shepperson, 1936), Library of Virginia.
53. Civilian Conservation Corps Newsletter, "The White Chimney Eagle" and "The Bomb" (Caroline County, Virginia August 23, 1939), Library of Virginia.
54. "The White Chimney Eagle."

55. "The White Chimney Eagle."
56. "The Bomb."
57. "The Bomb."
58. "The Bomb."
59. Olen Cole Jr. *The African American Experience in the Civilian Conservation Corps* (Gainesville: University Press of Florida, 1999), 13.
60. "The White Chimney Eagle."
61. Hanover, *Herald Progress,* May 16, 1935, May 30, 1935, 1.
62. Kiblinger Papers.
63. Hanover *Herald Progress,* March 25, 1937.
64. Hanover Herald Progress April 1, 1937.
65. This was a state-wide research project on the Virginia Rural Marginal Population conducted by the Virginia Agricultural Experiment Station in cooperation with the Works Progress Administration, Virginia State Planning Board, and other agencies.
66. Hanover *Herald Progress* December 1, 1938.
67. Hanover *Herald Progress,* 1 December 1938.The newspaper uses the term "underfed" but FDR actually said, "ill fed."
68. Editorial, Hanover *Herald Progress,* December 1, 1938.
69. Virginia Agricultural Experiment Station, "A Rural Sociology Report" (Blacksburg, Virginia); Virginia Polytechnic Institute, Virginia Agricultural Experiment Station, "Some Virginia Population Trends of General Significance," mimeo report (no. 9, 1939), 1.
70. Editorial, Hanover *Herald Progress,* December 1, 1938.
71. Virginia Agricultural Experiment Station: A Rural Sociology Report. A Manual on Rural Poverty, no. 11.
72. Hanover County did not have a high school for African Americans until 1950. Before 1950, there was a training school.
73. Virginia Agricultural Experiment Station: A Rural Sociology Report. A Manual on Rural Poverty, Appendix, 9.
74. *Who's Who in Colored America,* (New York: Thomas Yenser, 1933), 199. John M. Gandy, an African American, was a leading educator in the state and the president of Virginia State College, now university, from 1914 until 1942. When Hanover finally got a high school for African American students, it was named after John M. Gandy.
75. Virginia Does Care Report.
76. Virginia Does Care Report.
77. Virginia Does Care Report, p. 16.
78. Steven Manson, et al.
79. Virginia Does Care Report, pp. 16–17.
80. Girls School Report. 1919.
81. U.S. Census Records: From 1910–1950, the census gives farm ownership data that includes "negroes and non-Whites." During this period, the number of non-Whites in Hanover County fluctuated between zero and 24; with an average of 18. Farm ownership statistics are not available for 1960.
82. Virginia Does Care Report.
83. Gray interview; John Morris interview.
84. Virginia Does Care Report.
85. Virginia Does Care Report.

86. Marvin Wilson Schlegel, *Virginia On Guard* (Richmond: Virginia State Library, 1949), 1.
87. Schlegel, 1.
88. Schlegel, 2–3.
89. Schlegel
90. Schlegel, 147.
91. Schlegel, 139.
92. Home demonstration agents worked with families, especially mothers and daughters, to teach them proper food preparation, sewing, entertaining, etc. There were regular reports in the Hanover *Herald Progress* discussing programs put on by the white and Black agents.
93. Hewlett letter to J.F. Nicholas, Aug. 8, 1942. Negro Civilian Defense; Hanover-unprocessed; Box 50; 04/G/01/35/02, LVA.
94. Report of the Field Trips of James F. Nichols Hanover County Civil Defense, Box 18, Folder 4, RG 55 July 23–25 & 27, 1942, LVA.
95. Hanover *Herald Progress*, September 10, 1942.
96. Lawrence R. Samuel. *Pledging Allegiance*, (Washington, DC: Smithsonian Institution Press, 1997), 3.
97. Samuel, 20.
98. Samuel does not mention whether or not racial lines were crossed in the establishment of the leadership of the bond program. However, when developing a list of organizations and agencies to approach to ask to help get the word out to their membership, African American groups were included.
99. Hanover *Herald Progress*, December 25, 1941.
100. Hanover *Herald Progress* February 14, 1944.
101. Hanover *Herald Progress*, July 6, 1944.
102. Hanover *Herald Progress*, October 1, 1942.
103. Hanover *Herald Progress* October 1, 1942.
104. Samuel, xviii.
105. Hanover *Herald Progress*, March 4, 1943.
106. This promise of special accommodation may have been due, in part, to the need to adhere to the Public Assemblages Act, also known as the Massenburg Bill, so named after its sponsor in the Virginia House of Delegates. The Act, which had been passed in 1926, was the first in the U.S. "requiring the separation of White and colored persons at public halls, theaters, opera houses, motion picture shows and places of public entertainment and public assemblages." For a discussion on this Act and the history regarding the legislation see: J. Douglas Smith, *Managing White Supremacy: Race, Politics, and Citizenship in Jim Crow Virginia* (Chapel Hill: The University of North Carolina Press, 2002), 107–129.
107. Hanover *Herald Progress*, December 25, 1941.
108. Hanover *Herald Progress*, December 25, 1941.
109. Virginia War Dead Database, LVA http://www.lva.lib.va.us/whatwehave/mil/vmd/index.asp.
110. Jack Foner, *Blacks and the Military in American History* (New York: Praeger Publishers, 1974) 143.
111. Jack Foner, 144.
112. See photo of SeaBees in beach assault simulation, National Archives: https://catalog.archives.gov/id/535776.

113. John Gordon interview, October 15, 2004.
114. Floyd Dabney Jr. Speech at Providence Baptist Church Black History Month Program February 2007.
115. Kareem Abdul-Jabbar and Anthony Walton, *Brothers in Arms: The Epic Story of the 761st Tank Battalion, WORLD WAR IIs Forgotten Heroes* (New York, NY: Broadway Books, 2004), 6. Floyd Dabney, Sr. is pictured on p. 144.
116. Claudius Dabney interview.
117. Richmond *Times-Dispatch,* November 11, 1992.
118. Leisa Meyer, *Creating G.I. Jane: Sexuality and Power in the Women's Army Corps During World War II* (New York: Columbia University Press, 1996), 11.
119. Meyer, 6.
120. Hanover *Herald Progress,* September 3, 1942. See also https://digital.lib.uiowa.edu/islandora/object/ui%3Awwii_2311.
121. Martha S. Putney, *When the Nation was in Need: Black in the Women's Army Corps During World War II* (London: The Scarecrow Press, Inc. 1992), 154, 164, 167.
122. Hanover *Herald Progress,* September 3, 1942.
123. Hanover *Herald Progress,* May 6, 1943.
124. Hanover *Herald Progress,* October 18, 1945.
125. Richmond *Times-Dispatch* January 30, 1941.
126. Richmond *Times- Dispatch,* 1 February 1941.
127. Hanover *Herald Progress,* September 18, 1941.
128. Hanover *Herald Progress,* November 27, 1941.
129. See John Kneebone
130. Holy Bible James 2:20.
131. Hanover County Land Deed Book 50, p. 173.
132. Brown Grove is a predominantly African American community in Hanover.
133. Benjamin Jackson interview, October 24, 2005.
134. Jackson interview.
135. Jackson interview.
136. Genesis 31:49. The Mizpah is often used in the Baptist church as a benediction.
137. Gray interview. This County-Wide League is not to be confused with the white young adult women's organization of the same name.
138. Jackson interview.
139. Hanover *Herald Progress,* September 26, 1940.
140. Hanover *Herald Progress,* January 23, 1941.
141. Community members raised the funds to add the cafeteria.
142. Jackson interview.
143. Jackson interview.
144. Official Bulletin of The Negro Organization Society, Inc of VA 1956; Capahosic, VA; Reprinted in 1984 by the Moton Institute and Conference Center H.C. Young Press, Virginia Union University Archives.
145. Hanover *Herald Progress,* September 24, 1931, p. 3. There was no acknowledgment of the fact that Black families paid taxes that were supposed support public schools. In essence raising money and paying taxes was double taxation.
146. Hanover *Herald Progress,* January 19, 1933, p. 1. Financial status of the fundraiser was not provided.
147. Hanover *Herald Progress,* April 12, 1934.
148. Hanover *Herald Progress,* March 21, 1933.

149. Hanover *Herald Progress*, March 30, 1933.
150. Hanover *Herald Progress*, March 30, 1933.
151. Hanover *Herald Progress*, April 16, 1933.
152. Hanover *Herald Progress*, December 6, 1934.
153. Hanover *Herald Progress*, March 30, 1933.
154. Luther Porter Jackson Papers, Letter dates October 2, 1944 and April 13, 1947. Box 46, folder 3, Virginia State University.
155. Luther P. Jackson Papers.
156. William C. Berman, *The Politics of Civil Rights in the Truman Administration* (Columbus: Ohio State University Press, 1970), 84.
157. Luther P. Jackson Papers, Box 21, folder 10.
158. Luther P. Jackson Papers, Box 21, folder 10.

6. The Heat of Change

1. Morris, Wingfield, Parnell interview.
2. Morris, Wingfield, Parnell interview.
3. Morris, Wingfield, Parnell interview.
4. Morris, Wingfield, Parnell interview.
5. For an extensive discussion of African American church women see Higginbotham.
6. Morris, Wingfield, Parnell interview.
7. Morris, Wingfield, Parnell interview.
8. Morris, Wingfield, Parnell interview.
9. Morris, Wingfield, Parnell interview.
10. Carter interview.
11. Carter interview.
12. Litwack, *Trouble in Mind*, 226.
13. Carter interview.
14. See School Reports for Hanover County from 1870–1940.
15. The Hanover County Training school went to the eleventh grade and was not an accredited high school. Graduates received a certificate and not a diploma.
16. HCSB February 7, 1950.
17. HCSB February 7, 1950.
18. HCSB April 11, 1950.
19. HCSB April 11, 1950.
20. HCSB May 30, 1950.
21. Hanover *Herald Progress*, October 12, 1950.
22. Hanover *Herald Progress*, October 12, 1950.
23. William & Mary would follow suit in 1951 with the admission of Hulon Willis, Sr. to the Master's in Physical Education program and Edward Augustus Travis to the Law School.
24. Sweatt v. Painter, 339 U.S. 629 (1950) and McLaurin v. Oklahoma State Board of Regents, 339 U.S. 637 (1950). The first African American to take advantage of these court decisions was Gregory Swanson. He entered the University of Virginia Law School in 1950. He was not allowed to live on campus. He left the school in 1951. Before entering UVA, Swanson earned a law degree from Howard University in 1948. See Sarah Patton Boyle, *The Desegregated Heart: A Virginian's Stand in A Time*

of Transition, (Charlottesville: University of Virginia Press, 1962) for a discussion of Swanson's time at UVA. Also see the speech Boyle gave before Race Street Friends Meeting titled "The Lonely Crusade: A Virginian's Stand for Racial Justice" on December 13, 1963, LVA.

25. Grimes interview.
26. HCSB May 2, 1950.
27. HCSB May 2, 1950.
28. HCSB May 2, 1950.
29. HCSB July 7, 1950.
30. HCSB July 7, 1950.
31. HCSB July 7, 1950. The Board minutes do not elaborate on the concerns regarding Mr. Fleming; however, he was hired back for the next school year.
32. Hanover *Herald Progress* March 29, 1951.
33. Hanover *Herald Progress,* March 29, 1951.
34. HCSB October 9, 1951.
35. Ogletree, 111.
36. Hanover *Herald Progress,* Editorial May 17, 1951.
37. HCSB August 6, 1951.
38. HCSB February 12, 1953.
39. HCSB March 16, 1953.
40. Hanover *Herald Progress* July 9, 1953.
41. HCBS September 30, 1955.
42. Hanover *Herald Progress* January 27, 1955.
43. Hanover *Herald Progress,* January 27, 1955.
44. Hanover *Herald Progress,* February 10, 1955, p. 1.
45. Hanover *Herald Progress,* September 30, 1954.
46. Hanover *Herald Progress,* October 7, 1954. These same surveyors reported to the *Herald Progress* that they planned to survey Gandy alumni to see what paths they were following.
47. Hanover *Herald Progress,* October 7, 1954.
48. Hanover *Herald Progress,* February 17, 1955.
49. Hanover *Herald Progress,* February 17, 1955.
50. Hanover *Herald Progress,* February 24, 1955, p. 5.
51. Hanover *Herald Progress,* February 23, 1956.
52. HCSB March 1, 1955.
53. While it is not stated, these men were probably trustees of the church. Typically, it is the trustees in a Baptist church who deal with financial transactions.
54. HCSB March 25, 1955.
55. Editorial, Hanover *Herald Progress,* June 6, 1963; June 27, 1963.
56. A white man named John Gabbert of the Ellerson community in Hanover conducted a poll in Mechanicsville in June 1963. Gabbert, described in the *Herald Progress* as a "one-man nighttime and Saturday hobbyist," went door to door asking residents their opinions on certain questions. When asked about closing the schools, the informants said overwhelmingly that the schools should remain open. By this time, Hanoverians had the Prince Edward County example of impact of closing the schools.
57. Hanover *Herald Progress* June 15, 1963.
58. Hanover *Herald Progress,* September 5, 1963.

59. Ogletree, 131–132.
60. Virginia Department of Education, Record Group 27, Desegregation Files 1965–1970 ACC # 29479 Box 3, Assurance of Compliance Form, Hanover County File, LVA.
61. HCSB February 18, 1965.
62. Calvin C. Green interview, November 2, 2001.
63. Hanover *Herald Progress*, March 18, 1965.
64. Henry Marsh interview, November 25, 2002.
65. Department of Education Record Group 27, Desegregation Files 1965–1970 ACC # 29479, Box 3, Hanover Folder, Notice and Instructions to School Children and their Parents or Guardians, of Hanover County, Virginia, LVA.
66. *Charles C. Green, et. al v. The New Kent County, Virginia School Board* 391 U.S. 430 (1968) http://law.touro.edu/patch/Green/.
67. Hanover *Herald Progress*, August 8, 1968.
68. Green interview.
69. HCSB August 6, 1968; Hanover *Herald Progress*, July 11, 1968.
70. HCSB August 27, 1968.
71. Hanover *Herald Progress*, June 10, 1965, August 5, 1965, September 9, 1965.
72. Hanover *Herald Progress*, April 11, 1963; April 25, 1963
73. Hanover *Herald Progress*, May 14, 1964, May 21, 1964. In 1966, RMC accepted its first Black student, who transferred from Virginia Union in Richmond. Hanover *Herald Progress*, September 15, 1966.
74. Hanover *Herald Progress*, May 16, 1968.
75. Deborah Dabney Joseph interview. For discussion of the residential ordinance in Ashland see Chapter 4, p. 10.
76. Joseph interview.
77. Lift Every Voice and Sing tells the story of the Black experience in this country from slavery to freedom and was often sung as a means of resistance, strength, and protest after school desegregation. For more on this topic see Imani Perry's 2018 book, *May We Forever Stand: A History of the Black National Anthem*, UNC Press, 2018.
78. Hanover *Herald Progress* February 24, 1971.
79. Hanover *Herald Progress* February 24, 1972.
80. National Archives https://www.archives.gov/milestone-documents/voting-rights-act#:~:text=The%20Voting%20Rights%20Act%20had,African%20Americans%20registered%20to%20vote.

Epilogue

1. John Morris interview.
2. John Morris interview.
3. John Morris interview.
4. John Morris interview.
5. John Morris interview.
6. John Morris interview.
7. Interview with Renada Harris.

8. See Virginia Department of Historic Resources at https://www.dhr.virginia.gov/. Berkleytown, in Ashland, also written about here, is now on the state and national registries.
9. 2020 Census Report Social Explorer Hanover County Virginia accessed December 15, 2023. https://www.socialexplorer.com/tables/CENSUS2020/R13542883. These numbers do not include non-Hispanic multi-race people, non-Hispanic American Indian and Alaska native alone, non-Hispanic Asian alone, non-Hispanic native Hawaiian and Pacific Islander alone, or non-Hispanic other alone.
10. In the March 14, 2023, Hanover County School Board Meeting Minutes, Rachel Levy, PhD, an Ashland resident, expressed her opposition to the name change and suggested that over the years, assurances had been made the consolidated school would maintain the name John M. Gandy.
11. According to the Hanover County School Board Policy and Regulation Manual, "The Hanover County School Board shall solicit recommendations from the community for the naming of new schools. In reviewing recommendations, the following factors will be considered: geographic location, environmental features, and historical considerations" (145). The Accompanying Regulation says that "Requests for the naming of schools and facilities are periodically recommended to the Hanover County School Board. The division superintendent, School Board, or a committee thereof will consider such recommendations in a systematic manner, using the following guidelines: 1. The division superintendent or his designee shall solicit suggestions and/or recommendations from the community, including PTA's and/or PTO's. 2. Requests shall be in writing with reasons for the recommendation included in the statement. 3. Evidence of broad community support shall accompany the request. 4. Suggestions coming from School Board members, Hanover County officials or the administration and staff shall follow the same procedure. The School Board shall reserve to itself the right to designate the official name of any school or school building" (146)
12. May 9, 2023, Hanover County School Board meeting minutes.

BIBLIOGRAPHY

Archival and Manuscript Sources

Ancestry.com
Bureau of Refugees, Freedmen, and Abandoned Lands
Records of the Assistant Commissioner for the State of Virginia, LVA
Records of the Superintendent of Education for the State of Virginia, LVA
Civil War Pension Records, NARA
John C. Underwood Papers, LVA
Hewlett Family Papers, LVA
Luther Porter Jackson Papers, Virginia State University
Maggie Lena Walker Papers, Maggie L. Walker Historical Site, National Park Service
Negro Industrial and Agricultural Society of Virginia, LVA
Negro Protective Association Records, LVA
National Archives, Record Group 35, Records of the Civilian Conservation Corps, Entry 115,Division of Investigations, Camp Inspection Reports, Box 224, Folder P-78, NARA
National Archives. https://www.archives.gov/milestone-documents/voting-rights-act#:~:text=The%20Voting%20Rights%20Act%20had,African%20Americans%20registered%20to%20vote
Kiblinger Papers, LVA
Library of Virginia, the Virginia State Archives LVA
Patrick Henry Bicentennial Celebration Souvenir Program, LVA
Records of the Richmond Theological Seminary, Accession # AR-0008, Archive and Special Collections Department, L. Douglas Wilder Library, Virginia Union University, Archives (VUU)
Report of the Adjutant-General of the State of Virginia, LVA
The Negro Organization Society, Inc. Virginia Union University Archive
Virginia Department of Education, LVA

Virginia Manual Labor School of the Negro Reformatory Association of Virginia Biennial Report
Hanover County Industrial Home School for Colored Girls, Pamphlet, LVA
USDA Census of Agriculture Historical Archive 1870, Cornell University

Government Documents

Ashland Town Council Minutes
Hanover County Board of Supervisors Minutes
Hanover County Chancery Court Records
Hanover County Land Deeds
Hanover County School Board Minutes
Hanover County Taxation Records
Reports of the Superintendent of Public Instruction State of Virginia
Virginia Acts of the Assembly, 1867–1868
Virginia Acts of the Assembly, 1889–1890
Virginia Acts of the Assembly 1894
Virginia Acts of the Assembly 1897

Oral Histories

Beryl Thompson Carter
Ruth Winston Carter
Claudius Wilson Dabney
Jean Folley
John Gordon
Inez Winston Gray
Calvin Green
Robert and NaChay Grimes
Robert Grimes
Renada Harris
James Edward Henry
Benjamin Jackson
Dorothy Jones
Deborah Dabney Joseph
John and Doris Morris, Doris Wingfield, Berniece Parnell
Margaret Washington, Inez Gray, William Robinson

Published Sources

Alexander, Ann Field. *Race Man: The Rise and Fall of the "Fighting Editor," John Mitchell, Jr.* Charlottesville, VA: University of Virginia Press, 2002.
Anderson, William. "Speech before Virginia Bar Association Meeting." Ft. Monroe, VA, 1900.
Bailey, Samuel. "The Adjustment of Italian Immigrants in Buenos Aires and New York, 1870–1914." *The American Historical Review* 88, no. 2 (April 1983): 281–305.

Beito, David T. *From Mutual Aid to Welfare State: Fraternal Societies and Social Services, 1890–1967*. Chapel Hill, NC: University of North Carolina Press, 2000.
Bennett, Hugh H., and W.E. McLendon. *Soil Survey of Hanover County*. Washington, DC: GPO, 1905.
Berlin, Ira. *Many Thousands Gone: The First Two Centuries of Slavery in North America*. Cambridge, MA: Belknap Press of Harvard University Press, 1998.
Berman, William C. *The Politics of Civil Rights in the Truman Administration*. Columbus, OH: Ohio State University Press, 1970.
Blassingame, John. *The Slave Community*. New York: Oxford University Press, 1979.
Brenaman, Jacob Neff. *A History of Virginia Conventions*. J. L. Hill Printing Company, 1902.
Brown, Elsa Barkley. "'What Has Happened Here': The Politics of Difference in Women's History and Feminist Politics." *Feminist Studies* 18, no.2 (Summer 1992): 295–312.
———. "Womanist Consciousness: Maggie Lena Walker and the Independent Order of St. Luke." *Signs* 14, no. 3, (Spring 1989): 610–633.
Brundage, W. Fitzhugh. *Lynching in the New South, Georgia and Virginia, 1880–1930*. Chicago, IL: University of Illinois Press, 1993.
———. *The Southern Past: A Clash of Race and Memory*. Cambridge: Belknap Press, Harvard University Press, 2005.
Bureau of Public Administration. "Report on An Administrative Survey of Virginia's Training Schools." Charlottesville: University of Virginia, 1957.
Burrell, W.P., and D. E. Johnson. *Twenty-Five Years of the Grand Fountain of the United Order of True Reformers, 1881–1905*. Richmond, VA: Grand Fountain United Order of True Reformers, 1909.
Campbell, Otto C. "John Sargent Wise: A Case Study in Conservative-Readjuster Politics in Virginia, 1869–1889." PhD diss., University of Virginia, 1979.
Censer, Jane Turner. *The Reconstruction of Southern Womanhood, 1865–1895*. Baton Rouge, LA: Louisiana State University Press, 2003.
Chafe, William. *Civilities and Civil Rights: Greensboro, North Carolina, and the Black Struggle for Freedom*. Oxford University Press, 1980.
Cheek, William, and Aimee Lee. *John Mercer Langston and the Fight for Black Freedom 1829–1865*. Urbana: University of Illinois Press, 1989.
Chenery, William. *So It Seemed*. New York: Harcourt, Brace and Company, 1952.
Clermont, Kevin. *The Indomitable George Washington Fields: From Slave to Attorney Ziff Professor of Law*. Cornell University, 2013.
Cohen, Stan. *The Tree Army*. Missoula, MT: Pictorial Histories Company, 1980.
Cole, Olen, Jr. *The African American Experience in the Civilian Conservation Corps*. Gainesville: University Press of Florida, 1999.
Dabney, Floyd, Jr. "Speech before Providence Baptist Church Black History Month Program." February 2007.
Dabney, Wendell P. *Maggie L. Walker: Her Life and Deeds*. The Dabney Publishing Company, Cincinnati, OH, 1927.
Daniel, John W. "Speech before Virginia State Bar Association 'The Work of the Constitutional Convention.'" Hot Springs, VA, 1902.
Davis, D. Webster. *The Life and Public Services of William Washington Browne*. Richmond, VA: Mrs. M.A. Browne-Smith, 1910.
Diner, Hasia. *Erin's Daughters in America*. Baltimore, MD: Johns Hopkins University Press, 1983.
Du Bois, W. E. B. *Black Reconstruction in America 1860–1880*. New York: Atheneum, 1992.

———. *The Souls of Black Folk*. New York: Barnes & Noble Classics, 2003.

Earley, Charity Adams. *One Woman's Army: A Black Officer Remembers the WAC*. College Station, TX: Texas A&M University Press, 1989.

Ebenezer Baptist Church History, Ebenezer Baptist Church, Beaverdam, VA.

Egerton, John. *Speak Now Against the Day: The Generation Before the Civil Rights Movement in the South*. Chapel Hill: University of North Carolina Press, 1995.

Ely, Melvin Patrick. *Israel on the Appomattox: A Southern Experiment in Black Freedom from 1790s through the Civil War.* New York: Alfred Knopf, 2004.

———. *The Adventures of Amos 'N' Andy: A Social History of an American Phenomenon.* New York: The Free Press, 1991.

Feldman, Glenn. *Reading Southern History: Essays on Interpreters and Interpretation.* Tuscaloosa, AL: The University of Alabama Press, 2001.

Foner, Eric. *Reconstruction: America's Unfinished Revolution 1863–1877.* New York: Harper Rowe, 1988.

Foner, Eric, and Joshua Brown. *Forever Free: The Story of Emancipation and Reconstruction.* New York: Knopf, 2005.

Foner, Jack. *Blacks and the Military in American History: A New Perspective.* New York, NY: Praeger Publishers, 1974.

Franklin, V.P. "Hidden in Plain View: African American Women, Radical Feminism, and the Origins of Women's Studies Programs, 1967–1974." *The Journal of African American History* 87, no. 4 (2002): 433–455.

Gales, Melinda. "African American Churches in Hanover County, Virginia, 1865–1900." MA Thesis, VCU, 1999.

Genovese, Eugene. *Roll, Jordan, Roll.* New York: Pantheon Books, 1974.

Gillespie, Mary Gail. "Havens for the Fashionable and Sickly: Society, Sickness, and Space at Nineteenth Century Southern Spring Resorts." PhD diss., University of North Carolina, 1998.

Glass, Carter. "Speech for the Virginia Constitutional Convention: 'A Conclusive Argument Showing Why We Should Submit the New Constitution to the White Electorate.'" Richmond, VA, September 6, 1901.

Green, Hilary. *Educational Reconstruction: African American Schools in the Urban South, 1865–1890.* New York: Fordham University Press, 2016.

Griffin, William E., Jr. *One Hundred Fifty Years of History. Along the Richmond, Fredericksburg and Potomac.* Richmond, VA: Whittet & Shepperson, 1984.

Griffith, Elisabeth. *In Her Own Right: The Life of Elizabeth Cady Stanton.* New York: Oxford University Press, 1984.

Hahn, Steven. *A Nation Under Our Feet: Black Political Struggles in the Rural South from Slavery to the Great Migration.* Cambridge, MA: Harvard University Press, 2003.

Hall, Jacquelyn Dowd. "'You Must Remember This.' Autobiography as Social Critique." *The Journal of American History*, 85, no. 2 (September 1998): 439–465.

Hershman, James H., Jr. "Public School Bonds and Virginia's Massive Resistance." *Journal of Negro History* 52 (Autumn 1983): 398–409.

———. *Leon Bazile—Jim Crow's Jurist*. Virginia Forum, George Mason University, 2014.

Higginbotham, Elizabeth Brooks. *Righteous Discontent: The Women's Movement in the Black Baptist Church, 1880–1920.* Cambridge, MA: Harvard University Press, 1993.

Holt, Thomas. *Black Over White: Negro Political Leadership in South Carolina during Reconstruction.* Urbana: University of Illinois Press, 1997.

Holt, Wythe. *Virginia's Constitutional Convention of 1901–1902.* New York: Garland Publishing, 1990.

Hunter, Tera. *To 'Joy My Freedom: Southern Black Women's Lives and Labors After the Civil War.* Cambridge, MA: Harvard University Press, 1997.

Jackson, Giles. "Speech before Committee on Education of the Constitutional Convention of Virginia." Richmond, VA, 1900.

Jackson, Luther Porter. *Negro Office-Holders in Virginia 1865–1895 1865.* Norfolk, VA: Guide Quality Press, 1945.

Jabbar, Kareem Abdul, and Anthony Walton. *Brothers in Arms: The Epic Story of the 761st Tank Battalion. World War IIs Forgotten Heroes.* New York, NY: Broadway Books, 2004.

Jones, Jacqueline. *American Work: Four Centuries of Black and White Labor.* New York, NY: W.W. Norton Company, 1998.

Jones-Branch, Cherisse. *Better Living Their Own Bootstraps: Black Women's Activism in Rural Arkansas, 1914–1965.* Fayetteville: University of Arkansas Press, 2021.

———. *Labor of Love, Labor of Sorrow: Black Women, Work, and the Family from Slavery to the Present.* New York: Basic Books, 1985.

Jones, Winfield. *Story of the Ku Klux Klan.* American Newspaper Syndicate, 1921.

Kneebone, John, J. Jefferson Looney, Brent Tarter, and Sandra Treadway, eds. *Dictionary of Virginia Biography.* Richmond: Library of Virginia, 1998.

———. *Southern Liberal Journalists and the Issue of Race.* Chapel Hill: University of North Carolina Press, 1985.

Kunzel, Regina. *Fallen Women, Problem Girls: Unmarried Mothers and the Professionalization of Social Work.* New Haven, CT: Yale University Press, 1993.

Lassiter, Matthew, and Andrew Lewis, eds. *The Moderates' Dilemma: Massive Resistance to School Desegregation in Virginia.* Charlottesville, VA: University of Virginia, Press, 1998.

Layton, William. *Layton Looks at Life.* Washington, DC: W.W. Layton, 1996.

Lebsock, Susanne. *The Free Women of Petersburg: Status and Culture in a Southern Town 1784–1860.* New York: Norton, 1984.

Leonard, Cynthia Miller, ed. *The General Assembly of Virginia.* Richmond: General Assembly of Virginia, 1978.

Levine, Lawrence. *Black Culture, Black Consciousness: African American Folk Thought from Slavery to Freedom.* New York: Oxford University Press, 1974.

Link, William A. *A Country and a Lonely Place.* Chapel Hill, NC: University of North Carolina Press, 1986.

Litwack, Leon. *Been in the Storm So Long: The Aftermath of Slavery.* New York: Knopf, 1979.

———. *North of Slavery.* Chicago: University of Chicago Press, 1961.

———. *Trouble in Mind: Black Southerners in the Age of Jim Crow.* New York: Knopf, 1998.

Makosky, Donald, Kate Neckerman, and Carolyn Hemphill. *One and Two Room Schools.* Ashland, VA: Hanover County Black Heritage Society, 2001.

Manson, Steven Jonathan Schroeder, David Van Riper, Katherine Knowles, Tracy Kugler, Finn Roberts, and Steven Ruggles. IPUMS National Historical Geographic Information System: Version 18.0. Minneapolis, MN: IPUMS, 2023. http://doi.org/10.18128/D050.V18.0.

Marlowe, Gertrude Woodruff. *A Right Worthy Grand Mission: Maggie Lena Walker and the Quest for Black Economic Empowerment.* Washington, DC: Howard University Press, 2003.

McDanel, Ralph Clipman. *The Virginia Constitutional Convention of 1901–1902*. Baltimore: The Johns Hopkins Press, 1928.

McIlwaine, Richard. "Address before Democratic Members of the Constitutional Convention." Richmond, VA, 1902.

McMillen, Neil. *Dark Journey: Black Mississippians in the Age of Jim Crow*. Urbana: University of Illinois Press, 1989.

Meyer, Leisa. *Creating G. I. Jane: Sexuality and Power in the Women's Army Corps during World War II*. New York, NY: Columbia University Press, 1996.

L. H. Minor to Sir. 2 May [1862], M-458 1862. Letters Received, series 5. Secretary of War. War Department Collection of Confederate Records, Record Group 109, National Archives.

Mitchell, Mary H. *Hollywood Cemetery: The History of a Southern Shrine*. Richmond: Virginia State Library, 1985.

Moore, James Tice. *Two Paths to the New South: The Virginia Debt Controversy, 1870–1883*. Lexington, KY: University Press of Kentucky, 1974.

Morgan, Jennifer. *Reckoning with Slavery: Gender, Kinship, and Capitalism in the Early Black Atlantic*. Durham, NC: Duke University Press, 2021.

Morton, Richard Lee. *The Negro in Virginia Politics, 1865–1902*. Charlottesville: University of Virginia Press, 1919.

Ogletree, Charles, Jr. *All Deliberate Speed: Reflections on the First Half Century of Brown v. the Board of Education*. New York: W.W. Norton and Company, 2004.

Perdue, Charles, Thomas E. Barden, and Robert K. Phillips. *Weevils in the Wheat: Interviews with Virginia Ex-Slaves*. Charlottesville, VA: University of Virginia Press, 1976.

Perry, Imani. *May We Forever Stand: A History of the Black National Anthem*. Chapel Hill, NC: University of North Carolina Press, 2018.

Petty, Adrienne Monteith. *Standing Their Ground: Small Farmers in North Carolina since the Civil War*. Oxford University Press, 2013.

Putney, Martha S. *When the Nation Was in Need: Blacks in the Women's Army Corps during World War II*. London: The Scarecrow Press, Inc., 1992.

Rabinowitz, Richard C. *Race Relations in the Urban South*. New York: Oxford University Press, 1977.

Rachleff, Peter. *Black Labor in the South: Richmond, Virginia 1865–1890*. Philadelphia: Temple University Press, 1984.

Randolph, Lewis, and Gayle Tate. *Rights for a Season: The Politics of Race, Class and Gender in Richmond, VA*. Knoxville: University of Tennessee Press, 2003.

Redcay, Edward E. "Pioneering Negro Education." *Journal of Negro Education* 6, no. 1 (January 1937): 38–53.

Ridgeway, James. *Blood in the Face: The Ku Klux Klan, Aryan Nations, Nazi Skinheads, and the Rise of the New White Culture*. New York: Thunder's Mouth Press, 1990.

Roediger, David R. *Working toward Whiteness: How America's Immigrants Became White: The Strange Journey from Ellis Island to the Suburbs*. New York, NY: Basic Books, 2005.

Salmond, John A. *The Civilian Conservation Corps, 1933–1942: A New Deal Case Study*. Durham, NC: Duke University Press, 1967.

Samuel, Lawrence. *Pledging Allegiance: American Identity and the Bond Drive of World War II*. Washington, DC: Smithsonian Institution Press, 1997.

Scanlon, James. *History of Randolph-Macon College: A Southern History, 1825–1967*. Charlottesville, VA: University of Virginia Press, 1983.

Schlegel, Marvin Wilson. *Virginia on Guard*. Richmond, VA: Virginia State Library, 1949.

Schweninger, Loren. *Black Property Owners in the South 1970–1915*. Chicago, IL: University of Illinois, 1990.

Schwalm, Leslie. *A Hard Fight for We: Women's Transition from Slavery to Freedom in South Carolina*. Urbana: University of Illinois Press, 1997.

Scott, James. *Domination and the Arts of Resistance: Hidden Transcripts*. New Haven, CT: Yale University Press, 1990.

Shalf, Roseanne Groat. *Ashland, Ashland: The Story of a Turn-of-the-Century Railroad Town*. Lawrenceville, VA: Brunswick Publishers Corp., 1994.

Shibley, Ronald E. "Election Law and Electoral Practices in Virginia, 1867–1902." PhD diss., University of Virginia, 1972.

Shiloh Baptist Church History. Ashland, VA.

Smith, James Douglas. *Managing White Supremacy: Race, Politics, and Citizenship in Jim Crow Virginia*. Chapel Hill, NC: The University of North Carolina Press, 2002.

——. "Virginia during Reconstruction, 1865–1870. A Political, Economic and Social Study." M.A. Thesis, University of Virginia, 1984.

Smith, Lillian. *Killers of the Dream*. New York: Norton, 1949.

Smith, Susan Lynn. *Sick and Tired of Being Sick and Tired: Black Women's Health Activism in America, 1880–1950.* Philadelphia: University of Pennsylvania, 1995.

Snedden, David S. *Administration and Educational Work of American Juvenile Reform Schools*. New York: Teachers College Columbia University, 1907.

Sturkey, William. *Hattiesburg: An American City in Black and White*. Cambridge, MA: Belknap Press: An Imprint of Harvard University Press, 2019.

Tarter, Brent. "Funders." *Encyclopedia Virginia*. Virginia Humanities (December 7, 2020).

Tarter, Brent. *A Saga of the New South: Race, Law, and Public Debt in Virginia*. Charlottesville, VA: University of Virginia Press, 2016

Thom, Alfred Pembroke. "The Inevitable Readjustment of the Law." Delivered before the Virginia Bar Association. Old Point Comfort, VA, August 3, 1893.

Ture, Kwame, and Charles V. Hamilton. *Black Power and the Politics of Liberation in America*. New York: Random House, 1967.

Turner, Nicole Myers. *The Evolution of Black Religious Politics in Postemancipation Virginia*. University of North Carolina Press, 2020.

Tyler, Lyon Gardiner. *Encyclopedia of Virginia Biography*. Baltimore: Genealogical Publications, 1998.

Virginia State Federation of Colored Women's Clubs. *The History of Virginia State Federation of Colored Women's Clubs Inc*. Eastville, VA: Hickory House, 1996.

Virginia War Dead Database, LVA. http://www.lva.lib.va.us/whatwehave/mil/vmd/index.asp.

Wallenstein, Peter. "The Quest for Loving: Race, Sex, and the Freedom to Marry." Lecture at the Virginia Museum of History & Culture, Banner Lecture, 2015.

Watkins, T. H. *The Hungry Years: A Narrative History of the Great Depression in America*. New York: Henry Holt & Co., 1999.

Who's Who in Colored America. New York: Thomas Yenser, 1933.

White, Deborah Gray. *Ar'n't I a Woman? Female Slaves in the Plantation South*. New York: W.W. Norton & Company, 1987.

White, Evans C. and Rose B. *Eastern Hanover County Churches, Schools & Organizations: A Brief History "from a Black Perspective."* Hanover County, VA: WhiteBrook Printing, undated.

Wickham, Henry T. "Address before Joint Session of the General Assembly." Richmond, VA, February 23, 1940.

Wilhoit, Francis M. *The Politics of Massive Resistance.* New York: George Braziller, 1973.

Williams, Heather Andrea. *Self-Taught: African American Education in Slavery and Freedom.* University of North Carolina Press, 2007.

Williamson, Joel. *After Slavery: The Negro South Carolina Reconstruction, 1861–1877.* Chapel Hill: University of North Carolina Press, 1965.

Wise, John S. *The Lion's Skin.* New York: Doubleday, Page & Company, 1905.

Woodson, Carter G. *The Miseducation of the Negro.* Las Vegas, NV: IAP, 2010.

Woodward, C. Vann. *Origins of the New South, 1877–1913.* Baton Rouge, LA: University of Louisiana Press, 1971.

———. *The Strange Career of Jim Crow.* New York: Oxford University Press, 1974.

INDEX

A. Cappell and Company v. the Mutual Building Fund and Dollar Savings Bank of Richmond, 49
Africa, 17, 27, 91
agriculture, 19, 50, 70, 119, 125, 156, 161, 206. *See also* farms
Allen, Andrew, 147–48
Allen, Dorothy, 148
Allen, Liza, 147–48
Allen, Rev. T. M., 75, 104
Allen's Creek, 52
Allen's Pond, 147
American Guest, 74
Anderson, Rev. Stephen, 56
Anderson-McCormick, 57, 77, 189n11
Ashland Kiwanis Club, 121
Ashland Museum, 178
Ashland Riot, 81, 85
Ashland Town Council (ATCM), 89, 110, 192, 194–95
Ashland Train Station, 82, 87, 95, 95, 119
assassinations of Kennedys, Malcolm X, and Martin Luther King, 170
"Assurance of Compliance" agreement, 166

Banks, Lester A., 163
baptism, 26
Barrett, Janie Porter, 96–102
Beaverdam Fountain, Pin Hook, 61
Berkleytown, 106–7, 110, 129–32, 141, 170, 179, 203n8
Bethany Elementary School, 160, 164
Black History Month, 171
Bossieux, Captain C. G., 84
Boxley, Barbara Johnson, 150
BPS Club, 76–77
Brackett, Ellen, 67–68
Broadneck Plantation, 14, 40, 41
Brown, J. B., 52
Brown, Jesse, 22
Brown, Orlando, 21–22
Browne, William Washington, 58, 61, 64, 66, 79
Brown Grove, 137, 172, 177
Buckner, Willie, 110
Bundy, Eunice, 117
Bureau of Refugees, Freedmen, and Abandoned Lands. *See* Freedmen's Bureau
Burnett, B. C., 45, 47
Burton, Carrie Winston, 115, 137
Bushell, Grace, 119

Carter, Beryl Thompson, 105–6, 149–50, 154
Carter, Hill, 78
Carter, Julia, 32

Carter, Ruth Winston, 113
Carter, William, 48
Carver, George Washington, 109
Center, the, 178
Charity, J. L., 103
Chenery, William, 85–88, 102–3, 151
children, 25, 48, 71, 113
churches: Bethany Baptist Church, 110, 164; Brown Grove Baptist Church, 27, 95, 103, 137, 172, 175, 177, 199n132; Cold Spring Baptist Church (Southampton County), 27; Ebenezer Baptist Church (Chilesburg), 56; Ebenezer Baptist Church (Richmond), 26, 74; First Baptist Church (white), 113; First Union Baptist Church, First Shiloh Baptist Church, 27; Jerusalem Baptist Church, 29, 56, 65, 75; Mt. Salem Baptist Church, 74; New Bridge Baptist Church, 75; Rockhill Baptist Church, 75; Shiloh Baptist Church (aka Shiloh Freedmen's Church), 9, 29, 75, 95, 108, 140, 142; statistical information on, 74; Union Baptist Church Sunday School, 117
church finances, 27
civic church, 149
Civilian Conservation Corps (CCC), 119–25, 139, 147, 196n38, 196n51
Civil Rights Act of 1964, 166, 172
civil rights bill, 53
Clarke, Alexander, 70
Clarke, Charles, 70
Clarke, Eliza, 48
Clarke, William, 48, 70
Coleman, Frances, 45–48, 66
Coleman, George, 46
Coleman, John, 90
Coleman, Judson, 110
Colored Baptist Convention, 26–27
Colored Farmers Alliance, 127–28
Colored Shiloh Regular Baptist Association of Virginia, 26–27
Community Inn, 106
Confederate Army, 36, 45, 176
Conservative Democrats, 56
Conservative Party, 42, 44, 53
constitutional conventions of 1867–68, 37–42. *See also* Underwood Constitution

conversion experience, 146–48. *See* baptism
coroner's jury, 84
County-Wide League (Hanover), 95, 138, 149, 154, 193n51. *See also* junior league
Crenshaw, Charles, 46
Crenshaw, John B., 38–39
Crenshaw, Nathaniel, 46
Custer, General George Armstrong, 46

Dabney, Adele, 116, 119
Dabney, Claudius, 117, 170
Dabney, Henry W., 138
Dandridge, Richard, 45
Democrats, 53, 56–57, 77–78, 186n41
Denton, America, 15, 21–25, 32, 183–84
Denton, Dick, 15, 22–25, 183
Department of Health, Education, and Welfare, 166
Derricott, Matilda, 68
desegregation: *Davis v. County School Board of Prince Edward County, VA, Brown v. the Board of Education of Topeka, Kansas,* 158–60, 162–71; freedom of choice, 167–68; *Green v. New Kent County, Virginia,* 168; protest against, 171; Pupil Placement Board, 165; of staff, 119; of University of Virginia Law School, 153; of Virginia State University, aka Virginia Normal and Collegiate Institute (VNCI), aka Virginia State College, 57, 64, 71–74, 143, 151
Dinwiddie County, 57
Downtown Ashland Main Street Association, 178
Du Bois, W. E. B., 6, 83, 182n10

education: of Black/African Americans, x, 29–32; facilities, condition of, 110, 125, 153–57, 159–60, 165, 173, 177, 206; funding, 94–95, 141, 154; public districts, 52; teacher salaries, 52; training school movement, 94. *See also* desegregation; schools
Ellett, John, 49
Ellett, Sarah, 49
Emancipation Day, 61–64
Emancipation Proclamation, 66

Index

employment, 25, 67, 68
enfranchisement. *See* voting rights
entrepreneurs, Black: John Coleman, 90, 106, 109; Judson Coleman, 106, 109–10; Claudius Dabney, 117, 138, 170, 206; Floyd Dabney Sr., 133–34; Henry W. Dabney, 106, 109, 138; William M. Sullivan, 106; Clinton Winston, 58, 70–71, 94, 108; Johnny Clinton Winston, 94, 108, 149–50

farms, 4, 19, 33, 35, 39–40, 43, 46, 48, 50, 56, 61, 65, 68, 70–71, 83, 85, 88, 99–103, 110, 119, 126–28, 150, 156, 172, 177, 181–82, 206
Fechner, Robert, 120
Federation of Colored Women's Clubs, 101
Fields, George Washington, 13, 175, 178
Fields, James Apostle, 175
Fields, Martha Ann, 14, 175, 178
First Union Baptist Church, 163
Fleming, John, 139, 156, 161
Folly, Jean, 96
Fourteenth Amendment, 36–37, 127
Freedmen's Bank, 50
Freedmen's Bureau (Bureau of Refugees, Freedmen, and Abandoned Lands), 9, 18–22, 31, 32, 35–37, 39–41, 43–44, 52, 68, 131, 183n20, 183n25, 184n58, 185n11, 187n50. *See also* Freedmen's Court
Freedmen's Court, 21
funders, 53, 56
Funding Act of 1871, 53

Gandy, John Manuel, 127, 151
gender, 22–25, 51, 63, 78
Giles, J. P., 154, 164
Giles, Rev. B. S., 163
Gordon, John, 133
Graves, Mildred, 16
Gray, Inez Winston, 95, 108
Gray, William, 64
Gregory, Roger, 79
Grimes, Robert, 1–2, 8, 11, 115
Gwathmey, Robert, 164

Hall, J. Walton, 136, 141
Hampton Institute, 103

Hancock, Gordon Blaine, 142
Hanover County Black Heritage Society, 178
Hanover Tavern, 178
Harris, Alfred, 57
Harris, Samuel, 104
Haw, George, 82
Hayes, G. W., 64
health and healthcare, 56, 96; Eastern Lunatic Asylum, 41; National Negro Health Movement, 118; smallpox vaccination, 96; tuberculosis, 116, 119, 172
Henderson, Linwood, 110
Henry, James Edward, 116–17, 165
Henry Clay Elementary School, 179
Henry Clay Inn, 115
Henry Clay Spring School, 141
Hewlett, David, 69
Hewlett, Thelma, 144
Hickory Hill Club, 69
Hickory Hill Plantation, 26, 117
Hicks, Ethel Winston, 108
Hill, Oliver, 158
Hogg, Elizabeth (aka Tinsley), 49
Hunter, Lucian, 138
H. W. Dabney Funeral Home, 138

Independent Order of St. Luke, 92–94
Interstate 95, 172, 177

Jackson, Andrew, 42
Jackson, Benjamin, 137–40
Jackson, Lelia or Lillian, 137
Jackson, Luther Porter, 6, 143–45
Jackson, Walter, 137, 172
James, William, 38–39, 49
James Shelton Jr. v. Ella D. Hewlett, etc., 69
J. C. Bagby & Company, 70
Jerry, Sammie Lee, 132
Jerusalem Baptist Church, 29, 56, 65, 75
Johnson, Hannah, 15
Johnson, Mary, 110
Johnson, Robert Lee, 120
Johnson, Thomas, 162
Jones, Dorothy Gardner, 109, 115
Jones, Frances Williams Jackson, x, 155
Jones, Isabelle, 68
Jones, Leedom, 123

Joseph, Deborah Dabney, 3, 170
junior league, 138

Keitt, Anthony, 178
Kelley's Truck Stop, 176
Kilbourne Farm, 100

landownership, 69
Latney, Maria, 104
Lee, Harper, *To Kill a Mockingbird*, 179
Lee-Davis High School, 178
Lewis, John, 42–44
Lift Every Voice and Sing, 171, 202n77
Liza and Andrew (A.P.) Allen Park, 147–48

manufacturing, 50
marching bands, 97, 107, 112, 131
March on Washington for Jobs and Freedom, 165
Marsh, Henry, III, 167
Mathers, Mae, 117–19
Mathers-Dabney Fund, 119
McCue, E. O., 144
Merhige, Robert R., Jr., 168–69
Military training camp, 101
Mitchell, John, 64, 74, 81, 85
Moore, Martha Riis, 160–61
Moore, Rev. Eddie Moore, 142
Morris, Charles, 21
Morris, James, 83, 85
Morris, John, 104, 176
Mt. Zion Fountain, the, 58
Murphy, Ed, 21, 183n22
Murray, H. C. Walter, 144
Mutual Building Fund and Dollar Savings Bank, 49

National Association for the Advancement of Colored People (NAACP), 144–45, 149; Hanover County Chapter, 167
National Constitutional Rights Association, 78
Negro Citizen's League, 142–43
Negro Protective Association of Virginia, 77
Negro Reformatory Association, 193n66
New Deal, 10, 113–14, 118–19, 125, 128, 136, 192n44; Roosevelt, 114

Newman, E. W., 89
Nicholas, J. F., 130, 198n93
North Wales Plantation, 14, 66
Nutshell Plantation, 178

organizing: Black people finding strength in organizations, 50; Colored Farmers Alliance, 70; County-Wide League, 95, 138,141, 149, 154, 193n51; Hanover County School Board, 153–54; Junior League, 138; Laboring Mechanics, 50; Negro Citizens League, 142–43; Negro Industrial and Agricultural Society of Virginia (NIAS), 88; Negro Organization Society, 103, 138, 141, 143, 145; PTA, 162, 164; religiously affiliated organizations, 50; Sisters of Damon, 107; Sons and Daughters of Zion Hall, 66; South Anna Elks Lodge, 117, 129, 131–32, 143–44; Union League, 45; United Order of True Reformers, 58; unnamed political club, 142

Parnell, Bertha, 121, 146–48
Phillips, Rev. C. H., 61
Phillips, Stephen, 164
Plessy v. Ferguson, 83, 160
political parties. *See specific parties*
poll tax, 53, 56–57
Powell, Jacob, 42–44

Quarles, R. T., 58, 70

race relations, 34–36, 39–40, 54
Randolph, Rev. E. A., 64
Randolph-Macon College, 81–87, 109, 169
readjusters, 53, 56, 57
Reconstruction, 32–37; anti-enticement laws, 36; Black Codes, 36; civil rights bill of 1866, 36; Presidential, 35–36; Radical/Congressional, 23, 42; Reconstruction Acts, 37
Republicans, 36, 38–39, 53, 56
residential segregation, 89, 109
Richmond Institute, 55
Richmond Theological Seminary, 64, 75
Richmond Theological Seminary, 75
riot in Ashland, 81–87

Index

216

Roane, E. E., 154
Robert E. Lee statue (Richmond), 64
Robinson, Contee, 138, 143, 154, 156
Robinson, Ozwell, 156
Robinson, Rev. R. F., 61
Robinson, Spotswood, 158
Rogers, Edith Nourse, 134
Roosevelt, Franklin Delano, 114. *See also* New Deal
Roses in December, meaning of, x
Russell, J. Alvin, 129

schools: Bell Creek Middle School, 179; Bethany Elementary School, 160, 164; Hanover County Training School, 94, 117, 138; Hanover Reformatory for Negro Boys, 96–98, 193n66; Industrial Home School for Colored Girls, 96–102; John M. Gandy High School, 151–63, 165, 176; Lee-Davis High School, 165; May Day Celebration, 138; Mechanicsville High School, 178; Patrick Henry High School, 165; Pleasant Grove Elementary School, 96, 161, 163; Pole Green Elementary School, 163, 170; Providence Church School, 117; transportation, 138; Wickham School, 116. *See also* desegregation; education
Scott, Edward L. C., 84
Scott's Funeral Home, 140
SeaBees, 133, 198n112
Sheridan, General Philip, 46
Sheridan's Cavalry, 46
Smyth, John Henry, 193n66
social life, 76–77
Southern Claims Commission, 44
Spring Cottage, 56
Stebbins, Charles, Jr., 82–83, 85–87, 191n3
Stebbins, Charles, Sr. 82, 86–87
St. Luke Penny Savings Bank, 93
Stonewall Jackson Middle School, 178
Storrs, Peter, 33, 45–48, 66
Sullivan, William, 110
Sullivan's Auditorium, 107
Sutton, Leroy, 124

Taliaferro, Bessie, 162
Taylor, Anderson, 164

Taylor, William, 55–56, 61, 65, 79, 91
ten-point plan, 144
Thompson, Arlene, 166
Thompson, Harold, 166
Thompson, J. Conroy, 150
Thompson, Stephanie V., 166–67
Timberlake, William, 47
Tinsley, C. F., 59
Tinsley, Jane, 48
Tinsley, Joseph, 48
Toler, Burrell, 38–39, 49–50
Toler, Sally, 49
Tonkins, Vashti, 135
Trevillian, Bill, 83, 85
True Reformers, 58–65, 70, 78, 91
Truman, Harry S., 144
Tucker, Samuel, 168
Turner, Nat, 27
Tyler, John Hoge, 84

Underwood Constitution, 44
Union Army, 14, 16–17, 32–33, 46, 48, 66
Union Baptist Church (Beaverdam), 61
Union League, 45
Untold Stories: Growing Up in Ashland/Hanover-Black and White Experiences (event), 178

violence, anti-Black, 42–44
"Virginia Does Care," 127–29, 153
Virginia General Assembly, 96
Virginia League of Counties, 126
Virginia State Gazetteer and Business Directory, 70
Virginia Union University, 141–42
voting rights, x, 3–6, 8–9, 28, 32, 37–42, 44, 50, 57, 64, 67, 77–79, 81, 83, 85, 87–89, 103, 110–11, 114, 126–27, 131, 136, 140, 143–45, 148–51, 157, 161, 172
Voting Rights Act of 1965, 172

Walker, Gilbert C., 44, 52
Walker, Maggie Lena, 92, 102
Wallace, John, 35
Waller, Rachel, 55
Walton Election Law of 1894, 77
Ware, James R., 92
Weatherless, Rev. James, 41, 186n33

Index

Webb, David B., 162
Wegman's supermarket, 177
Wells, Ida B., 59
Wheatley, Phyllis, 9
whipping post repealed, 56
White, L. C., 103
White, Taylor, 45
White Chimney Eagle, 122–23
white people, kept out of leadership positions in Black church, 26
Wickham, Williams C., 69
Wingfield, Lelia, 68
Winston, Amy, 48
Winston, Charles, 69
Winston, Clinton, 58, 70–71, 108
Winston, Johnny Clinton, 108, 150
Winston, Lee, 131
Winston, William Henry, 14, 48, 66, 175–76
Women's Army Auxiliary Corps, 134
Woodson, Carter, 6
Woolfolk, James, 143
Works Progress Administration, 15, 119, 127, 197n65
Works Projects Administration (Works Progress Administration), 127
World War II, 129–36
Wright, William, 70

Young Men's Christian Association, 107

RECENT BOOKS IN THE
Carter G. Woodson Institute Series

*The Struggle for Change: Race and the Politics
of Reconciliation in Modern Richmond*
MARVIN T. CHILES

*A Little Child Shall Lead Them: A Documentary Account of the Struggle
for School Desegregation in Prince Edward County, Virginia*
BRIAN J. DAUGHERITY AND BRIAN GROGAN, EDITORS

*We Face the Dawn: Oliver Hill, Spottswood Robinson,
and the Legal Team That Dismantled Jim Crow*
MARGARET EDDS

*Keep On Keeping On: The NAACP and the Implementation
of Brown v. Board of Education in Virginia*
BRIAN J. DAUGHERITY

*Schooling Jim Crow: The Fight for Atlanta's Booker T. Washington
High School and the Roots of Black Protest Politics*
JAY WINSTON DRISKELL JR.

The Punitive Turn: New Approaches to Race and Incarceration
DEBORAH E. MCDOWELL, CLAUDRENA N. HAROLD, AND JUAN BATTLE, EDITORS

Freedom Has a Face: Race, Identity, and Community in Jefferson's Virginia
KIRT VON DAACKE

Gabriel's Conspiracy: A Documentary History
PHILIP J. SCHWARZ, EDITOR

Rambles of a Runaway from Southern Slavery
HENRY GOINGS, EDITED BY CALVIN SCHERMERHORN,
MICHAEL PLUNKETT, AND EDWARD GAYNOR

Whispers of Rebellion: Narrating Gabriel's Conspiracy
MICHAEL L. NICHOLLS

Word, Like Fire: Maria Stewart, the Bible, and the Rights of African Americans
VALERIE C. COOPER

Strategies for Survival: Recollections of Bondage in Antebellum Virginia
WILLIAM DUSINBERRE

Criminal Injustice: Slaves and Free Blacks in Georgia's Criminal Justice System
GLENN MCNAIR

Segregation's Science: Eugenics and Society in Virginia
GREGORY MICHAEL DORR

The Segregated Scholars: Black Social Scientists and the Creation of Black Labor Studies, 1890–1950
FRANCILLE RUSAN WILSON

Bitter Fruits of Bondage: The Demise of Slavery and the Collapse of the Confederacy, 1861–1865
ARMSTEAD L. ROBINSON

Migrants against Slavery: Virginians and the Nation
PHILIP J. SCHWARZ

Black Prisoners and Their World, Alabama, 1865–1900
MARY ELLEN CURTIN

Rituals of Race: American Public Culture and the Search for Racial Democracy
ALESSANDRA LORINI

"Rearing Wolves to Our Own Destruction": Slavery in Richmond, Virginia, 1782–1865
MIDORI TAKAGI

Enterprising Southerners: Black Economic Success in North Carolina, 1865–1915
ROBERT C. KENZER

Free Blacks in Norfolk, Virginia, 1790–1860: The Darker Side of Freedom
TOMMY L. BOGGER

A House Divided: Slavery and Emancipation in Delaware, 1638–1865
PATIENCE ESSAH

A New Plantation South: Land, Labor, and Federal Favor in Twentieth-Century Arkansas
JEANNIE M. WHAYNE

Limits of Anarchy: Intervention and State Formation in Chad
SAM C. NOLUTSHUNGU

Fire This Time: The Watts Uprising and the 1960s
GERALD HORNE

Virginia Landmarks of Black History: Sites on the Virginia Landmarks Register and the National Register of Historic Places
CALDER LOTH, EDITOR

Cultivation and Culture: Labor and the Shaping of Slave Life in the Americas
IRA BERLIN AND PHILIP D. MORGAN, EDITORS

The Color of Their Skin: Education and Race in Richmond, Virginia, 1954–89
ROBERT A. PRATT

Power and the Praise Poem: Southern African Voices in History
LEROY VAIL AND LANDEG WHITE